TWENTY-FIRST CENTURY
PSYCHOANALYSIS

TWENTY-FIRST CENTURY PSYCHOANALYSIS

Thomas Svolos

KARNAC

First published in 2017 by
Karnac Books Ltd
118 Finchley Road
London NW3 5HT

British Library Cataloguing in Publication Data

A C.I.P. for this book is available from the British Library

ISBN-13: 978-1-78220-503-6

Typeset by V Publishing Solutions Pvt Ltd., Chennai, India

www.karnacbooks.com

For my friends and colleagues sitting at the table at the banquet of analysts, especially Maria Cristina Aguirre and Alicia Arenas,
And,
For Bufflehead, always and forever.

CONTENTS

PART VI: *ENCORE,* ENCORE: CONCEPTUAL EXTRACTS
FROM *SEMINAR 20*

PART VII: REMARKS ON PSYCHOANALYSIS

PART VIII: REMARKS ON THE
MENTAL HEALTH FIELD

ACKNOWLEDGEMENTS

"Jacques Lacan, reader" was first published in *Hurly-Burly, the International Lacanian Journal of Psychoanalysis* in 2012, and in *Open Letter: A Canadian Journal of Writing and Theory* in a special issue "Negotiating the Social Bond of Poetics" and is reprinted with permission.

"Terrible events and their relation to the universal trauma of subjectivity" was first published in *Analysis* in 2004 and is reprinted with permission.

"Fundamental fantasy as the axiom of the unconscious" was first published in *Journal for Lacanian Studies* in 2004 and is reprinted with permission.

"Introducing the symptom" was published in 2005 in the online journal *International Lacanian Review* and is reprinted with permission.

"The supposed-to know-to read-otherwise" was first published in *Psychoanalytical Notebooks* in 2012 and is reprinted with permission.

"Introducing the new symptoms" was first published in the *Bulletin of the New Lacanian School* in 2008 and is reprinted with permission.

"Ordinary psychosis" was published first in *Lacanian Ink* in 2008 and is reprinted with permission.

"Ordinary psychosis in the era of *sinthome* and semblant" first appeared in French translation in *Semblants et Sinthome*, published by Collection rue Huysmans in 2009, and is reprinted with permission.

"Knowledge" in Part 6: *Encore, encore* first appeared in 2013 in *Echoes: Lacanian Psychoanalysis* and is reprinted with permission.

"The Specificity of psychoanalysis relative to psychotherapy" was first published in *Ornicar? Digital* in 2002 and is reprinted with permission.

"Neurasthenic psychoanalysis and the Name of the Father" first appeared in the *NLS—Messager* in 2006 and is reprinted with permission.

"Countertransference is the symptom of the analyst" first appeared in *The Symptom* in 2006 and is reprinted with permission.

"There is no situation in the United States" was published in the *NLS—Messager* in 2005 and is reprinted with permission.

"The American plague" was first published in *Psychoanalytical Notebooks* in 2005 and is reprinted with permission.

A shorter version of "The crumbled building blocks of evidence-based medicine" appeared in *Focus*, an online journal of the Creighton Center for Health Policy and Ethics, in 2008 and is reprinted with permission. The full version of the paper first appeared in French in *la Lettre mensuelle* in 2009 and is reprinted with permission.

"Depression screening as the latest avatar of moralism in American public mental health" was published in *Re-Turn: A Journal of Lacanian Studies* in 2010 and is reprinted with permission.

Thomas Svolos is a psychoanalyst and psychiatrist, and a member of the New Lacanian School and the World Association of Psychoanalysis. He practices in Omaha, Nebraska, where he serves as Professor of Psychiatry at the Creighton University School of Medicine.

PREFACE

If psychoanalysis will survive in the twenty-first century, my wager is that it will be Lacanian psychoanalysis. Now, today, the survival of psychoanalysis is very much in question—the fall or decline or failure of psychoanalysis, especially in the United States, is accepted now as a fact, and issues associated with the historical trajectory of psycho-analysis, not just Lacanian, and not just in the United States (though that is a focus of mine) will be touched on throughout many of the chapters below. That said, even Jacques Lacan himself, at the peak of his influence in Europe, when psychoanalysis was a dominant discourse in Western European society, did not believe that psychoanalysis would triumph (in fact, as I will argue in this book, the desire of psychoanaly-sis to triumph in the United States was the very cause for its downfall), and merely posed questions about the possible survival of psychoanal-ysis, when future subjects, in the face of the growing anxieties in the world, would want, rather, something else (which he identified as reli-gion; Lacan, 2013, p. 64). That said, a statement of a wager on Lacanian psychoanalysis in the United States is perhaps an odd starting point for a discussion of psychoanalysis, given that Lacanian psychoanalysis, at least as a clinical practice, is only just barely established in the United States.

With this book, I hope to articulate why I would like to bet on a possible future for Lacan and psychoanalysis in the US. This argument is developed from different perspectives and in different forms—distinct, yet related paths of inquiry. Some of the papers, especially the first two chapters, will directly address this question through an examination of the reception of Lacan in the US and a review of some of the ways in which Lacanian psychoanalysis offers a unique response to some of the more pressing clinical, or subjective, demands of our time (Indeed, in that sense, chapter 1 functions also as a general introduction to the book itself, introducing and providing context for many of the concepts developed in greater detail in later chapters).

Much of the book, parts 3–5, stages this in a different way, through explications of specific ways Lacanian concepts have developed as a reading of the clinical—and indeed even broader psychic and social— phenomena of our moment in history. My belief is that now, in the twenty-first century, we are in a particular historical era, postmodernity, with its own social and economic and cultural logic, but also with features that might be identified in the psyche, or the subjective field. Psychosis—an increasing clinical phenomenon—and addiction— itself oft described as a veritable contemporary epidemic—are given longer treatment, but other chapters will address central concepts such as trauma, fantasy, the symptom, the body, and transference— approaching these concepts from the standpoint of this historical moment.

My development of these concepts is of course Lacanian, but I want to specify it further as Millerian, in that I have found the work of Jacques-Alain Miller the most vital entry point for an approach to Lacanian psychoanalysis and the reading of the texts of Lacan, in addition to which I want to acknowledge Miller's own contributions to psychoanalysis—say, in the development of concepts such as extimacy, generalized foreclosure, and the notion of ordinary psychosis. For me, as a young clinician, working in my clinical practice at a certain point in my formation as a psychoanalyst, my discovery of the literature associated with Miller and those working together with him in the Schools of the World Association of Psychoanalysis (WAP) was critical in orienting me in my practice, through their written work but more importantly by inspiring me to reach out to Miller and other Members of the Schools of the WAP. For, I assert that it is not through texts, but, most importantly, through the life of the School itself—that unique collectivity through which psychoanalysts gather in a process of what we might call continuous formation or the continuous reinvention of our practice in the face of the very changing nature of the psyche itself—that what we might ineptly call the "theory" and the very praxis of psychoanalysis can evolve to meet the demands of those who come to us with requests for help. It is to the work of and through exchanges with Miller and colleagues that I owe much of my inspiration, and these texts are an effort to bring Millerian psychoanalysis into the American psychoanalytic discourse. I want to add, though, that this is not a systemic or general introduction to Lacanian psychoanalysis in the Millerian orientation, however. Psychoanalysis is transmitted, well, above all through psychoanalysis itself, and supervision, and cartels, and our various encounters—Congresses, Study Days, and especially the Testimonies of the Pass—and not through texts. Texts, however, may serve as the entry point to psychoanalysis, especially for students, how one is introduced to psychoanalysis—but texts such as this are merely residues of that work, derogatorily referred to by Lacan with the neologistic *poubellication*, derived from a union of publication with *la poubelle*, the trash can (Lacan, 1978a).

Furthermore, the psychoanalytic experience of the twenty-first century will not be a general or universal experience, but what Lacanians refer to as singular. And, in a parallel manner, each of these texts themselves represents singular encounters with problems that I was struggling with, and an attempt to craft a response, in the context of my clinical work and in my collaboration with others in the School. This is something different from how academia or the universities works, or the American psychoanalytic institutions. And, this informs the very form of this book, which is not systemic in its presentation, in as much as psychoanalysis is not a system.

With that in mind, let me note that the book can approached in varied ways. One might elect to read it from beginning to end. That said, each of the chapters is freestanding in its own right, and not dependent on an other: each could be read on its own. Alternatively, one might even read this as a type of *Bildungsroman*, and read the chapters in absolute chronological order of production, to find the subtle shifts in perspective reflective of my own evolving formation as a psychoanalyst. For, it is fair to say, for a book composed over a long period of time, an earlier composed chapter may have an intrinsic value not necessarily reflective of how I might approach such a topic today (and, indeed, say, the chapter on fantasy, Chapter Five, is an effort to stretch an earlier, Freudian explanatory metaphor to cover a more contemporary phenomenon—an effort that stretches the nineteenth century metaphor past the breaking point—but in psychoanalysis, it is failure that really matters).

The context for these chapters, many delivered as papers in meetings, varies—and that is reflected in a varied character or style of the chapters themselves. With a few exceptions (perhaps mostly the section on *Seminar 20*), these were delivered to an audience of diverse background and familiarity with the work of Lacan. Thus, my hope is that while the book will most logically end up in the hands of a reader with some familiarity with Lacan, a dedicated general reader with some persistence will get something out of the reading experience (and, as way of guidance for a reader less familiar with Lacan—Chapter Seventeen might be a good starting point to situate the Lacanian orientation in contrast to other psychoanalytic currents or psychotherapies, before starting at the beginning).

The section on *Seminar 20* is an attempt to extract three critical concepts from Lacan's *Seminar 20*, a seminar that is well known in the Anglophone world due to its early translation and that is a critical seminar at the point of transition of Lacan into the final phase of his work and delineation of his separation or disjunction from aspects of Freud's work. I might also add that it is indeed the work of the later Lacan, say from *Seminar 20* forward, that has, in some ways, the most relevance to my particular claim for the place for Lacan in addressing the psyche of the twenty-first century, as will be developed in several chapters.

The book will close with two sections of reflections, delivered from the Lacanian psychoanalytic orientation. The first is a set of remarks on psychoanalysis itself—the distinction of psychoanalysis from other mental health therapies, the distinction of Lacan, and some comments on specific matters in psychoanalysis. The second of these sections is a series of interventions on the greater so-called mental health field, certain tendencies in medicine today and their impact on clinical practice, and the unique perspective on these issues brought by psychoanalysis.

PART I

INTRODUCTION

CHAPTER ONE

Twenty-first century psychoanalysis*

What is the future of psychoanalysis? What psychoanalysis might we have in the twenty-first century?

I would like to start my remarks with a reference to a way in which Lacan defined psychoanalysis in *Seminar 17*, as a discourse or a social bond that might exist between speaking beings. This definition places psychoanalysis within the realm of speech and language. And indeed it is with words that we practice.

This definition transforms a whole series of debates about the "identity" of the psychoanalyst. For example, I supervise residents in a psychiatric clinic. When they talk about their clinical work, from time to time, clearly the words spoken between patient and the resident psychiatrist can be described as something happening within the discourse of psychoanalysis. The psychoanalytic discourse can exist without either of those participating being aware of it, and, as discourse, it existed before Freud, who described it for the first time.

*"Twenty-first century psychoanalysis" was presented at the University of Chicago on May 19, 2013, at "Which way forward for psychoanalysis?"—a Conference sponsored by the Society for Psychoanalytic Inquiry.

On the flip side of that, just because a person has been named as psychoanalyst is no guarantee that the speech that that individual engages in with his or her patients should be understood as psychoanalysis. I can look in the mirror and think to myself, "I am an analyst," but as we learn from the first lessons of Lacan regarding the Imaginary, such recognition always carries within itself the potential for misrecognition. The attribution of identity is a separate matter from spoken discourse.

This basic approach to psychoanalysis has implications for the institutional questions that are often posed about psychoanalysis. In some psychoanalytic groups, it is Imaginary rules that define the process by which a person is named a psychoanalyst—numbers of sessions or supervisions, being present in a class (even one about neuroscience!), and so forth. The Schools of the World Association of Psychoanalysis, however, acknowledge Lacan's famous statement that the analyst authorizes himself or herself. Any two people may engage in spoken discourse that could be structured as psychoanalysis. But, while the speech of any two people may fall within the discourse of psychoanalysis, it is an ethical responsibility of the analyst to conduct himself or herself with those who come for help in such a way that is consistent with psychoanalytic discourse. The best that we can do as a School of psychoanalysts is listen to those who wish to join our School and determine if we can offer a guarantee, of course never certain, that we believe the potential member is able to sustain that responsibility.

And, further, in contrast to some groups who award their highest honor to the training or supervising analyst, which is largely a function of age and scholarly activity and clinical experience, in our Schools the greatest honor is awarded to those analysts of the School who are able to put something of their experience of psychoanalysis into words, to say something new about psychoanalysis, to extract something from their experience that can be transmitted to colleagues through their Testimonies and thus move our practice forward.

While we describe the practice of psychoanalysis itself as something we do as analysts with the spoken word, we must on the other hand recognize the significance of those developments in the last work of Lacan that reframe the practice as one of reading—a shift from listening to words to the reading of the text of the analysand, a reading of the unconscious, a reading of the symptom. The genius of Freud was to recognize that those seemingly meaningless phenomena of the patients that he saw—dreams, slips, symptoms, and so forth, are, in fact, a kind of text that is to be read by the analyst.

Freud, we must say, had a very particular way of reading these texts. They are always read through the perspective of the Oedipus complex. It is hard for us in our current moment to recognize the shock that this reading of Freud had on his patients and on society. Freud's formulations relating to sexuality, infantile sexuality, and the ways in which he believed this was structured through the Oedipal complex—some of which are accepted now as fact in many disciplines—were difficult for the society around Freud to accept.

From a clinical perspective, though, many of the first people who came in to see an analyst felt a dramatic relief, a significant diminution in the suffering of their symptoms as these symptoms were deciphered through Freud's reading. To me, there are two different issues in play here with Freud's work. First, there is the hypothesis that Freud introduces regarding the unconscious (and hypothesis is what it remains). In Lacan's classic formulation, the unconscious is that set of signifiers—the "treasure trove of signifiers," (2006a, p. 682) as he put it—that form the backdrop against which the unconscious formations such as dreams, symptoms, and slips may be decoded. In the work of Lacan of the 1950s, the truth to the unconscious formations is found in the unconscious (Let me add parenthetically, that in the later work of Lacan, more relevant today in practice, as further developed by Jacques-Alain Miller, in addition to this aspect of the unconscious as signifier—the transferential unconscious—there is also a Real unconscious, what we might describe as the libidinal dimension of the unconscious). The second issue with Freud relates to the Oedipal complex. It seems to me that Freud used this concept to master the unconscious, to organize it, to structure it. It was, we might say, his law of the unconscious, and in the first decades of psychoanalysis it was powerful in the elucidation of meaning and in its therapeutic efficacy as an interpretive key.

This did not last long however, and by the 1920s, Freud and his colleagues were already lamenting the loss of therapeutic efficacy of psychoanalysis and the persistence of symptoms in the patients of that era who came in for psychoanalysis, even after long periods of psychoanalysis. The Oedipal interpretations were no longer working. Where before, Oedipal interpretations were able to reduce or eliminate the symptom, now analysts struggled more and more with the fact of the resistance of symptoms to interpretation. The hermeneutic aspect of psychoanalysis lost its power; indeed, psychoanalysis is not a hermeneutics (or, better said, hermeneutics is only one facet of psychoanalysis).

We should note that the moment when patients begin to come into their sessions no longer complaining of meaningless symptoms or troubling dreams, but rather come in complaining of unresolved Oedipal wishes, is the moment where the Oedipal reading will, without a doubt, fail. The analyst must read otherwise. When the symptoms were meaningless, an Oedipal meaning was an Other reading. But, when the Oedipal hypothesis becomes part of the world (as a result of the very success of psychoanalysis itself), an analyst may no longer use it to read Otherwise, for it is already incorporated into the unconscious. The unconscious is not a stable phenomenon, the Jungian position, but articulates with the society in which people live. And society itself absorbed the first Freudian lessons.

We must fast forward all the way to the Lacan of the late 1960s and 1970s to reach a point where the residual repetitive effects of symptoms are no longer sign of the failure of psychoanalysis, but become the grounds for the basis of another way for psychoanalysis to work.

It is the moment of the 1960s and the advent of what we now call postmodernity that puts psychoanalysts in a situation where they are confronted with a different society and a change in the unconscious. Authority—paternal authority and the Name of the Father, a key concept for the Lacan of the 1950s—no longer organizes society—the "master narratives" in postmodernity are no longer trusted, as Lyotard described it (1984). As for postmodernity, I will add that Fred Jameson's work in this area (see especially Jameson 1991, 2015) is presupposed throughout.

I would characterize three responses of psychoanalysts to the 1960s. On the one hand, in the face of a clear decline in paternal authority, a weakening of authoritarian structures in many forms, there are movements in psychoanalysis that seek to reassert the power of the father, of Oedipus. This is what we might term a conservative, or, perhaps better yet, a fundamentalist response from psychoanalysis. In the face of a social change with regard to authority, there is a reaction to prop it back up.

There is a second response, which is that which celebrates the unconscious and the overthrow of authority. Rather than using Oedipus to tame the unconscious, the unconscious, in the form of the drive object, is placed at what Jacques-Alain Miller refers to as the zenith of society (Miller, 2005). Society is no longer organized around the Ideal, previously derived from the father, but by the drive object. This argument from psychoanalysis aligns well with Fred Jameson's comment regarding the colonization of the unconscious by capitalism in postmodernity, as these drives are often linked no longer to the old Freudian part objects, but rather ready made drive objects created by society, consumer objects. The drives are something to be identified with, and to pursue without any restriction, thus the development of addiction as the paradigmatic psychic state of our current moment. It is the proposal of Deleuze and Guattari against Oedipus and in praise of schizophrenia that is the most clearly articulated intellectual version of this response (1983).

Lacan's response marks the third response. Lacan responded to this moment of the 1960s in a way that remains relevant today. The act of reading the symptoms will no longer make the symptoms go away as it did a century ago. However, we must not simply celebrate the symptom, for it is certainly a source of pain and suffering and, to go back to the Freudian formulation, is linked to the death drive. I would say that the task is not to enjoy the symptom (as, say, with the Deleuze, or with the addictive push so present in our society today), as much as find a way to live with the symptom. How might we help our patients find a way to live with the symptom, with their particular symptom, their unique symptom, their partner, in a world where the old rules no longer hold sway?

Instead of Oedipus rex, a single Oedipal formulation that rules over all of psychic reality for everyone, I would state that we are now in a world of A-topos rex. There is no longer a general Aristotelian Topos or rule or argument for all, but a kind of lack of rule in which all must try to find their way.

The consequences of this in the clinic are immense. It is clear, for example, that a century ago, Freud did not know what to do with psychosis. He placed that psychiatric category outside the realm of psychoanalysis. Psychoanalysis has been grappling with that ever since. Lacan's first response to the question of psychosis in the 1950s was to apply his linguistic formulations of the time in such a way to define psychosis as what we might refer to as a refusal of Oedipus—foreclosure (1993; 2006a, pp. 445–488). However, in the 1970s, with his study of Joyce, we have a novel, and what will become quite useful, formulation of psychosis (2005). Namely, Lacan tackled the question of how

James Joyce used his very particular symptom, writing itself, as a way to prevent him from falling into psychosis, from an acute psychotic episode. The hypothesis is that Joyce used his symptom as a way to evade or avoid psychosis. At this moment we move from the symptom as only a source of suffering to the symptom as something that may provide the possibility of stabilization, of finding a place in the world.

In our current moment, with so many debates and discussions in the psychiatric clinic regarding the seemingly impossible task of diagnosis—debates over bipolar disorder, autism, and so forth are so common in the psychiatric world today as psychiatrists face a proliferating variety of clinical presentations—the psychoanalytic reformulation of these questions in terms of the particularity of the psychic structure for each patient offers a clinical path that meets the demands of the time.

Let me add that if, in the old Freudian world, it was only within the erogenous zones that one would find the drive or libido or jouissance, we must note that in the case of psychosis, language does not have the same mortifying effect on the body. Speaking beings in the world of psychosis experience drive or jouissance outside the paths as specified by Freud. And, in the final work of Lacan, we find a redefinition of the relationship of speech and language such that signifiers are identified as having both a significatory and also a libidinal value (Lacan, 1998a). Thus, even words, in particular words of love, have an aspect of the drive or jouissance.

And, it was not only psychosis that baffled Freud. Freud also struggled with the desire of women or the question of what Lacan refers to as sexuation. Freud's formulations on this matter are not completely without value, but seem so convoluted—the negative Oedipus complex and so forth. For Freud, the key to sexuation, to the difference between the male and female, was a matter of biology, of nature, of a difference in the genitals. For Lacan, the question here is not one of nature. For the speaking being, sexual identity, or gender identity, is a function of language or even logic, and not biology. Man and woman are signifiers. This is not to deny biological sexuality or genetics, but rather to point out that the fundamental fact of sexual identity for the speaking being is not a function of nature. We see this very clearly in transsexuality.

But, even further, there is nothing natural about sexuality itself for the speaking being. What is an instinct with an animal, in the encounter with language and society, becomes the drive for the speaking being. The drive is a function of the impact of language on the body. We see this the most in the case of trauma, which has nothing to do with terrible events as such, though these may have traumatic impacts of their own, but with the way in which language leaves a mark on the speaking being.

And, when it comes to the issue of sexuality as a relation to an other, to one's intimate partner, we find Lacan's most famous formulation on the matter, *il n'y a pas de rapport sexuel*, which we might translate as "there is no sexual relationship" or "there is no sexual harmony" or "there is no sexual ratio," indicates that for every speaking being, sexuality is something that is struggled with in one way or another. Thus, there is no natural or harmonious relation between two speaking beings with regards to sexuality. There is no sexual utopia. Speaking beings will often act as if there is (why not?), but that is only a fantasy. Note, however, that we also have love—what seems to me now one of the most fragile things in today's world—that allows us a way of bringing another speaking being into our lives. As analysts, we must assist those who come to us to find a way to struggle through the challenges of sexuality in the world today without rules.

In this brief survey, I've tried to point out the ways in which we see an unconscious that changes. It is even one that changes in response to psychoanalysis itself. Though it is not the unconscious of old, in the Lacanian world we still believe in the unconscious in whatever new forms it may take. Some analysts, however, have lost their faith, have lost this belief in the unconscious. They feel a need to turn to science to find the unconscious in the brain, in different parts of the brain or different neuronal structures. That side of the neuropsychoanalytic project, where analysts look to science for proof of their discipline, is a departure from psychoanalysis itself, as the unconscious does not exist as such. That is not to say, however, that scientists may not want to make use of psychoanalytic formulations. There is a lawless quality to science, and it will mine psychoanalytic texts for hypotheses that it may try to use in the advancement of scientific knowledge. But, that is a different matter.

I want to close with a very brief vignette that may elucidate something about interpretation in this post Oedipal psychoanalysis, where it is not our goal to put meaning to the analysand's words, to give an example of an analyst at work in this new world, to give an example of interpretation in a post-hermeneutic era. This is a story recounted in a documentary that includes an interview with Suzanne Hommel, who was in analysis with Lacan in 1974 (Miller, G., 2011). One piece of background to the story is vital, namely that Suzanne was a young girl when her country was occupied by the Nazis. In this documentary, she spoke of a session with Lacan when she was talking about a dream. She said to Lacan that she woke up every morning at five o'clock, adding that Gestapo came to get the Jews from their homes at five o'clock in the morning. She states that at that moment Lacan jumped up from his chair, walked over and gave her an extremely gentle caress on her cheek. She immediately understood this as the way in which Lacan had changed Gestapo to *geste à peau*, which in French means a gesture on the skin. She described it as tender, as an appeal to humanity. It did not take away her pain, but turned it into something different, something she could live with, and had an effect she remembers. She talks about how she can still feel the caress on her skin forty years later.

PART II

ON THE LEGACY OF JACQUES LACAN IN THE UNITED STATES

CHAPTER TWO

Jacques Lacan, reader*

L ike most Americans and most people of my generation, or those younger than me, I never met Lacan, never saw him, never heard him speak. When we talk about Lacan's Legacy, I think there is a gulf between the notion of a legacy among those who knew Lacan, who heard him, who went into analysis with him; and those without that personal connection. If, like me, you have no personal experience of the man, I think you will have missed something important about him, something associated with his corporeal existence. In Commandatuba, Jacques-Alain Miller (2005, p. 15) noted that whenever he hears an analysand of Lacan's relate one of Lacan's interpretations, it is always done in Lacan's tone of voice. That piece of the Real, which is present there in the voice—the voice in as much as the voice is something beyond the words spoken—the most memorable thing about the seminars of Lacan, according to Philippe Sollers (Sollers, 2011, p. 3)—is something that most Americans, and most young people, will never have access to. So, a certain gulf exists, a gulf in time and, for those of

---

*"Jacques Lacan, Reader" was first presented at Barnard College, Columbia University, on September 30, 2011, at a Paris-USA Lacan seminar on "Lacan's legacy."

us in the United States, a gulf in space between those who knew Lacan and those who did not know him.

That is not to say, however, that even for the young and the Americans, there is no legacy of Lacan's—only that it will not be based on the same relationship.

I first encountered the name Jacques Lacan in a classroom, at Duke University, in the middle of the 1980s, in a class on "Literary historiography" taught by Fred Jameson. For those born in this country, this would not be an unusual place to have first encountered Lacan—in academia, in a classroom. Lacan's initial reception in this country was among academics, which is, in fact, actually literally true. Lacan visited the United States on three occasions, almost always speaking to academic, not clinical, audiences. The most well known trip is certainly the trip to Baltimore, to a conference on "The languages of criticism and the sciences of man," the famous meeting on Structuralism, held at Johns Hopkins University in 1966. Much less well known is that Lacan did a tour of, I believe, six American universities earlier that year, on a trip organized by Roman Jakobson. Lacan spoke about it in his seminar on March 23, 1966 (Lacan, 1966). Finally, there was the famous set of trips in 1975, to Yale, Columbia, and MIT. And, it was the academics, largely, who first wrote about Lacan: the 1977 issue of *Yale French Studies* dedicated to Lacan was an important event in the reception of Lacan in the United States, published the same year as the first Lacan translations. There was little interest in Lacanian psychoanalysis among clinicians at that moment.

Some clinicians look upon this reception of Lacan in the United States in a negative light—a sign of failure in some way—and can be dismissive at times of the intellectual appreciation of Lacan's work. The story of psychoanalysis in the United States, and the issue of Lacan, must, however, be read carefully. Even before Lacan, Freud was quite skeptical of what Americans wanted to do with psychoanalysis. Indeed, while Freud felt a warm welcome by Americans, he was concerned about the impact of the United States on psychoanalysis itself. In *An Autobiographical Study*, Freud noted that "[Psychoanalysis] has not lost ground in America since our visit; it is extremely popular among the lay public and is recognized by a number of official psychiatrists as an important element in medical training. Unfortunately, however, it has suffered a great deal from being watered down" (1925d, p. 52). Lacan too was explicit in his statements linking the development of the, put simply, anti-Freudian ego psychology that came to dominate mid-century psychoanalysis to the wartime immigration of many psychoanalysts to the United States, writing in 1960 that:

> The academic restoration of this "autonomous ego" justified my view that a misunderstanding was involved in any attempt to strengthen the ego in a type of analysis that took as its criterion of "success" a successful adaptation to society—a phenomenon of mental abdication that was bound up with the ageing of the psychoanalytic group in the diaspora of the war, and the reduction of a distinguished practice to a label suitable to the "American way of life." (Lacan, 2006a, p. 685)

In a meeting of his seminar on June 23, 1965, Lacan (1965) took up the issue of psychoanalysis in the United States more explicitly, assigning the young Jacques-Alain Miller the task of discussing an article that had just appeared in *Diogenes* by the American psychoanalyst Norman Zinberg on "Psychoanalysis and the American Scene" (Zinberg, 1965). Zinberg, best known for his work on addiction, surveys the place of psychoanalysis in all domains of the United States: medical and therapeutic, intellectual, literary, cinematic, cultural, educational, even legal—and comes to the conclusion that psychoanalysis has been both an incredible success in the United States, working its way into all aspects of this country, and, at the same time, a failure, because of the way in which psychoanalysis has been absorbed into the United States. The failure relates to the way that psychoanalysis was "used" in the United States, as a way in which one might buy happiness through the experience of a psychoanalysis. For Zinberg, something particular changed about psychoanalysis in its rise in this country, becoming yet one more path by which, through the deployment of money, one might exercise an American citizen's right to the pursuit of happiness, something I will come back to.

I am struck by a very particular reading here of American psychoanalysis: namely, that it was the rich and the knaves—approaching the psychoanalyst not from a position of suffering or guilt, but as a technique that might better equip them to get what they want—that, in a sense, define this American perspective on psychoanalysis. We might say that the American psychoanalysts, the ego psychologists, created a practice for two groups of people who have what in an older language we might call "relative contraindications" to psychoanalysis. If Lacan has suggested we consider refusing a psychoanalysis to the rich and knaves, I think we could say that in America, psychoanalysis was distorted into a therapeutic practice precisely for the rich and knaves.

And, thus, from this perspective, we might see one dimension of what Lacan's Legacy is, with regard to the United States, namely in a stance that I would describe as a refusal or reluctance or skepticism with regard to the possibilities of psychoanalysis in the United States. Now, of course, there are Lacanian psychoanalysts in the United States, and we even have a fledgling group here. But, it is undoubtedly true that Lacanian psychoanalysis has not had the "success" here in the United States that it has had in France, Europe in general, Argentina, and other Latin countries. My hypothesis is that this "failure" of Lacanian psycho-analysis in the United States is indeed a legacy of Lacan's, a recognition of the true failure of the "success" of Freud and psychoanalysis in the United States. The very failure of Lacanian psychoanalysis to establish itself in a big way in the United States is, in fact, a necessary precondi-tion for any possible development of Lacanian psychoanalysis in the United States.

It is, however, against the backdrop of this successful failure of Lacanian psychoanalysis as a practice in the United States, that we can examine the success of Lacan in American academia and intellectual life. My thesis is that Lacan, in this regard, was a success in American academia because of the interest of academics in Lacan as what I will term here a Reader. What Lacan developed, in his praxis as a psycho-analyst, of Reading the unconscious, or, Reading a Symptom, a praxis informed not only by his work with his analysands but also by his study of psychoanalysis, and also of logic and philosophy and, of course, lin-guistics, was of the greatest interest to academics, whose own work might be constructed as a Reading (a criticism, or critical reading) of a text, some cultural product, or social formation. I believe that in the face of the failure in the clinical domain, there was a success of Lacan in the United States, a success based on the recognition by the American academics of Jacques Lacan, as a Reader.

I want to use this word Reader in a very particular way. It is not only related to books, though, after having read many of Lacan's seminars, it seems clear to me that Lacan had a passion for books—he talks often of looking for particular books, the pleasure of finding a book, different editions, and so forth. And, there is no doubt that he was "well-read." This surely is not unrelated to what I want to say. And the importance of linguistics for Lacan plays a role here as well, beginning with his earliest work, with the emphasis on the unconscious as "structured like a language;" an importance that carried through even to the end of his work, say, for example, in "l'Étourdit" (Lacan, 2001), with his emphasis on the role of equivocation in interpretation, to be found on the homophonic, grammatical, and logical planes. But, Reading, for Lacan, is not merely the use of linguistics for some deciphering operation, finding the meaning of a dream or a symptom in some hypothesized unconscious. There is a dimension of that in psychoanalysis, and indeed it is the fundamental aspect of Freudian psychoanalysis. But, as even Freud recognized in *The Interpretation of Dreams*, with regard to what he called the "navel of the dream," (Freud, 1999, p. 88) there is an "unreadable" dimension to the subject—be it identified as primary repression, or the Real as that which is impossible to speak (but which insists nonetheless), or the *hors-sens*, that which is meaningless. For Freud, as Jacques-Alain Miller put it in "Reading a symptom," this "unreadable" was a limit, an endpoint to the process of interpretation in the classical Freudian sense of producing meaning. But, this is not the case for the Lacanian process of Reading, which involves also a Reading of that which is beyond meaning, of what Miller calls the "signifying materiality" of the letter (in contrast, say, to a notion of listening to the semantic possibilities of a phoneme). In Miller's words:

> Interpretation as knowing how to read aims at reducing the symptom to its initial formula, i.e. the material encounter between a signifier and the body, the pure shock of language on the body. So, admittedly, to treat the symptom you have to pass through the shifting dialectic of desire, but you also have to rid yourself of the mirages of truth that this deciphering brings you and aim beyond, at the fixity of jouissance and the opacity of the real. (Miller, 2011, p. 152)

This is the very unique dimension of Lacan as a Reader, not only what he is often credited with, namely a rigorous formalization of the Freudian process of Reading through the incorporation of linguistics (an act of Reading, I might add, that is still critical in psychoanalysis today— every analysis proceeds through the shifting dimensions of meaning), but through the development of this second aspect of Reading, of Reading that which is impossible to read.

Lacan himself, in a session of his *Seminar 25* of December 20, 1977, drew attention to this dimension of reading, in rewriting transference as the subject-supposed-to know-to read-otherwise:

> There is surely writing in the unconscious, even if only because the dream, [...] the *lapsus* and even the *Witz* are defined by being readable. A dream, it happens, one doesn't know why, and then, *après-coup*, it reads itself; a *lapsus* also and everything that Freud said about *Witz* are truly notorious for being linked to this economy that is writing, an economy different from speech. The readable, knowledge consists in that. And in the end, it's not much. That which I said about the transference I timidly advanced as being the subject [...] supposed to know. And what does that mean? The supposed-to know-to read-otherwise. The otherwise in question, it is truly that which I write [...] in the following way: S(A). Otherwise, what does that mean? (Lacan, 1977b, session of December 20, 1977)

To put it quickly: the Freudian act of reading consisted in finding the Oedipal meaning in what to his analysands were the meaningless stuff of their lives—the dreams, symptoms, bungled actions, and so forth. For the Freudian analysand, their unconscious formations had no meaning, and Freud read them otherwise, as rich in Oedipal signification. For Lacan, to read Otherwise is to Read the very signifier of the lack in the Other, to be able to read something in a place where the Other lacks, where it fails to give meaning.

I think that the American academics were able to grasp something of this, but it seems clear to me that this Lacanian Reading would be rejected by the American clinical community. So much of American clinical practice has nothing to do with Reading. In the case of Cognitive-Behavioral Therapy, a model for many psychotherapies: a patient arrives, makes a complaint—"I have no energy"—and is immediately identified as "depressed." There is no attempt to find any meaning in the complaint of the sufferer, but merely to give a name to it, not a name specific to the person drawn from the very discourse of suffering, but a name that is drawn from a short list of names—depressed, obsessive-compulsive, panic disorder, and so forth. And, for each name, there is a script, which the CBT therapist will pull out, and speak. Many therapists are not only not readers, they are not even listeners, they are just speakers. The person suffering is spoken of—"you have depression"—and then spoken to—"replace your bad thoughts with this set of good thoughts." But, even currents in American psychoanalysis are not so different from that. Yes, the clinician may listen, and there will be a lot of exploration of meaning, but the meaning delivered is always at the level of meaning, and spoken from a script, be it the old Freudian script of the Oedipal Complex, or some newer one, say incorporating various pre-Oedipal sequences in the distribution of meaning to the discourse of the analysand.

This act of Reading that Lacan left us has value beyond the work in an individual psychoanalytic session. Let us look at the clinical field in a more general sense. Clearly, over the last decades, non-Lacanian clinicians throughout the mental health field have noted changes in the ways in which people present for care—new symptoms, different means of expressing suffering, or, to put it in an overt medical discourse, a shift in psychopathology. When one surveys the changes in the ways in which these clinicians approach this, we see a dramatic increase in the use of diagnoses such as bipolar disorder, attention-deficit disorder, and even autism and Asperger's Disease. Some critics have noted that these diagnoses are not being applied in the proper way, that these clinicians are sloppy or just wrong in their diagnoses. I think that it is instructive to compare this development in the non-Lacanian clinical field with a development in Lacanian psychoanalysis. In France, in the 1990s, the École de la Cause freudienne held a series of three meetings devoted to what were described as unusual cases, unclassifiable cases, and unusual psychoses that did not develop in the classical, Schreberian fashion. These meetings—case presentations and discussions—published in a series of three books—*Le Conciliabule d'Angers* (l'Instance de réflexion sur le mathème analytique, 2005a), *La Conversation d'Arcachon* (l'Instance de réflexion sur le mathème analytique, 1997), *La Psychose Ordinaire* (l'Instance de réflexion sur le mathème analytique, 2005b)—led to the proposition of a new concept in psychosis, that of Ordinary Psychosis. I think that it is instructive to compare these two different developments. I argue that the non-Lacanian clinicians were confronted with similar phenomena. They recognized what they were hearing in the words of their patients. We might even say that they could read it—that is, recognize something different—however, they then forgot about it when it came to developing a diagnostic approach and treatment. These clinicians were, to put it bluntly, bad readers—they read something in their work, but instead of recognizing it, they forgot about it and just applied their same old approach in a misapplication of diagnosis. Philippe Sollers (2011, p. 5) has developed a wonderful word in French for this—*oublire*—which, through the transposition of two letters—manages to evoke both *lire*, to read, and *oublier*, to forget. It is reading, without remembering. These clinicians are reading clinical phenomena, but forgetting it when it comes to diagnosis. The work of the École, in contrast, demonstrated a reading in which the psychoanalysts read and remembered what they saw, and created a new concept to facilitate their work. This is another way in which I think we must recognize a legacy of Lacan in reading—one broader than just what happens in an individual psychoanalysis.

To finish: It is important to specify again that "reading," as I am using the word, has nothing to do with books as such. That said, in a session, an analysand began with a reference to a children's book that she is very fond of. She made an offhand allusion to the book. She noted that this was a book she read often in her childhood and continues to read now as an adult. Whenever she wants to feel a certain way—about herself, about the world around her—she reads this book. She is not reading the book critically, but to obtain a particular affect, some jouissance. The book is an older book, not a book of our contemporary or hypermodern society. The book is not a so-called postmodern consumer object—a song, music video, or movie. It is not a *lathouse*, as Lacan put it in *Seminar XVII*, a scientifically constructed consumable object (2007, pp. 150–163). Yet, I believe that this analysand is using this traditional object in the precise way in which one uses a *lathouse*, as a means of access to a particular jouissance. She is not listening to her reading, but rather, forgetting what she reads, in the jouissance-effect itself of this repetitive reading, a type of what is now called addiction. Lacan linked this use of an object to a time in history, to when he was speaking in the 1960s. We might call this time a post-Oedipal world, a world no longer organized around a single Name of the Father, a social phenomenon noted by Lacan as far back as the 1930s in the text on Family Complexes—in his comments on the decline of the paternal *imago*. This historical development represents a significant shift in the Symbolic order for sure. Indeed: this was the very theme of one of the early twenty-first century Congresses of the World Association of Psychoanalysis: "The Symbolic order: No longer what it used to be, what consequences for the treatment?" So, yes, we can describe this as a temporal shift—a historical shift in the Symbolic order. But, I think we can also understand this post-Oedipal world, this shift, in a spatial way. Let us look at the very contracts under which societies organize themselves politically. In the United States, at the moment of the Revolution, the Founders threw off King George, disposed of his authority, both as a person and as a political concept. At least, they thought they were doing that: we must note the strong desire of a faction to have made Washington King and also the common designation for him as the father of the Country. But, it was certainly a break, the significance of which can be found in the Declaration of Independence: "We hold these truths to be self-evident, that all men are created equal, that they are endowed by their Creator with certain unalienable Rights, that among these are Life, Liberty, and the pursuit of Happiness." I think Jacques-Alain Miller was spot-on, in an interview (2003, p. 110), to link today's lifting of interdictions and the notion of a right to a drive and to one's own jouissance to the very American concept of the right of the pursuit of Happiness. It is important to note that this notion of Happiness has less to do with being happy—in our current sense of having a happy mood—than in the right to take advantage of one's property—one's belongings and, indeed we could say, one's body itself, a form of property. The original concept of these three rights can be found in John Locke's *Second Treatise on Government*, and were picked up by Samuel Adams, who, in the *Rights of the Colonists* wrote: "Among the natural rights of the Colonists are these: First, a right to life; Secondly, to liberty; Thirdly, to property; together with the right to support and defend them in the best manner they can" (Adams, 1906, p. 351). The Happiness of the Founders is not something along the lines that everyone has a right to be in a good mood, thus, but rather something along the lines of a right of enjoyment—of a thing, an object, a property, a body, which of course brings us very close to jouissance, which, as Lacan noted in the first few paragraphs of *Seminar 20*, has a close relationship to the law (1998a, pp. 1–4). It is in this sense that I would assert that this post-Oedipal world might also be understood spatially, it has appeared at different moments in different societies and countries in our world, and I would argue the United States has a special place in this regard.

Thus, my analysand, we could say, was enjoying her right to obtain a certain jouissance from this object, in a context in which, I would say, there is an affinity between a moment in history (postmodernity, or post-Oedipal society) and a place in history (the United States). And, again, I would state that while she was indeed doing this through reading the book, this is not the sense of reading that I have associated with Jacques Lacan. In the session in which the book was talked about, though, I attempted to read her reading of the book in this precise Lacanian manner. For, after getting her to accept at face value the significance of her use of this book, and after she spoke some about the place of this book in her life, and why she turns to the book now, I was able to make an interpretation—a reading of her reading—regarding her identification with one of the characters in the book, and the way in which—following a slip of the tongue she made with regard to her naming one of the other characters in the book—her stated attraction to men identified with that character in the book was seen as a screen for another more "true" desire for men identified with yet a different character in the book. This simple interpretation—a deployment of signifiers of the characters of the book in a series of ego and object identifications—had quite the shock effect on the analysand, in shifting her perspective on the configuration of her desire, leading her to read her desire for men otherwise, *autrement*, to take up again this formulation of Lacan's, in a way that was disconcerting to her. But, at the end of the session, she went back to the affect itself she associated with the book, the reason that she repetitively seeks the book out now many decades after she first read it, a piece of jouissance that remained after all the interpretive work earlier in the session, and she talked about her bodily experience when first reading that book as a very little girl, her identification with her mother at that precise moment, something she found difficult to put into words, but about which she said: "When I read this book now, I am there."

PART III

LACANIAN EXPLICATIONS

CHAPTER THREE

From the father to a father*

J acques Lacan made a very particular use of the "father" in his work in the 1950s, and I would like to start with this notion of the Name of the Father and the place of that in psychic structure. Let me first set the stage for this. Sigmund Freud, the founder of psychoanalysis, half a century before, proposed that psychoanalysis is only for patients who are neurotic, those who do not have psychosis. He felt that patients with psychosis directed their psychic energy inward—narcissistically— and not outward, in the direction of others—such as a psychoanalyst. Without such an investment of energy outwards to others such as an analyst, the interpretations or the interventions of an analyst could have no effect. This view about the psychoanalytic treatment of psychosis was called into question by a group of mostly British analysts working at the time of Lacan's interventions on psychosis in the 1950s. They were expanding psychoanalysis to work with psychotic patients and also with children, and indeed, we could hypothesize that their work with children—in this regard, especially their research into the observation

---

*"From the father to a father" was presented at Carlos Albizu Univeristy in Miami, Florida, on May 3, 2012.

of children with their mothers—inspired their hypotheses on psychosis, centered as they were on the bond between the mother and the child.

Lacan, on the other hand, was very cautious with regard to the treatment of psychosis, and he had reservations about the work described above. From a strictly clinical perspective, he felt that subjects with psychosis did not do so well when treated with an analysis in the same way as those not psychotic. Indeed, he also noted that when people with an unrecognized psychosis are taken into psychoanalysis, the treatment can trigger an acute psychosis—lead to the development of an acute psychotic break. He was also concerned about the ways in which his colleagues hypothesized the cause of psychosis as a function of the parenting, in particular the mothering, of the child who develops a psychosis. He studied psychosis intensely for a year in his third Seminar and set out his findings in a text whose title is worth examining in its own right: "On a question preliminary to any possible treatment of psychosis" (1993, 2006a). The title is very precise: there is no assured treatment of psychosis, only a possible treatment of psychosis. And, before that can even be considered, there is a question that must be addressed. That question has to do with the psychic structure of psychosis—how do we describe or understand the logic of the psyche in psychosis, in its distinction from neurosis? Lacan is very clear on this point—the issue is not one of the cause of psychosis, but rather the structure of the psyche in psychosis.

Lacan, at this point in his teaching (but, see the chapters below on Ordinary Psychosis for further elaboration and development) describes the psychotic structure most concisely as a foreclosure of the signifier of the Name of the Father. I want to describe in some detail this seemingly complex formulation, derived from his work on psychosis (1993; 2006a, pp. 445–488), but also from his yearlong seminar in 1957–1958 (Lacan, 1998b). For the neurotic, or non-psychotic, subject (and, in the Lacanian orientation, there is no normal as such—in the 1950s, Lacan conceptualized the psyche as either neurotic or psychotic in structure), we have the following situation: There is a child. This child is confronted with the desires of the mother (which we may understand specifically as the mother as a person in the most traditional nuclear family mother–father–child, or more generally as the primary caregiver or nurturer for the child, regardless of gender or age or family structure—more on this later). The mother, the caregiver, has words she uses in her care of the child and those words are clearly associated with desires on the part of the mother in relation to the child. What is it that motivates the existence of the mother in this situation, for the child, in particular her coming and going? She is here, and then she leaves. In a first moment, the child believes that it is he—he is the object that causes the desire of the mother. It is he that gives meaning to the existence (the very presence or absence) of the mother in the world.

Now, Lacan takes this idea a step further and describes it using terminology from linguistics, which are necessary to review to transmit the full impact of Lacan's work. Lacan adopted the linguistic terminology of the Swiss linguist Ferdinand de Saussure. Saussure proposed that words—what he called linguistic signs—are comprised of two parts: the signifier, the sound of the word—broken into units of sound known as phonemes; and, the signified, which is the meaning of the word. For most all words, however, the signifier and the signified, however, do not have a necessary relationship, but one that is unfixed and based on the use that the speaker makes of the words and the way that they are heard, in the context of other signifiers—it is a system of linguistics not based on any necessary relationship of the sound to meaning (and further, by extension, to the object referent of the sign) (1994). To take a very simple example, on hearing the signifier, the sound (and this has to do with speech and not the written word), "there," it is not clear if this refers to "there," as opposed to "here;" or, to "their," as the third person plural possessive pronoun; or, "they're," the contraction of "they are." The signifier does not obtain its meaning, its signification, without something else, namely other signifiers. Indeed, this is true for any sentence, which does not obtain its signification, its meaning, until the sentence is over. Let us take this simple example: "I love you," with no period yet to end the sentence: this seems to have a straightforward meaning. "'I love you,' she said to me." Adding another phrase changes the meaning of the utterance completely, regarding who is the lover and who is the beloved. "'I love you,' she said to me with a sarcastic grin [.]" Now, with the sentence over and the addition of the period and the completion of the sentence, the meaning changes completely.

If we go back to the situation with the child, another way of formulating this is that the child is surrounded by the signifiers of the Other, the signifiers, or the discourse, of the Mother (again: not the person, but the function). As a child, without a grasp of language, the child is trying to make sense of the signifiers, trying to identify the signification or the meaning that is associated with them. In other words, the child is surrounded by signifiers, but the signified is not present—sound without meaning. A desire from the mother, the Other, is articulated in those signifiers—clearly those around the child using this language, these words, want something form the child (for example: to eat, to be quiet, to smile, to sleep, and so forth). There is a stream of signifiers, the child is surrounded by them, but without any signification, meaning. For those who have learned a second language as an adult, it is perhaps not so difficult to put oneself in this situation. At this first moment, the child believes that he is the object of desire of the Mother—it is he who is the object of all the discourse, all this speech. Lacan will write this position with the small Greek letter phi, φ, which is a matheme, an abbreviation, for the phallus. Phallus here is not the penis, not the biological body part, but rather something that has something to do with desire—a sign of desire, let me simplify. As a small letter, it is what is called the Imaginary phallus. But, I think more importantly, as with the large and small letter "S" for signifier and signified, respectively, we might conceptualize this as the signified. The signified is missing, and the child places himself as object, as phallus, φ, in this place of the signified, to give signification to the discourse of the Mother.

As the child's notion of the world expands, in a later moment—in the traditional nuclear family with regard to the presence of siblings and a father—he becomes aware of the existence of others in the world that he sees as rivals—rival objects for the mother or, in this linguistic sense, rivals whose existence also gives meaning to the signifiers of the mother. This is what drives the whole range of emotions of aggression, hatred and jealousy at what Lacan calls the Imaginary level and plays out in the relation of child to child, and, at first, of child to father (there will be different aspects of the father articulated here—see the chapter below on Love for further development of this).

Then, another moment arises, with what we might call the realization and acceptance by the child of the Name of the Father. The Name of the Father is, in a sense, a different solution to the question of the desire of the mother or the meaning of the signifiers of the Other. The answer to the question of the desire of the mother is not the child, as the Imaginary phallus for the mother. Rather, it is a name that names and solves the question of the desire of the mother and, in doing so, at the same time, establishes a logic for the meaning of the signifiers in the Other. There is a particular aspect of the French phrase Name of the Father that is worth noting here. The phrase in French is *le Nom du Père*. This phrase literally translates to Name of the Father. But, it is a homonym for *le Non du Père*, which would be the "No" of the Father. This homonym captures another dimension of what is at stake. This would be the fact that the function of this Name of the Father is also to prohibit the child from taking the position as the Imaginary phallus, φ, for the mother. Or, more broadly, a certain jouissance—drive satisfaction, libidinal satisfaction—is prohibited—in other words, the child cannot take the position as the object of the desire of the Mother. The structuring or symbolizing function of language and the organization of speech and also of the body that are brought about by acceptance of the Name of the Father are corollary to a prohibition of certain libidinal satisfactions, one way of conceiving castration in the Lacanian orientation. This is the mortification of the body by language brought about through the entry in the Symbolic order organized by the Name of the Father.

The Name of the Father in this sense provides a structure of signification to the child, to the psyche, in such a way that provides the child with not only a name with which to signify the desire of the mother, but a possible signification for questions regarding sexual identification (or, the logical roles of male and female), the place of the Mother and Father, and the child's own sense of being, through an identification to or with the Name of the Father. The Name of the Father is not a concept out in the open, though, but one identified through its effects that can be found in the unconscious. In other words, meaning and signification are not provided through an image, through an object, or through a "person" of the father, but through a signifier—a name—that organizes the world for the child. The organization is not at an Imaginary level— with love and hate, and rivalry and jealousy regarding who is closer to or further from some ideal object, or to some Imaginary phallus, φ. Rather, the organization of the world is at a Symbolic level, where this structuring signifier provides meaning for the child regarding his being in the world. At this point, the child acquires the answer as to what organizes the desire of the Mother—it is the Phallus. But, this is not the Imaginary phallus, the child imagining that he is the image or object of what the mother wants. Rather, this is the Symbolic phallus, capital Greek phi, Φ, that the father has—that which is the key to the maternal desire. This is not something that the Father *is*, but something that the Father *has*, and which can be transmitted to the child (Lacan will later develop this concept as a transmission of a particular choice with regard to the otherwise overwhelming demand of the anonymous

Other [which we might further simplify as the "yes" of the Father to compliment the "no" of the earlier stage], which subjectifies, as it were, the Other and opens a path of subjectivity for the child [Miller, 2014b, p. 17]).

I would like to emphasize here that Lacan's concepts here revolve around a notion of the Name of the Father, and not a notion of the Father as such. It is the name, the signifier, that is at stake in this theory. Lacan makes a further specification regarding the Father that I would like to highlight—a distinction between two Fathers, as it were. The first Father is what he refers to as the Real Father. This is the Father as present at the second moment I stated above as the Imaginary, the moment of sibling rivalry. Well, the sibling is not the child's only rival for the mother, but the Father is as well—this Father as rival. This is the Father who the child will realize has the mother, the "Great Fucker," Lacan notes, the one who is castrating, in the sense that this is the Father who does not allow the child to be the Imaginary phallus for the mother (1992). Castration is the fact that we do not have the object of jouissance for the mother. At the end of this story, though, what is left of the Father, once the Name of the Father has been installed, what is left is what Lacan refers to as the Imaginary Father, the one who messed the kid up. Because, at the end of the story, the Father never lives up to this Real Father. The Father is not the Imaginary phallus for the mother either. He is fallen as well—fallen from some ideal. And that ideal, which is the origin of the superego, is something regarding which the child reproaches not only itself, but also the Father—for failing. And, for Lacan, this is linked to hatred, the most basic hatred, of myself and of this Imaginary Father, and further for God himself, for handling this all so badly, as Lacan puts it (the clinical consequences of this will be spelled out in the later chapters on "Knowledge" and "Love"). If you go back and read Freud's case histories, the neurotic subjects all complain of the failure of the Father.

I want to pause here, however, to digress for a second to develop something about foreclosure—and why Lacan felt that this theory was relevant in some ways with regard to the question of psychosis. Lacan's theory on psychosis—at least his theory from the 1950s—is that while the neurotic subject, the non-psychotic subject, accepts the Name of the Father and is given access to Phallic signification, the psychotic subject refuses, or forecloses, the Name of the Father and does not have access to Phallic signification. This foreclosure explains some of the clinical phenomena we see in psychosis. For example, the difficulties with regard to issues of meaning—"thought disorganization," to use the more psychiatric lexicon—are a function of the failure of the installation of the Name of the Father as a signifier to organize or structure the psyche of the psychotic subject through a certain fixation of the signifier to the signified. And, the problems with regard to body image and sexuality in psychosis can be linked to the fact that the Symbolic phallus is absent in psychosis. This is something that can be developed, but let me finally add that while psychoanalysis in its most classic form is indeed not indicated in psychosis, psychoanalysts in the Lacanian orientation have created ways to work with psychotic subjects (see the later chapters on Ordinary Psychosis).

I want to touch now on the words of my title here: from *the* father to *a* father. To do so, though, I want to begin by noting one thing. This concept of the Name of the Father does not have anything to do with the father as such, with the father as a person. Lacan was adamant on this point. Lacan is quite critical of those who look at certain traits of the parents as the key in the matter of psychic structure: mocking the concepts of his contemporaries who link the psyche to parenting, in a blame that passes "from the frustrating mother to the overfeeding mother" (2006a, p. 481) and also the "thundering father, the easy-going father, the all-powerful father, the humiliated father, the rigid father, the pathetic father, the stay-at-home father, and the father on the loose" (2006a, p. 482). Lacan states that "we should concern ourselves not only with the way the mother accommodates the father as a person, but also with the importance she attributes to his speech—in a work to his authority—in other words, with the place she reserves for the Name of the Father in the promotion of the law" (2006a, p. 482). I would emphasize here a point that is very important. For some people, the problems of the child can be identified in the parenting—the ways in which the parents raise the children or how they act as people. There were some very destructive ideas that resulted from this, such as the idea that in their actions, certain parents—mothers especially—cause the pathology or suffering of their children.

Lacan is introducing here a much more subtle point, one relating to the speech or discourse that surrounds the child. What is critical is not the persons of the parents involved, but rather the discourse (set of words) of the Other that surrounds the child and whether or not the child will choose to recognize or to refuse, to foreclose, a name within that discourse. This is why I would emphasize again this notion of the Name of the Father as key here, as opposed the Father as person, as a living being. For Lacan, language here is the key to the process. This move by Lacan shifts psychoanalysis away from Freud, with his emphasis on the relationship of the child to the actual mother and father as a person. For Lacan, I am arguing that the key has to do with language and the function of language on the body. Lacan adopted the vocabulary of mother and father in the 1950s to describe it, but already he is moving away from the person of mother and father to a new conceptualization. Indeed, my hypothesis regarding Freud is that Freud's theories that revolve around interactions between the father, mother, child, and sibling in a traditional, heterosexual parented, Western nuclear family, might well just be seen as a very special case of the general principles that Lacan articulates. An analogy here is the physics of Newton and Einstein. Newton's physics described well the motion of bodies that we can see in our world with our naked eyes. As physicists went on to discover and describe very big things like universes and very small things like atoms, they found Newton's rules did not apply. Einstein and other modern physicists created a new set of theories to describe everything from an atom to an apple to a universe. In other words, Freud's hypothesis is merely a special case in which the impact of language, the organization of discourse, and the prohibition of a certain jouissance are functionally completed by persons playing very particular and well-established roles within the family.

I would like to develop another historical point: it may also be that the Symbolic phallus—the signifier of the desire—was also more universally designated a century ago in Freud's time, at least in western countries, when the Church had a stronger hold on society, when there was perhaps a greater psychic uniformity than what we see in the twenty-first century, if I might put it like that. In this regard, I would say that in some ways, perhaps Freud represented a very particular special case or special instance of what Lacan developed. This is what I wanted to evoke in the title of this chapter—"From the father to a father." There was a moment, to a certain extent at least, though even here there is something of a myth, where the function of the father was more universal, and perhaps even more commonly personified in the person known himself as the father. That function of the Name of the Father, now, is much more particular, particular for each subject, and can be fulfilled in very unique and individual ways, ways not necessarily dependent on a particular person playing a particular role.

Indeed, within Lacan's own work, the terms shift: by the end of Lacan's work, "mother" and "father" are less present. The notion of the master signifier, the *sinthome*, and even the notion of the One will, in the final work of Lacan, come to hold aspects of the function of the Name of the Father, but these are points that I will develop in later chapters. It is critical here to note how Lacan's turn to linguistics and his reformulation of Freudian principles in the twentieth century sets the stage for the more radical reformulations of psychoanalysis for the final phase in his work.

I do want to make some comments though about this function of a father, as I have put it, and the family in our current moment in history—our postmodern world, or hypermodern world, as Giles Lipovetsky puts it (2005). Some of my comments here I have derived from a talk on "Hypermodern families" given by our French colleague Pierre-Gilles Guéguen (2011). First, speaking about the notion of the family, I would agree with Guéguen that the family, as a concept, is not a psychoanalytic concept as such. It is rather, a legal term, one regulated by social custom and laws, which of course vary from place to place and from time to time. Clearly, now, in the United States and elsewhere, we are in a situation where the traditional family—the so-called nuclear family with father, mother, child, and sibling—is no longer the only recognized type of family. We have single parent families, and families that are not heterosexual, but homosexual or with transexual partners. And, the production of the child in such families is not only through the sexual intercourse of a biological man or woman, but can involve hormonal manipulations and a variety of possibilities, in which the source of biological material (egg and sperm) and the body which brings the fertilized egg to the point of a newborn (in the case of surrogate mothers) may come from individuals that are different from the person or persons raising the child. All of these possibilities are brought into existence by science and these new reproductive practices, as well as the new organizational possibilities for a family structure, are obviously matters of great public and legal debate. Psychoanalysis is neither for nor against what is happening here. At least, not psychoanalysis in the Lacanian orientation in which I practice. There are other practices—within psychoanalysis and the greater psychotherapeutic world—that wish to intervene here. Certainly, there are psychoanalysts who argue that we need to preserve the old family structure. There are psychoanalysts who intervene to preserve families through couples counseling or to advocate for certain practices in parenting, practices that can be traced back to analysts within both the ego psychology and the object relations tradition. And, there are analysts and therapists who identify themselves as for one position or place as it may be defined legally—and promote a certain view on these political debates.

As I have tried to describe, Lacan took a very different approach even decades ago to these very contemporary questions. As I stated, the Father is not the father as a person, but the Name of the Father. The Mother may even be understood in many ways as the Other, as the discourse or language that surrounds the subject. In as much as in the first formulation, Lacan retains use of the name Father and Mother, even at that point in his work, they can be understood as functions, functions that could be played by any particular person. The discourse of the Mother, the words, surrounding the child could come from anyone—a heterosexual female, or Mother, or a hetero male, in the case of a male who is the primary care giver or nurturer for a child; or, it could come from a homosexual or transgendered parent; or another family member; or someone or some group of people employed to raise a child. The key is that the child is surrounded by words, or the discourse, of the Mother who cares for it. The Name of the Father has to do with a signifier promoted within that discourse. It need not necessarily come from the Father, the Church, or the State—but could be from somewhere else. Even in the new communities of today—social structures organized around identities, such as the gay rights movement, or particular modes of jouissance—there still exist master signifiers, or Names of the Father, that can have some structuring function. In *Where Has the Name of the Father Gone Today?*, Éric Laurent has carefully delineated how to pinpoint this father function (2006). For Lacanians, it matters not whether one is a biological male or biological female or some other biological category. And, for the child, the source of DNA is not necessarily an important question for the psychoanalyst. So, to talk about the Name of the Father today, for us, is not linked to any kind of return to a mythically ideal time of the father, or, say, to any particular religious or ideological tradition. A task in a psychoanalysis may be to identify what Names of the Father may be functioning in the discourse surrounding the child, as the discourses are structured in some way.

I want to quote from Laurent's text. He states that:

> beyond tradition, beyond the world of the religious or the traditionalists, who have their own name of the father, which protects them from anxiety, we all have to invent some kind of father, some kind of guarantee, for ourselves: with the transmission of the particular sin of our father. He never transmitted an ideal to us. He never transmitted the fact to us that an existence could be inscribed in the function, in the function at the level [points to the "for-all" formula on the board] $\forall x$ —that could be for all—we have to invent something for ourselves. Starting from existence, starting from the fact that anybody could be our father, in a certain sense, he was "anybody," but particularized. (2006, p. 83)

I believe this is the task that we confront in analysis with regard to the question of the father. Can we help those who come to see us for help to construct those signifiers—the names of the father—that have had a significatory—and significant—function in their lives? For, in psychoanalysis, the meaning of suffering is not pre-determined, as it is in other psychotherapies. The meaning is constructed by the patient, by the analyst, during the psychoanalytic experience. At the end of an analysis, the patient may indeed—in taking responsibility for his destiny through a decided desire—drop his reproach against the Imaginary Father who messed him up. He can, as Lacan said, do without him—he can also construct a name of the father that he can make use of.

CHAPTER FOUR

Terrible events and their relation to the universal trauma of subjectivity*

In clinical discussion, I often here about trauma, about how someone has suffered through a traumatic childhood or upbringing, or how certain traumatic things have happened to someone as an adult. This trauma is often divided, nicely segregated, into sexual, physical, or psychological trauma, and the categorizations now include both positive and negative manifestations of trauma, both abuse and neglect. The subjective category advanced most often as the correlate of this is the victim—the person is a victim of trauma. And, finally, the therapeutic work is often described as a processing, or working-through, of what to that point has been unresolved trauma. The processing can take the form of remembering the traumatic event, the therapist bearing witness to it, and reformulating material that is remembered.

This theoretical orientation is often seen as in conflict with psychoanalysis. Freud, identified as one of the early discoverers of the importance of trauma, is also seen, through his rejection of the Seduction

---

*"Terrible events and their relation to the universal trauma of subjectivity" was presented at a "Special workshop on trauma and terror" sponsored by Creighton University in Omaha, Nebraska, on February 1, 2002.

Theory, as an opponent of those who work within this trauma studies orientation. This is interesting to me, for the very first thing that strikes me about trauma work, at least how I sketched it above, is its great similarity to the work of the early Freud, and even some resemblance to psychoanalysis proper. There are differences as well.

But before getting into that, let us begin with a look at one of the founding texts of the Trauma Studies movement, *Trauma and Recovery*, by Judith Herman (1992). Let us look, in particular, to Herman's description of Freud's work. Herman starts with an appreciative evaluation of Freud's work from the mid 1890s, particularly the thesis advanced in "The aetiology of hysteria".

The critical clinical issue that Freud addressed in that essay was not trauma, but hysteria. Patients with hysteria were for the most part women, though Freud argued, against considerable resistance from his peers, for the existence of male hysteria, with a range of medical, neurological, and psychiatric symptoms that were, at the time, felt to be resistant to medicine's efforts at both understanding them and treating them. Freud, in contrast to those who prescribed a variety of active treatments—physical therapies, massage, spa time, rest cures, electrical treatments, and so on—listened to his hysteric patients. He asked them to speak and allowed them to talk to him and respected that which they told him. After listening to a series of these cases, Freud drew a number of conclusions, which he presented before his colleagues in a talk titled "The aetiology of hysteria." In it, he wrote that:

> [...] the symptoms of hysteria (apart from the stigmata) are determined by certain experiences of the patient's which have operated in a traumatic fashion and which are being reproduced in his psychical life in the form of mnemic symbols. What we have to do is to apply Breuer's method—or the one which is essentially the same—so as to lead the patient's attention back from his symptom to the scene in which and through which that symptom arose; and, having thus located the scene, we remove the symptom by bringing about, during the reproduction of the traumatic scene, a subsequent correction of the psychical course of events which took place at the time. (Freud, 1896c, pp. 192–193)

Furthermore, not only do hysterical symptoms result from traumatic experiences, but, he continues, "no hysterical symptom can arise from a real [this is, current] experience alone, but that in every case the memory of earlier experiences awakened in association to it plays a part in causing the symptom" (Freud, 1896c, p. 197). And, finally, he concluded, "at the bottom of every case of hysteria there are one or more occurrences of premature sexual experience, occurrences which belong to the earliest years of childhood, but which can be reproduced though the work of psycho-analysis in spite of the intervening decades" (Freud, 1896c, p. 203). These premature sexual experiences included outright sexual assaults from strangers, assaults or seductions from parents or nurses or others, and sexual encounters of children with one another.

This description of Freud, from well over a century ago, is fresh, vivid, evocative, and is not unfamiliar—so close it is to many of the standard notions in contemporary work on the psychological treatment of trauma disorders. Herman speaks very favorably of this work: this is Freud as the brave explorer, as she sees it (1992, pp. 10–14). And the description of such a thesis as brave is indeed fitting, as Freud's presentation of this paper in 1896 to the Vienna Society for Psychiatry and Neurology was received extremely poorly. Freud himself acknowledges such, even considerably later in his career after his positive reputation was well established, and what written records that exist of this presentation apparently support this representation (1985, pp. 184–185).

The conclusion to be drawn here is that, in spite of the desire of certain orientations—particularly within trauma studies—within the mental health field to distance themselves from Freud and psychoanalysis—and shortly I will specifically reference some of Herman's critique of Freud—, the very terms of the work they do are directly drawn from Freud's work, a debt that often goes unacknowledged. All too frequently, we see, in an effort of those who have followed Freud, such a felt need to distance themselves from him, that the overwhelming debt to him for his contributions is not recognized.

Freud, as is well known, then went ahead and abandoned this thesis—which is commonly known as the Seduction Theory, and replaced it with a range of other explanations. The most common version of the story is that Freud dropped the Seduction Theory and replaced it with the Oedipus complex. No longer did a terrible, but contingent, external experience define the origins of the particular neurotic symptomatology he confronted in the consulting room. Rather, a certain universal psychic structure—an internal, universal, and necessary feature of the human psychic structure—was the critical key in his work. In Herman's view of the story, the negative response Freud received from his Vienna colleagues and the threat of the loss of professional business led him to abandon this theory. As she sees it, Freud recognized that, given the common frequency of neurosis in the population, the incidence of child molestation in one form or another must be equally large, because that was the only cause of neurosis. She states this disturbed him and his sensibility as a member of the very Viennese social class has was seeing in consultation. Furthermore, this led him to develop significant worries regarding his practice. In the face of this conclusion, he backed down, and dropped this thesis. To her, this should be understood as a "recantation" on Freud's part and a "breach of alliance" between Freud and his patients. Herman seems to blame this in part on Freud and in part on his society, which constricted his ability to pursue certain lines of inquiry (1992, pp. 13–20).

The major evidence she advances here is the September 21, 1897, letter to Wilhelm Fliess. A close reading of the letter, however, reveals a slightly different story from that advanced by Herman. Freud writes:

> So I will begin historically where the reasons for my disbelief [in the Seduction Theory] come from. The continual disappointment in my efforts to bring a single analysis to a real conclusion; the running away of people who for a period of time had been most gripped [by analysis]; the absence of the complete successes on which I had counted; the possibility of explaining to myself the partial successes in other ways, in the usual fashion—this was the first group. Then the surprise that in all cases, the father, not excluding my own, had to be accused of being perverse—the realization of the unexpected frequency of hysteria, with precisely the same conditions prevailing in each, whereas surely such widespread perversions against children are not very probable. The [incidence] of perversion would have to be immeasurably more frequent than the [resulting] hysteria because the illness, after all, occurs only where there has been an accumulation of events and there is a contributory factor that weakens the defense. Then, third, the certain insight that there are no indications of reality in the unconscious, so that one cannot distinguish between truth and fiction that has been cathected with affect. Fourth, the consideration that in the most deep-reaching psychosis the unconscious memory does not break through, so that the secret of childhood experiences is not disclosed even in the most confused delirium. (1985, pp. 264–265)

The first thing to note here is that Herman bases her reading of this critical letter on the expurgated edition of Freud's letters to Fliess edited by Marie Bonaparte, Anna Freud, and Ernst Kris and published in 1954. The version of the letter in this edition does not include the statement I quoted above from the Masson edition of 1985 regarding Freud's own self-analysis (Freud, 1954, pp. 215–216). The logic Freud gives is that if his description of the logically necessary character of incestuous trauma in the aetiological cause of the neurosis is right, then he himself must have been abused by his father—which he felt was not true. Furthermore, based on his contemporary theories of etiological causation of different pathologies, he felt it could not be true—the resultant effect would be a different distribution of pathology. Finally, it should be noted that while Freud abandoned that theory of sexual trauma as the necessary cause of hysteria and neurosis, he by no means disregarded stories of sexual trauma or denied that they could have effects on an individual. The case of the Rat Man here is notable. In this, perhaps most complete of all of Freud's case histories, there are several episodes of sexual activity forced onto the Rat Man as a child and their impact is discussed by Freud (Freud, 1909d).

A much more convincing, and, in some sense more highly critical, interpretation of this turn away from the Seduction Theory is offered by Mikkel Borch-Jacobsen (1996). Following a very close reading of Freud's letters and published material from the 1890s, Borch-Jacobsen concluded that Freud abandoned the Seduction Theory when he realized that the true source for the various stories of abuse and molestation was suggestion by Freud himself. Noting the gradual shift in the nature of the stories and the agent of the molestation over a period of several years and the ways in which that reflected Freud's changing theories, and several somewhat elliptical comments by Freud himself on the suggestive power of the particular therapeutic approach he was using, Borch-Jacobsen asserts that Freud dropped the theory when he realized his patients were simply following—in the suggestible way of hysterics—the various explanatory schemata he himself was introducing. Furthermore, Borch-Jacobsen argues that as soon as he dropped the Seduction Theory, Freud stopped hearing these various stories of abuse. One of the most striking aspects of this whole period of suggestion is that, for some time, as documented by his own readings, Freud was interested in witch hunts and stories of diabolic activity of one sort or another, stories which were soon to be repeated in the very clinical material he was gathering. These stories of satanic and ritual abuse bear an uncanny resemblance to the recent examples of such stories. At the time, even Fliess accused Freud of implanting material in his patient's minds. Freud went on to reject these theories, describing his work of the time as suggestive therapy, and separate from psychoanalysis.

Thus, psychoanalysis originated with this shift of Freud away from the Seduction Theory and a shift away from suggestion as a mode of treatment. Keep in mind that suggestion was and remains an immensely powerful form of treatment. In its late nineteenth century modality in the form of hypnotism, it caused all sorts of shifts in symptoms, behaviors, and so forth. And today, still, it remains as the theoretical foundation of many of the psychotherapies. In as much as cognitive therapy "works," it works by the therapist suggesting to the patient that he is wrong, for example, to feel depressed and that he ought to replace his current outlook on himself and the world with a different one. And even medications themselves exert tremendous effects through suggestion. The so-called placebo effect—that, for example, the majority of people given a sugar pill in randomized controlled studies will be "cured" of their depression—is merely another manifestation (The current state of suggestive therapies will be developed more fully in the final two sections).

Like many of these contemporary examples of suggestive therapy that exert their suggestive effects in a way the practitioner is unaware of—most psychiatrists, in prescribing medications, do not think that a significant part of the benefit of their prescribing is due to their suggestive powers—, Freud was unaware of his suggestive effects, which extended not just to therapeutic effects—effects that were short-lived, as we see from Freud's own comments—but also to the very historical material his patients presented with. Freud should be given credit, however, for recognizing this effect he had on his patients and for modifying his theories and technique in the creation of psychoanalysis.

But what of these modifications? I think that they must be understood in several different dimensions. The first has to do with a modification in his understanding of the unconscious itself. My sense is that for the early Freud, the unconscious acted as something of a recording device, simply inscribing the material that was presented to it. Thus, with the Freud of the Seduction Theory, when Freud encountered unconscious material presenting stories of seduction, he assumed that these were simply recordings or representations of what had happened previously. And, in a sense, they were, except that they were representations put into the unconscious only recently by Freud. Thus, the universal presence of these stories led Freud to doubt their universal truth, and in his future work they appeared as contingent, accidental facts, and not in every case. The possibility that they could exist in the unconscious—could appear in unconscious formations—led Freud to the belief that the unconscious was not simply inscribing reality, various perceptions experienced by the patients, but could also be inscribing what, in the letter quoted above, he describes as "fiction cathected with affect." Thus, the unconscious content, the material elicited through psychoanalysis, is not a simple audio-visual representation, as it were, of the history of the patient, but includes what most would tend to describe as subjective, or internally produced, content, though content heavily invested. This is what will later turn out to be a critical dimension of fantasy.

A second modification relates to his theory of sexuality, or what we might term his invention of a theory of sexuality in the *Three Essays on the Theory of Sexuality* (Freud, 1905d). In this signal contribution, which introduces the Drive (poorly translated as Instinct, as in Sexual Instinct, in the Strachey translations), he described the presence of sexual drives during infancy (a revolutionary assertion at the time), and surveys a range of sexual practices from infancy through puberty. Freud laid out a description of the critical functions that dominate, as it were, that very internally produced material that operates so strongly on the child. Inasmuch as the unconscious now had to take into account a full range of internally produced excitations—to turn to Freud's language from his first forays into psychology—this work defined the varied nature of those excitations. Freud advances these theories without any recourse to his notion of the unconscious or to Oedipus, which is not mentioned once in the text in his original 1905 edition, and only in a few footnotes in later editions. I mention this because the typical reproach to Freud is that he abandoned the Seduction Theory for the Oedipus complex, suggesting that he immediately substituted a necessary attraction to the father for a necessary abuse from the father. While it is true that Freud first writes of the Oedipus complex shortly after the turn away from the Seduction Theory, in a letter of October 15, 1897, to Fliess, it makes minor appearances over the next two decades only to assume a greater prominence in his work in the 1920s (1985, p. 272).

This is very significant, for the findings of Freud on infantile sexuality are, in the most general sense, now fairly well accepted, and that is largely the most critical shift that occurred with the shift from the

Seduction Theory. Freud's recognition that there is, to use this poor terminology again, "internally driven" sexual activity on the part of the child, and that this is the critical factor in psychoanalysis, was revolutionary and is now widely recognized, uncontroversial, and also rarely attributed to Freud.

All of this is not to say that the turn to the Oedipal complex did not occur, and that Freud did not in many ways—particularly later in his work—replace a theory of trauma as the universal and necessary precondition for neurosis with one in which the Oedipal complex, as a universal and necessary intra-psychic structure or developmental stage, played the same role. In fact: he certainly did, and—contrasting Freudianism as such an Oedipally bound theory with psychoanalysis proper—I have written elsewhere about the deleterious effects of this on psychoanalytic theory and practice (2001; Chapter Seventeen). My point is rather that Freud vacillated between an adherence to psychoanalysis—a theory and praxis based on a subject's contingent, not necessary, encounter with the Drive and with the Outside World, what Lacan will formulate as the Other—and adherence to Oedipus, which served some role for him.

In any case, it is clear that by the turn of the century, while Freud did in fact continue to hear stories of abuse and seduction, these stories were not universal and did not have any absolute explanatory role. But Freud returned to trauma, again, two decades later, in the aftermath of World War I, when he and others were forced to confront what was then termed traumatic neurosis, what is now described by many as Post-Traumatic Stress Disorder.

His first writings on this center around the issue of appropriate treatment for traumatic neurosis. Psychoanalysts exerted a strong presence in directing psychological treatments—within the military psychiatry departments—of traumatic neurosis. One of the major forms of treatment at the time was a form of electrical therapy, where the traumatized patient, in a syndrome that included paralysis of the extremities, was treated with shocks to affected extremities applied without any anesthesia and which seemed to work by making the treatment worse than the condition it treated (Freud, 1955c). Psychoanalysis presented the wartime psychiatrists with an alternative, one which seemed more successful and without the painful and what would be now termed inhumane aspects of the electrical treatments. The wartime neuroses, however, provided the analysts with a certain set of theoretical questions, for it seemed that though the treatments were successful, they presented a challenge to the very theory on which they were based (Freud, 1919d). For in the war neuroses, there was no obvious sexual drive issue at stake, the eruptions of the drive, particularly in childhood, being seen as the greatest threat to the stability of the organism and the cause for repression and symptom formation. Freud's initial response to the matter, the elaboration of a series of distinctions between the peaceful ego and the war ego, were unsatisfactory.

Freud takes the issue up again in what is certainly his most significant later theoretical formulation, *Beyond the Pleasure Principle* (Freud, 1920g). Freud's exposition here is worth reviewing at some length. He starts with several general comments about the traumatic neuroses: the need to distinguish them from organic lesions, as results of some type of mechanical injury (e.g., the theory of concussion); their similarity in symptomatic presentation to hysteria, though with a greater severity of pathology than most cases; and, the great suffering that results from them. He then goes on to elaborate three critical features, not obvious from simple enumerations of the syndromic presentation, that have a significant role in his theorization of traumatic neurosis. The first is that the element of fright or surprise plays a critical role in developing a traumatic neurosis. In other words, while an individual may experience many different terrible things, it is the one that is unexpected that will lead to the neurosis. Or, alternatively, many individuals might experience the same event, but those that are surprised by it, did not expect it, will subsequently develop the neurosis. In more Lacanian terms, we might say that trauma is a function of contingency (as opposed to necessity). The second observation is that if an individual suffers a wound or injury at the time of the traumatic event, it is less likely that he will not go on to develop a neurosis. The final observation comes from analysis, namely that an individual with a traumatic neurosis will, in his dreams, return to the traumatic event. This surprised Freud, as it ran counter to the central theory of dream formation, that dreams enact the fulfillment of a wish, indicating to him that dreams can function outside of the pleasure principle.

Freud then proceeds—after enumerating other observations of the repetition of non-pleasurable actions—to offer a complete reformulation of his earlier metapsychological theories. He starts with a new psychic model. In it, consciousness is described as a border between the inside and the outside, and is thus made up of perceptions (from the outside) and sensations (of the inside). In response to excitation, the organism evolves either consciousness of the excitation (the perception or sensation) or a memory trace (recall the discussion above), which cannot be perceived in consciousness, which must be available to observe new excitations, and is thus deposited in a layer right next to consciousness. In consciousness, the excitatory trace of the perception or sensation expires in the very process of becoming conscious, but when deposited it somehow remains with the memory trace.

Freud relates this to a very simple model of the body itself as a vesicle, with consciousness located outside on the skin, or outer surface, and leans on biology to note that the embryological origin of our central nervous system is itself in the ectoderm, the outermost layer of embryological tissue. He states that consciousness, because of constant excitatory impulses, becomes hardened, so as to make it resistant to potentially harmful impulses. In a sense, the outer layer becomes dead, much like the skin is dead, so as to protect the inner layers, which only receive modest levels of energy as filtered through the dead layers. In fact, protection against stimuli is almost more important than reception of stimuli. There is no dead shield, however, to protect from the sensations coming from within. Usually, consciousness is able to deal with them, but if they are too strong, and this is significant, they are projected outside, so that the shield can be mobilized against them.

With this model in place, Freud goes on to describe trauma as that which breaks through the protective shield. This break of the shield results in an inflow of excitatory impulse excessive to the system. The pleasure principle, which ordinarily reigns over the system in gradually discharging excess energy through binding the energy and motor action, is unable to function properly. The amount of energy let into the organism, and the continued inflow of energy into the system through the breach in the shield, require the organism to direct all of its energy into the binding of energy let into the system. Freud continues to assert that the greater the amount of existing bound energy within the system (which we could roughly formulate as the extent to which the system has previously symbolized, to use the Lacanian term, earlier perceptions and sensations), the greater the system's ability to further bind the energy let in through the breach. In other words, the greater the development of symbolization already existent within the organism (say, the typical adult versus the infant), the greater facility the organism will have in binding the break. Furthermore, he notes that if the system has a higher level of anxiety, it is somehow operating at a higher level of cathexis, and will thus more effectively bind the breach and be more resistant to a breach in the first place.

Freud is now in a position to revisit the traumatic dreams, whose function he now reformulates as that of stimulus binding. They function to bind the impulses that the system was unable to bind when first confronted with them, and some of this binding process works through the creation of anxiety, whose very absence was a partial cause of the breach in the system at the time of the traumatic event. This process of stimulus binding must take place before the impulse can occupy a so-called normal place within the psychic apparatus and thus function according to the pleasure principle. The implications of this are radical, namely that dreams themselves, independent of their function of wish fulfillment and sleep maintenance (diverting drive impulses that might disturb sleep), once had, and still at times in the individual continue to have, a completely different function, that of stimulus binding.

We can now put this revised topographical model to work and redefine trauma in relation to it. We can start by noting that trauma can be understood as a breach in the structure in the ego. Something is experienced—either a sensation or a perception—that is too much for the ego to handle, so to speak. This something is thus not either registered in consciousness, and thus affectively extinguished, or properly registered in a memory trace, and put into memory. It has such an excessive quantity of energy or affect associated with it that the energy travels through the psychic system unbound, as Freud would say. Now, this event could be either a sensation, or an internal excitation; or it could be a perception, an external excitation.

The first point I wish to advance following from this construct of Freud is that the Drive—specifically the Sexual Drive and its various manifestations—is, in fact, experienced as a universal trauma for all neurotics. The encounter of the subject with the Drive—with the subject's physiological and psychological immaturity constitutive of our species itself, this altricial state universal for all humans—ensures that the Drive impulses are experienced as an excitement beyond the ability of the system to register consciously or to bind into memory. The sexual Drive in this sense can only be experienced as traumatic and it is a universal trauma. And, as Freud noted above regarding the projection of excessive energy outside the organism, the Drives themselves have what Lacan will develop as a special topological status and are experienced as coming from outside the body, allo-erotic, such as in Lacan's reading of the case of Little Hans and his experience of his *wiwimacher* (Lacan, 1994).

I would, however, add that though the Drive is internally generated, as it were, to return to Freud's schema here, one key to understanding it is the way in which it is given a partial symbolization, largely through the role of the Other. Thus, for a child, for instance, a certain drive impulse is experienced, but it is the Other, in the form of the parents, that might give a name to that, in the ways in which the drive behavior is linked to a part of the body that is then named by a parent. The Other is also responsible for a certain (Symbolic) valuation given to the Drive, through the various demands and prohibitions made concerning certain behaviors associated with different drive impulses. The issue is not just that the Drive impulses are completely overwhelming. It is rather that with the subject's experience of them, an entire process of binding—what Lacan would call symbolization—is put into place. Freud noted this in the *Three Essays* where he links the epistemophilic drive—the Instinct for Knowledge—very closely to the development of the sexual drives (Freud, 1905d, pp. 194–197). Much of what is experienced is, in fact symbolized, partly through direct statements from the Other, partly through symbolizations gathered in passing, but the process is never complete, is always only partial and unsatisfactory. Freud goes on to say that there are two particular aspects of sexuality that are universally incomplete: "the fertilizing role of semen and the existence of the female sexual orifice—the same elements, incidentally, in which the infantile organization is itself undeveloped" (Freud, 1905d, p. 197). Thus, we see here a Drive experience that is partially symbolized, but always there is a remainder, an unsymbolized leftover, that represents this unbound energy, following from Freud's metaphor. We can propose that the unbound, or unsymbolized, remainder is what Lacan will proceed to describe as the Real as remainder, a certain leftover of the symbolization process.

There is one other aspect of this process worth noting, which is the very critical role of the Symbolic Other just at the moment of the eruptions of the Drive and the wealth of symbolization occurring in response to it. For, in fact, clinical experience demonstrates that these periods of intense Drive formation subsequently become linked to the developing desire of the subject, which makes logical sense in that desire itself is organized around the very remainder of the Real that is not subject to symbolization. And, furthermore, for the early Lacan, in the classical phase of his teaching, desire itself is structured around the way in which the Name of the Father, or what will become the Paternal Metaphor, organizes the desire of the child. The child initially is in a state of pure Drive: he experiences the Drive directly, without mediation through symbolization or binding. This experience has to be understood as not just unbound, but also without boundaries, in the sense that the Child has no sense of ego, or self, as distinct from the outer world, or the Other. This is captured as well in the initial Mother–Child bond, where there is no distance between the two. In this phase, the Child experiences a boundless jouissance, a certain Drive oriented relationship to his body and the body of the Mother. Well, language, through the agency of the Father, comes to disrupt this. The first stage, alienation, the "No!" of the Father, alienates and forms the ego, as separate from the mother and begins a process of naming and symbolization of the Other now delineated. Once distinguished from her, the Child becomes aware of the Mother, as a subject in her own right, and thus as subject to language, with desires of her own, things she wants that seem to go beyond what she says to the Child. This void the Child becomes increasingly aware of in the Mother—the Castration of the Mother—is threatening and overwhelming for the Child, and, through the second process known as separation, that desire of the Mother is named as the Name of the Father (Lacan, 2006a, pp. 445–488). In this schema introduced by Lacan in the 1950s, we see that it is by the Father—as bearer of the Symbolic order—that the state of jouissance, or immediate Drive saturated existence, is ordered (see the previous chapter for a description of this from a different vantage point). In a sense here, we can see that the discreet Drives, as linked to the erogenous zones, are only brought into existence through the channeling of the all encompassing Drive state through the process of symbolization, bringing out the very close relationship between the seemingly disparate phenomena of the internal, the sensation, and the external, the perception. The extreme importance of this in clinical work was only noticed by Freud late in his work. In *Group Psychology and the Analysis of the Ego*, which was written immediately following *Beyond the Pleasure Principle*, Freud introduces this in the famous chapter on "Identification" (Freud, 1921c). In this chapter, Freud speaks of the importance of Identification, and how the first Identification of every subject is with the Father, which forms the basis for all subsequent Identifications. Furthermore, the mother, as fundamental repressed object-choice, is not necessarily the source material for symptoms. In what Freud refers to as more regressed circumstances, an individual whose presence appears in the unconscious by means of identification might contribute more to symptom formation than material introduced into the unconscious as repressed object choice. Furthermore, relations to objects may, in certain situations, appear as ego identifications, identification superseding the importance of object relation. Importantly, this can occur through the identification of a single trait in the identificatory content, which serves as what Lacan will go on to describe as the unary trait. Thus, Dora develops the symptom of cough in as much as it serves as a relation of identification with her father, who had a similar cough. The cough itself might suffice to provide the point of identification here. One of the reasons this is so important is that it demonstrates some of the logic for the presence of the father in unconscious fantasy formations associated with trauma. An identification with the Father—what Lacan reformulated as an Ego-Ideal—forms the very core of the unconscious.

I want to make one additional theoretical remark before leaving this subject. Since introducing this notion of the ego as a sphere, responding to internal and external stimuli, it should be clear that Freud himself— in the remarks noted above—and others since him have commented on the very problematic notion of that metaphor, particularly the great congruity or continuity between the so-called inside and the so-called outside, in contrast to the ego. The clinical comments of Freud, about how certain very deep unconscious processes involve a great shifting between the two zones of inside and outside, through introjections and projections of identifications and object relations, and the more general comments about the critical role of the Other in the very construction of the Inner all suggest a great problem in this model, which seems, on the surface, so to speak, to be a very easily acceptable one. I think that it is this very problem that compelled Lacan to find alternatives, something he himself alluded to in introducing his own final attempt to reformulate this, his use of knot theory in his late seminar *R.S.I.* (Lacan, 1975b). Lacan's earliest formulation of this is his notion of "extimacy," introduced in *The Ethics of Psychoanalysis* (1992; see also Miller, 1988). He uses the term there to describe the Thing, *das Ding*, adopting this term from Freud to distinguish the Real object, outside of the Symbolic and language, the object of jouissance, from *die Sache*, the thing represented and created through language. The Thing is thus the monstrous object of incestuous desire, forbidden to the subject. In using extimacy to describe this object of the Real, Lacan is trying to bring out its "intimate exteriority," something that is both inside of and outside of the subject. Four years later, Lacan attempts to use non-Euclidean geometry, specifically figures such as the torus and the Klein bottle, to schematize the subject (Lacan, 1962). The final effort, the use of Knot Theory promulgated in *R.S.I.*, drops interiority and exteriority entirely, in a theory based on the nature of the topographic relationships between loops of string.

Now, I wish to take these theoretical formulations and explore the ways in which they might work themselves out relative to the 2001 attacks on the United States, particularly the events of September 11. Before I do so, though, I want to repeat that, in the life of the child, certain internal sensations—namely those associated with the Drive—form the basis for what we might term the Universal Trauma and the formation of the unconscious itself; that those very internal perceptions are irreparably linked to the external world, through the very figure of the Other; and, that certain events in the external world itself, such as incest or other terrible events, can set the pattern of Trauma in motion, just as Freud described it in his model.

Adults, too, can face terrible events, and, again, Freud's formulations would certainly apply here as well. Namely, to the extent that an event is perceived as excessive, such as those of September 11 and the subsequent anthrax attacks, and is in fact too much for the subject to make sense of, some of the affect and energy associated with it will remain free-floating and result in subsequent traumatic symptoms. And, here, again following Freud, I think that the context of surprise is significant, that part of the traumatic effects of these recent terrible events—which are certainly terrible under any standard, regardless of whether they cause one traumatic symptoms—result from the element of surprise, that many did not believe something like that possible, at least not possible in this country. Indeed, on a social level there are other terrible events occurring in many other parts of the world, social antagonisms that work themselves out through the most violent means, and those are known to a certain extent in this country. Social antagonism, particularly violent antagonism, is, however, seen as a foreign thing, not a feature of American civilization, always elsewhere. Thus, though many Americans are at least peripherally aware of the great violence in the world, this is not something that they experience as concerning them. Thus, the surprise of the events of September 11.

And, it is interesting that one of the key features of these recent events is the very difficulty in properly naming them. If there is any indicator of some difficulty with symbolization at the social level, it could certainly be seen in the months following the events of September 11 in the very failure of a proper name to develop for the events of that day. Varied terms proliferated in the media—attacks, terrorism, new war, even bombing, in spite of the fact there were no bombs involved. In Lacanian terms, we could say that the events of September 11 are traumatic to the extent that they remain in the Real register and resist symbolization. They thus provoke anxiety and exert a strange, monstrous impact on people, felt both as an external force and an internal disruption—the very two sets of complaints often heard after the attacks. They are extimate, in the sense Lacan used the term, a traumatic Thing. In that sense, they will remain unique, and thus the difficulty assigning a proper Symbolic status to them. If they had such a status, the attacks could be compared to social violence elsewhere in the world, or to other moments of violence within this country at other times in its history, but that process has just begun on a social level. Without such comparison and contextualization, which require symbolization, we can recognize that these events remain in the register of the Real.

A comment that I heard someone make immediately after September 11 is that the World Trade Center buildings represented powerful phallic symbols and that some of the impact of the attack resulted from this. I think that this is a mistake. The destruction at the Pentagon seemed no less horrifying and, had the Pentagon been completely destroyed and only part of the World Trade Center complex been damaged, I do not sense that the traumatic character of the attacks would be any less so. The mistake here relies on the visual appearance of the World Trade Center as tall erect structures and the simple assignment of a phallic character to them. More significant is that both the World Trade Center and, perhaps even to a greater degree, the Pentagon represent important points of Symbolic identification. Built upon the identification with the Father at the core of the unconscious are other layers of identification with structures of authority and institutional power and here, for many individuals, the World Trade Center is a symbol of New York, financial power, and capitalism, and the Pentagon a symbol of the strength of the United States, both very recognizable and, through their very simplicity, providing a single point of identification for many. Thus, the attacks on these structures marks perhaps not a trauma as much as a loss. Two objects in the world—the World Trade Center towers and the Pentagon—objects that evoke significant identifications on the part of many, were attacked, one destroyed and the other damaged. This loss of the object might perhaps best be seen as a loss that evokes a whole pattern of mourning. Thus, in the time immediately after the attacks, some individuals turned inwards, caught up in repetitions of the loss in the isolation of their homes watching television repeat the attacks in the days afterwards. We also saw a certain inhibition of activity, much as Freud described in the case of mourning the loss of a loved one (Freud, 1917e). We might say that this reaction is best described not so much as a trauma, but a process of mourning at a social level. While some may go on to a syndrome of traumatic neurosis from such an event, we could say the other concerning result would be the slide into melancholia, or depression.

We might, however, approach these terrible events from another perspective. There is the commonplace psychoanalytic insight that unconscious fantasy is unconscious because of a subjective desire present in it that the subject does not want to claim responsibility for. Furthermore, in clinical work, we often see that the progressive realization, or satisfaction, of such fantasies can cause the greatest anxiety in the analysand. In his short essay on the recent events titled *Welcome to the Desert of the Real*, Slavoj Žižek has built upon that to articulate an insight into a social fantasy that, in a sense, laid the groundwork for some of the subjective discomfort. Žižek writes:

> When we hear how the bombings were a totally unexpected shock, how the unimaginable Impossible happened, one should recall the other defining catastrophe from the beginning of the twentieth century, the sinking of the *Titanic*: this, also, was a shock, but the space for it had already been prepared in ideological fantasizing, since the *Titanic* was the symbol of the might of nineteenth century industrial civilization. Does not the same hold for these attacks? Not only were the media bombarding us all the time with the talk about the terrorist threat; this threat was also obviously libidinally invested—just recall the series of movies from *Escape From New York* to *Independence Day*. That is the rationale of the often-mentioned association of the attacks with Hollywood disaster movies: the unthinkable which happened was the object of fantasy, so that, in a

way, America got what it fantasized about, and this was the biggest surprise. (Žižek, 2012, p. 18)

While an individual may not want to confront his unconscious fantasy, relying on ego and object relations to sustain him in the world, it is important to note that fantasy itself is a cover-up, a defense, or a reaction to a certain Void in the Symbolic order itself, what Lacan terms the lack in the Symbolic (2006a, pp. 671–702). Put into the schema sketched earlier, the lack in the Symbolic is the very lack or desire in the Mother which is only settled for the child with the assignment of the Name of the Father as the Desire of the Mother. This lack or void at the level of the Mother is her own castration, which the child perceives, and which is threatening to him, and to which he responds with a desire organized around a certain unconscious fantasy. That lack in the Other can be symbolized, and, as a Void, a certain unnamable, is something encountered within clinical practice, a point of exquisite pain and anxiety within the clinical context. Another way of conceiving the events of September 11 might be to say that this represented a symbolization of that very lack in the Other at the level of the social itself, a monstrous void, a point without meaning, around which all the Symbolic activity circulates: all the talk, all the commentary.

I would like to end this presentation with one additional formulation, what is probably Lacan's most well known formulation on trauma, from the section on "unconscious and repetition" in *The Four Fundamental Concepts of Psychoanalysis*, his 11th seminar (1977a). In attempting to address the notion of repetition as a fundamental part of the unconscious, Lacan advances the notion of *automaton*, as a way of describing the Symbolic order as a network of signifiers, organized necessarily as a repetitive machine, having the status of an automaton in a science fiction sense. Once something gets into the system, it gets taken up and repeated over and over, this insistence being what Lacan identifies as a fundamental aspect of the unconscious. This is indeed what Freud was alluding to when he spoke of a failure of the unconscious to respond, in a sense, to his treatment, it kept insisting—thus the repetition compulsions that were one part of impetus to his *Beyond the Pleasure Principle*. Together with this notion of the *automaton*, Lacan introduces what he terms *tuche*, which means luck, or accident, or chance. For Lacan, the *tuche* is the encounter with the Real, the impossible, unexpected event that the subject was not prepared for and, whether good or bad, shocked the system. For such an event to become traumatic, it must be inscribed into the unconscious in a particular way. In other words, this contingent event turns into a repetitious necessity as it enters, so to speak, the *automaton* of the unconscious. This separation is key—for the traumatic event itself thus has both a Real and a Symbolic dimension. And this distinction, and the way it redefines the work of psychoanalysis, has, as Dany Nobus has pointed out in a fine reading of this, a critical impact on treatment (Nobus, 2000). For Lacan, the Unconscious itself is organized around repetition and the fact of repetition will not disappear through the treatment. Thus, in distinction to the Freudian model alluded to above and even some of the Lacanian concepts I have made reference to, the mere symbolization of the traumatic event, its narrativization, will not rid it of its impact. The impact will remain as long as the Symbolic structure in which it is inscribed is stable. The critical difference with psychoanalysis is that, through the elucidation of the Symbolic structure within the analysis, the Symbolic is articulated and, to a sense, reconstructed. The material operating at an unconscious level is replaced with different content, different material, and the repetition continues, but no longer organized around a particular traumatic content. Through analysis, the unconscious signifiers that mark the core of unconscious content around which these repetitions are organized get replaced, as it were, with a different set of signifiers, no less repetitious, but not necessarily organized around a certain traumatic event. And the terrible event returns, as it were, to the realm of a contingent encounter, some piece of bad luck, with perhaps some alleviation of the suffering associated with it. This is part of what is curative in psychoanalysis, and it is this that psychoanalysis has to offer to those suffering from trauma.

CHAPTER FIVE

Fundamental fantasy as the axiom of the unconscious*

The notion of Fundamental Fantasy—the relationship of the subject to the *object a*, the object-cause of desire—certainly represents one of Lacan's critical creations within the theory of psychoanalysis, and its so-called "traversal" likewise is often described as one of the definitions of the very end of a psychoanalytic treatment. After a survey and reformulation of a Freudian model of the unconscious, I wish to use the Freudian model to explore in this paper the Lacanian Fundamental Fantasy through an expansion of it to include the use of Wolfram's cellular automaton—as a model (or perhaps even analogue) for the rendering of Fundamental Fantasy.

I wish, here, to formulate a model for what this Fundamental Fantasy might be, one built upon Freud's first model. I want to begin with the unconscious, the unconscious much as it is developed by Freud in the *Interpretation of Dreams* (and of course back to the "Project" or, more informally, the December 6, 1896, letter to Fliess) as a series

---

* "Fundamental fantasy as the axiom of the unconscious" was delivered at the 5th Annual Affiliated Psychoanalytic Workgroups Conference, "Fundamental fantasies: *Écrits* and after" at Duquesne University, in Pittsburgh, Pennsylvania, on May 16, 2003.

of inscriptions or traces made (Freud, 1895; Freud, 1985; Freud, 1999). Freud speaks of them in this letter to Fliess as stratified, as, perhaps, being laid down in a series one after the other. I wish to argue that we could imagine such a process as organized around a type of Symbolic structure, the simplest version of which would be a binary series where the unconscious would be represented by the totality of such inscriptions coded into a binary representation and stored in layers. This very reduction of the Symbolic into such a binary system follows work advanced by Lacan himself in his *Presentation of the Suite* at the end of the *Purloined Letter* paper—this appendix less concerned with the "actual" truth of such a model in some sort of biological sense (as too am I—I do not propose this as a model of the functioning of the brain) than with its utility in demonstrating a certain Symbolic inertia inherent (shall I say fundamental?) to the very functioning of the Symbolic itself, which he used to advance a certain demonstration of repetition automatism, and we might even say the later Automaton of *Seminar 11* (Lacan, 2006a; Lacan, 1977a; see also, the previous chapter). In fact, a more truthful conceit here might be to view these inscriptions as less of the binary significations (signifiers) themselves (laid down in a series of layers), than of a series of inscriptions of the very connections between different signifiers—the signifiers somehow all present within the unconscious, but the layering being patterns of their relationships. This revised model evokes both the contact barrier Freud introduced in the *Project* as well as the work of contemporary neuroscientists such as Gerald Edelman, who have advanced notions such as neural networks working in the path laid out in the 1940s by D. O. Hebb, whose eponymous rule defined that when two neurons are stimulated by a similar source, a connection develops between them (Edelman, 1992; Palombo, 1992; Pally, 2000). My hypothesis regarding the Fundamental Fantasy will apply, however, regardless of the choice of models advanced above.

Let me add, though, that while Lacan does not endorse a concept of the unconscious as trace, and even moved away from the concept of the unconscious as such (to be replaced by the notion of the speaking being, the *parlêtre*; Miller, 2015), I propose this chapter as an exercise in the way in which this older conceptual model could be modified on the basis of Wolfram's work, with greater or lesser success, to take into account more contemporary clinical phenomena.

So—we have this model of the unconscious, where the various phenomena are encoded into a Symbolic system—whether binary or not, though I will use this simple version for the time being—and recorded as a series of inscriptions (or, inscriptions of connections). Thus, keeping with the binary system, the unconscious is a series of pluses and minus arranged in layers.

What can we say about the clinical utility of such a system? First of all, the very nature of the Symbolic inscription mechanism provides a certain set of inherent limitations that produce repetition, as Lacan demonstrated in the postscript to the "Purloined letter" paper cited above. I think a number of more basic observations still can be made. First, for any given individual, I believe this process of inscription only begins at a certain age and is, especially at the beginning, incomplete and filled with gaps. This is, of course, what Freud initially designated in his clinical work as infantile amnesia, namely that memory and the unconscious only begin to be formed at a certain age and that the earlier the age, the more fragmentary the representation.

Now, of course, such an inscription of the unconscious does not exist in the brain as such (as something we can see, can map out), but we assume it exists, or we must suppose that it exists for many other things to be true. This is essentially the argument Freud makes numerous times: the unconscious is necessary to explain dreams, parapraxes, and other unconscious formations; to explain symptoms; and, even to explain other aspects of our "personal experience" as Freud puts it in his 1915 paper "The unconscious" (Freud, 1915e). It is a necessary hypothesis. So it is a thing, a Place we might even say, the Other Scene Freud puts it elsewhere, and we know it by its effects. This notion of the unconscious as a necessary supposition is important, for the same argument is often made that the Fundamental Fantasy is also such a supposition, with a citation of the second stage of the development of the fantasy in *A Child is Being Beaten* frequently given as the example for that (Freud, 1919e). I wish to argue that these suppositions—of the unconscious and of Fantasy—are of a completely different nature and that some of the confusion in various technical issues regarding interpretation derive from this.

To demonstrate this difference, I wish to introduce a model, something of a metapsychological model, we might use to grasp fantasy. This model is derived from the work of the mathematician and physicist Steven Wolfram, whose research in the fields of cellular automata and complex systems theory has culminated in the publication of *A New Kind of Science* (Wolfram, 2002). In particular, I wish to take advantage of his work on cellular automata—whose very title is itself suggestive of the use I will make of it.

Imagine a piece of graph paper, with rows of empty squares—the cells—which we will code in a binary fashion, assigning each cell in a row a color white or black. We will start with a certain assignment of colors to the first row (in his example—he colors the middle square black with the others all white), and then develop a rule for how the colors of the subsequent rows will be assigned based on the surrounding cells. There are a certain relatively limited number of rules, given the two options for coloration of each cell and the limited number of immediately surrounding cells with which to construct the rule. If one programs out all these rules, with a similar starting configuration, a number of discrete types of patterns result. One is a simple pattern of repetition, with an easily identifiable result (e.g., a line going down or across the graph paper, or every cell colored black or white, etc.). A second is a nesting of patterns with a larger series of patterns, a slightly more complex, but still regular repetitive sequence—the so-called fractal patterns (such as triangles within triangles). A final is a pattern which does not seem organized in the simple sense of the first two, nor completely random, but an amalgam of the two—randomness with certain irregular areas of order. These patterns—when visualized, clearly have a certain amount of order to them, but using traditional, linear mathematical and statistical analysis are completely random. This final pattern type represents a complex system, the very type of phenomenon that has gotten so much attention over recent years as scientists have reached a type of limit to the power of linear equations for the explanation of certain types of natural phenomenon. Most popularly known as chaos theory, these developments seek to evolve an entirely new type of representational system for types of natural phenomena that could not be described in the older system. The interesting contribution of Wolfram here is that these very complex systems—which cannot be represented using traditional linear representational systems—can be described quite simply with this Rule, which sets out the system of regularity and randomness so easily visualized.

This demonstration of cellular automata is quite interesting, for it bears a remarkable similarity to that of some notions of Lacan's, particularly some of the work in the *Presentation of the Suite*, and the concomitant reduction of the Symbolic order to a binary structure (Lacan, 2006a). It is in fact this that I will take as a model of the unconscious itself. Now, one other aspect of this that speaks to its usefulness as a model is the way in which we can observe repetitive patterns in the different ways in which these grids develop, and, particularly, the irregularly regular patterns that represent the complex aspect of complex—nonlinear—systems theory. I will come back to the importance of that shortly.

In the application of such a model to the unconscious, there are several aspects of clinical phenomena that such a model will need to account for. The first is that this process of inscription of the unconscious—the registration of these representations, or connections—begins only at a certain point and thus the unconscious, inasmuch as we are going to somehow (at least here for a moment for the sake of this argument) make this a memory function, only begins at a certain age. I think that it is likely that there are memory functions that exist outside of the unconscious, but that those memory functions are not represented in a Symbolic manner, are not encoded in this way (in other words, there are many modalities of memory in play—the unconscious only one of them). My guide here is the notion of functional hierarchy Freud adopted from John Hughlings Jackson and which was so influential in the formative stages of his psychoanalytic work, as has been demonstrated by Mark Solms in collaboration with Michael Saling in his analysis of Freud's monograph *On Aphasia* from that period (Freud, 1953; Solms & Saling, 1986; Jackson, 1996). Using this, we might indeed say that the pre-verbal infant has memories of various sorts, and clearly memory and even recognition exist even in the newborn, who, it has been demonstrated, will recognize the voice of parents or others heard while in utero, or will quickly recognize and move to the nipple of the mother preferentially over other actions. Such memory—if we are going to call it that—is similar, in a sense, to the memory of animals, and exists at a level (is this the Real? the Imaginary?) and through mechanisms that are not mediated through the unconscious.

At a certain juncture, however, there is a certain encounter of language and the Real, the primal *tuche* we might say, that leads to Primary Repression and the inscription of material in the unconscious through the act of repression. Now, at that moment, the process of registration is not flawless, and there are the gaps of memory—of registration—that Freud initially observed in his work with hysterics and which continue for a number of years. Thus, in addition to the infantile amnesia, we have the fragmentary character of memory which is structural itself, which I will argue can be represented by a fragmentary recording in the unconscious itself—blank spots in the grid model we have advanced. Thus, we can say there are three types of "failings," as it were, of the unconscious. The first is the discordance of the unconscious as memory with other levels of what we might term animal memory. The second is a failing of the unconscious to record everything from the beginning. And the final is a failing at the critical moment of origin of the unconscious itself, a structural failing inherent to language itself.

It is in the context of this lack at the level of the Other—of these "failings" of the unconscious—that we could read some of Lacan's formulations regarding fantasy. For example fantasy as a "dramatization of the Other" which led Lacan in *Television*—in a section, a response to a question of Miller's on racism, of the broadcast that was not transcribed in the written text—to the creation of the neologistic *autrasme*, joining fantasy and the Other (Lacan, 1973). Without an obvious coherence at the level of the inscriptions or linkages of the unconscious, the unconscious presents with an ahistorical and repetitious—even mechanical—character—a synchronic structure of significatory processes that do not cohere—in a sense—in any dramatic form. There really is no place for a subject in this process when it is limited to this level alone as this is a pure signifying machine. Fantasy, however, introduces the subject here—brings him on stage—and does it through the introduction of the object itself, this being—of course—object *a*.

I believe that an inspiration here for Lacan may have been the work of Heidegger, and I wish to highlight in particular Heidegger's essay on *European Nihilism* that was brought to my attention by Fredric Jameson's *A Singular Modernity* (Heidegger, 1987; Jameson, 2002). The issue in particular is Heidegger's reading here of the *cogito*, which can be found in particular in the chapter "The Cartesian cogito as cogito me cogitare." Heidegger suggests that the proper reading—translation—of *cogitare* is not "thinking" but rather "representation," the German *Vorstellung* so important in Freud's work itself (with "propose" or "present" given as alternatives). Heidegger argues that the very act of thinking is thus—to follow the Latin roots—to take hold of, to take hold of something, to bring it before oneself: thinking is representing in the sense of creating a thing about which one thinks, a form of construction, another word quite important on the issue of fantasy to which I will return later. Thus, in the very act of thinking—or representing—an object is created. And the subject, interestingly, for Heidegger is not the substantial subject or ego formation, the philosophical subject, as it were, but rather a type of secondary process to this: to be best understood formally as a place from which such an object construction might be possible, a sort of empty place, produced by the object.

I wish to quote Heidegger here:

> If one heedlessly translates *cogitatio* with thinking, then one is tempted to believe that Descartes interpreted all modes of human behavior as thinking and as forms of thinking. This opinion fits in well with the current view concerning Descartes' philosophy, the view that it was "rationalism"—as if what rationalism is did not first have to be determined from a delineation of the essence of *ratio*, as if the essence of *ratio* did not first of all have to be illuminated by the already clarified essence of *cogitatio*. With respect to the latter, it has now been shown that *cogitare* is representing in the fullest sense, that we must conjoin in thought the following essentials: the relation to what is represented, the self-presentation of what is represented, the arrival on the scene and involvement of the one representing with what is represented, indeed in and through representing. (Heidegger, 1987, p. 109)

Thus, I think when we see Lacan speak of fantasy as a dramatization of the Other, I think we must see it as the way in which it brings the Other—and thus the subject himself—into being (this can be with a capital B in the Heideggerean sense), puts the whole operation on stage (on the scene, Heidegger states). In this sense, the reduction of fantasy through the use of the algorithms to the subject-object relationship is a brilliant move, cutting through the morass of phenomenological description exemplified for example in Susan Isaacs' seminal paper (Isaacs, 1948).

And it is further in this sense that we must see the creation of the very concept of Fundamental Fantasy—for my argument here is that the addition of *object a* to Lacan's formulations in the 1960s is a critical inflection point in his thought (one of his epistemological breaks, in the Althusserian sense), which we can say is even graphically represented in the addition of the upper level of the Graph of Desire to the lower level that characterized his earlier work—as linked to the relationship of fantasy to the signifier of the lack in the Other, which can be read at the level of the unconscious itself. In other words, it is with respect to the sense of gaps, failures, or lacks in the unconscious that the fantasy is articulated and which brings the subject to being. Thus, when Lacan refers to fantasy in the *Subversion of the Subject* as the "stuff of the *I* that is primally repressed," I think we can read this as an allusion to repression's non-representability in the unconscious (or perhaps the very failure of language itself as Other)—or a certain fundamental barrier to representation—filled out with the fundamental fantasy (Lacan, 2006a, p. 691).

Thus, relative to the various notions of failures or gaps in the unconscious articulated above, we can see the fantasy.

But this, to me, is not nearly as interesting and productive as the formulation of *Seminar 14*, in the final session of 21 June 1967, where Lacan states the following regarding the function of fantasy (I will quote here at length Cormac Gallagher's translation):

> I mean in your interpretation and more especially in your general interpretation [a phrase I wish to come back to] that you give of the structure of one or other neurosis, which ought always, in the final analysis, be inscribed in the registers that I gave, namely: for phobia, anticipated desire, for hysteria, unsatisfied desire, for obsessional, impossible desire. What is the role of phantasy in this order of neurotic desire? Well then, truth-meaning, I have said. That means the same thing as when you mark with a capital T—a pure convention in the theory given, for example, of such and such a set—when you mark with the connotation of truth something that you call an axiom: in your interpretation the phantasy has no other role, you have to take it as literally as possible and what you have to do, is to find in each structure, a way to define the laws of transformation which assure for this phantasy, in the deduction of the statements of unconscious discourse, the place of an axiom. (Lacan, 1967)

It is here that I would like to articulate the importance of the work of Stephen Wolfram, for it models this notion of axiom that Lacan proposes for phantasy—which we might approximate as a type of statement about the system (in this case, as Lacan writes: the "statements of unconscious discourse") from which the system itself can be deduced—in other words—a statement from which all other aspects of the statements can be deduced or derived—but which is not present within the system itself (not represented intrinsically within the system, is not a "statement of the unconscious")—or—to shift back to this other conceptual framework—is primally repressed and not only not represented, but not representable within the system (I must observe here a certain amusement with Lacan's choice of "axiom" to describe this notion, for an aspect of the traditional definition of axiom—its self-evident quality—is certainly not applicable to the unconscious itself, let alone a non-representable aspect of the unconscious: the Fundamental Fantasy. Turning to the Greek root definitions—"that of which one is thought worthy" or "that which is thought fit"—this choice of axiom becomes rather inspired [Liddell, 1889]).

Well, again, this is precisely what Wolfram has presented a model for. In as much as we can represent the unconscious as a series of discursive statements or inscriptions of connections, which could somehow be represented in binary terms on a grid, in the manner in which Wolfram presents these cellular automata, the Fundamental Fantasy is precisely the rule—the axiom—which defines the very patterns represented.

Furthermore, this axiom—the Fundamental Fantasy—is most notable for not being directly present in the representations itself—the very terms of the Fundamental Fantasy, the subject and the object, are not represented as such in the unconscious, thus their status as Real, or, axiomatic. I think that this is most critical, for it is very indicative of the fact that fantasy –Fundamental Fantasy—will not appear as such within the formations of the unconscious, within the very unconscious material that we work with in clinical work. This is critical for it indicates, in a sense, that the technical operation in play with our work with fantasies will be quite different from that in our work with the unconscious itself. Thus, in our work with unconscious formations, we are mapping out—in a sense—the unconscious through the collection of material indicative of the unconscious—this would be filling in the grid of the cellular automata. In working with the fundamental fantasy, however, we are operating with an axiom—a type of algorithmic formula—which can be deduced from the very grid itself, but is separate from this grid.

This distinction—and the clinical applications that follow from it—align quite well with a series of critical technical issues addressed by Jacques-Alain Miller in his 1994 lecture "E = UWK: towards the 9th International Encounter of the Freudian Field" (Miller, 1995). In this paper, Miller offers a reading of Freud's paper *Constructions in Analysis*, highlighting several points (Freud, 1937d). The first is the distinction

Freud makes within *Constructions* itself between interpretation and construction. Interpretation is directed to specific elements in analytic work—the "material" we work with in analysis—some formation of the unconscious. In this sense, I would say, that with interpretation we are working at the level of the unconscious, to a type of mapping of the unconscious that occurs at the level of the particular formation in question. With construction, however, we are at a completely different technical level, because what is involved is not a particular unconscious formation—its content, the associations it brings on and so forth—but multiple elements of the analytic material brought together in a particular way—and here the term "general interpretation" Lacan used in the quote above is quite to the mark. It is a type of assembly of many elements put together and given to the analysand. In this respect, it involves not any particular unconscious formation, but some amalgam of them not present in any one in particular, but which somehow ties them together. Furthermore, Freud emphasizes how constructions are linked to this primal or original repression spoken above. There is some fact of repression forever inaccessible—for Freud some aspect of very early history—or the very signifier of lack in the Other as noted above—that is constructed and given to the patient. In this sense, the construction provides that very same function of "dramatization of the Other" noted before, filling in for the very gaps within the Other itself.

Most important as well, this brings to light a technical distinction we must be aware of in our clinical work regarding the difference between interpretation and construction. In fact, it strikes me that often the two get quite confused, both with regard to the proper object of the technique as well as the agent associated with it. Thus, I think it is quite right to point out that interpretation is the work of the analysand. The analysand produces unconscious formations, and our obligation in the treatment is very much to attend to those formations—not so much that analysts offer interpretations as to their meaning and signification and so forth—but so that the analysand continues to speak and interprets, making the connections and linkages (to keep to our model) or highlighting the inscriptions of the unconscious itself. A common response of non-Lacanians to the Lacanian practice relates to this very emphasis on the various non-verbal interventions, from the various noises to the whole issue of the cut of the session itself. Even when addressing something named as interpretation, however, for example, when we speak of the oracular interpretations, I think it is best to state that these are not interpretations as interpretations in a certain classically understood way (giving a meaning), but a different type of intervention which leads to the production of interpretations, much as Lacan spells this out in the first session of *Seminar 19: D'un discourse qui ne serait pas du semblant* (Lacan, 2006b). It is not to us to make these interpretations, for they are made only within the speech of the analysand at the level of the unconscious itself.

With constructions, however, we are operating at a completely different technical level in which we are obligated to produce the construction. As Freud puts it, the analysand produces emotions, remembrances, associations, and so forth (or at least if we are doing our job as we should), and the analyst—what do we produce? Well, much is made often of the fact that we produce interpretations, but—as I argued—this is mistaken. We are obliged to produce constructions. This work of ours is difficult, usually late in the course of analysis when a sufficient amount of unconscious material is present. Freud empha-sizes how it is deductive and can involve even guesswork in the way in which we patch together different fragments from here or there in the analysis to fill in a certain hole in the unconscious (in the sense I used above). Miller points out how, with Lacan, a certain decisive shift takes place, however, where this knowledge is—in a sense—divorced from memory, how the logical connection between the two is no longer a necessity, and there, I believe, is the place where we must insert fantasy in all its importance. For fantasy here—particularly in this Wolframian and axiomatic deployment I have sketched out above—takes on this precise role. It is deduced from the unconscious itself, it is not necessar-ily intrinsic to the unconscious in the sense that it has (or even can be) verified in any sense relative to the so-called reality of the patient, and it is produced by analysts through a type of analysis of all the uncon-scious material presented as a type of necessary solution to this. What we construct is the Fundamental Fantasy.

Let me note, however, that our production of the Fantasy does not necessarily lead to its articulation within the session, as a form of ver-bal intervention. But rather that, through our construction, a certain direction is given to the very interventions that we make. As we listen within the session, a wide range of material is produced, and we must make decisions regarding what material we will respond to with an intervention—be it a punctuation, oracular interpretation, or session cut. Declining the position of the master, we do not provide interpretations as such. However, and in distinction to some readings of Lacan, we still give the treatment a direction, and it is our ongoing working construction that provides such a direction for our interventions: the intervention may be different from no other, but we are guided to it by our construction, which follows the very logic of the transference, where we assume the very position of *object a*: in as much as we can identify how we are in that position within the transference (itself supported by the Fantasy), we are able to direct the treatment.

What are some of the clinical implications of this?

The theoretical importance of fantasy and what I have tried to elaborate as its technical accompaniment in constructions give a certain structure and direction to the treatment. If an analyst takes interpretation as the only technical maneuver, there is no way to define the process (and also the end) of the analysis in any sort of technical manner. The unconscious remains there—unperturbed by the course of the analysis—with a continued production of material—of unconscious formations—for interpretation. The interpretive process itself is endless, and in this sense I do not think that it is mere coincidence that Freud raises the question of the end of analysis at a point in his career very close to his elaboration of construction. For it is construction—in particular the construction of the fundamental fantasy—that provides not only a certain direction to the treatment, but even a sort of conceptualization of the end of the treatment—the different experience of the drive characterized by Lacan in *Seminar 11* as the definition of the traversal of the Fundamental Fantasy at the end of analysis (Lacan, 1977a).

And we see this in our very work. We will see analysands, for many sessions, for weeks, months, years; we see certain patterns—certain signifiers which repeat in various ways within the patient's unconscious formations. Now, through the interpretive work, we might lead the patient to make connections among these signifiers, relate them to things within his past history, and so forth. This work, of course, is important and in a sense we might even say makes up the bulk of our work. But a certain point arises, where the question is not so much how these different signifiers connect, or relate, or—more often from the analysand—carry meaning? At a certain point the question shifts more to that of "why?" Why is this signifier so important? What causes this signifier to play such a significant role? At this point, the work is shifting from that of meaning, of signification, to the issue of cause—and there we have ventured into the domain of fantasy, in particular in the way in which fantasy relates to *object a* as object-cause of desire.

Put differently, the subject can be seen here as created—both in the Heideggerean sense of a place to which these various signifiers are addressed, and at a different level as a particular point of identification as *semblant*—by an object cause, which can be deduced or constructed through a type of analysis of the signifiers themselves, in particular a certain type or mode of partial drive function for which they are selected. For example, it might be in relation to signifiers of production, of possibility, of revulsion that the analyst can identify the object cause is shit; or it might be that the matter of gaze is central in the desire of the subject to get a certain look; and so forth for the entire series of possible partial drives—oral, anal, scopic, or invocatory. In any case, our obligation is to identify that object—to sift through the material and find the *object a* which satisfies the question of "why?" in these unconscious formations.

Fortuitously, we are at times given the aid in our work of a childhood scene remembered—a pattern I have seen in a number of cases, where the child is named—which, when repeated through the analysis, can take on a certain privileged status, in the sense that that name—which can take on a certain master signifier role—is invariably linked to *object a*, in the way in which it is taken on by the subject to support a certain cause. Thus, for example, this name—which functions as a point of identification, an Ideal, to which the patient will strive—most notably through the symptom itself—is not, in a sense, randomly chosen. There is a question of "why?" related to this Ideal around which identifications are repeated: the very ones around which are organized the symptom itself—why was *this* taken on as an Ideal? The answer relates to a certain satisfaction—a certain drive quotient—which we might say was not relinquished by the analysand: not repressed (and thus not found within the unconscious and its formations—the return of the repressed), but instead chosen—a certain parcel of jouissance not sacrificed—a remainder. The Ideal is created (again, as with Heidegger) to continue that very satisfaction (And I think it is useful here to view Lacan's formulation of Imaginary Castration from the early 1960s as a type of negative staging of a deprivation of this very satisfaction). This choice—I argue—is the very choice of neurosis: indeed it is the very choice of which neurosis—that we cannot recover through memory or any kind of historical reconstruction, but only through its logical necessity: this is the choice of this subject. And it is precisely in this sense that the construction and traversal of the fantasy and confrontation with the partial drive at the end of analysis is the exact same point as the identification with the symptom, in the sense that subject identifies himself in this original choice of symptom. And further, it is only at this point, with the reassumption of this fundamental choice—this very point of identification with the symptom—to which we bring the subject in analysis—that the subject again has some measure of freedom.

CHAPTER SIX

Introducing the symptom*

I want to start this out with a look at rectification. Rectification—incidentally, the same word in French, with all the same connotations as best as I can tell—is a briefly utilized concept in Lacan's work. There are certainly enough of these, but the curious thing about rectification is that Lacan gives it special privilege in "The direction of the treatment and the principles of its power," one of his few papers that explicitly deals with issues of psychoanalytic technique. In *Direction of the Treatment*, Lacan in fact offers a schematic of psychoanalytic treatment, a schematic drawn from his close readings of Freud's clinical cases, in which a psychoanalysis has three logical stages—"a process that begins with rectification of the subject's relations with reality, and proceeds to development of the transference and then to interpretation" (2006a, p. 500). I want to draw attention to rectification in that—in contrast to the more frequent discussions of the theory of the end of analysis—rectification is precisely a concept introduced by Lacan in reference to the beginning of analysis, and one which, as we shall

---

* "Introducing the symptom" was presented at the Sixth Annual Conference of Affiliated Psychoanalytic Workgroups, "Working with the symptom," September 24–26, 2004, hosted by Creighton University in Omaha, Nebraska.

see, has a special relationship with the Symptom—the psychoanalytic Symptom here, of course, not the simple phenomenological iterations from psychiatry.

This term refers to a particular technique that Lacan identifies in the Dora case and the Rat Man case. With regard to the former, it is the famed first dialectical reversal in which Freud brings Dora to realize that not only is she not the mere innocent victim propelled into a terrible position by various malevolent forces in the world (the position Lacan further characterized as that of the "beautiful soul" from Hegel's *Phenomenology*), but, rather, she in fact orchestrated through her "connivance" the very situation about which her complaints resound (Freud, 1905e). With reference to the latter case, it is Freud's intervention in a quick read of the Rat Man's psychic reality—based on a series of facts regarding the conditions of the parents' marriage, the critical role of money and debt, the turning away from one's true love—an intervention in which Freud repositions the Rat Man's various "impasses" and difficulties and his very flamboyant obsessions in the context of his relationship to his father and his belief about his father's disapproval of a desired marriage, an intervention all the more remarkable in that—while it worked within the analysis—it was nonetheless "untrue," in that his father was not alive at the time of the presumed statement on his part (Freud, 1909d).

In the previous chapter, I conveyed some thoughts on technique in which I stated—following a distinction first evoked by Jacques-Alain Miller—that while it is the analysand's work to provide interpretation—to give meaning, as it were, to the varied unconscious formations that evolve in the course of our work—it is our work as analysts to provide a construction, a construction of the fundamental fantasy. Well, to this delineation on technique—on both the level of logic of and agency within the treatment—to this delineation of two different interventions, I believe we need to add another, a third level of intervention, and that is what Lacan articulates as rectification, and which I would also clearly direct as the work of the analyst, a directing that I will elaborate here, hopefully less on the basis of some prescriptive *savoir*, but rather a Joycean *savoir-faire*, which we might apply in our work. Analysts do not interpret, but we may provide rectification—to initiate the treatment—and construction—to initiate the close of the treatment.

Now, the thing about this rectification is that it evokes nothing less than a "wild" psychoanalytic intervention, the very kind of "brusque" intervention that Freud specifically expressed reservation about (Freud, 1910k, p. 121). But a careful reading of the texts reveals that these particular technical interventions of Freud's—while certainly brusque and decisive—have less to do with a building up of meaning, but a certain breaking down of meaning in the form of the solidified ego and object representations inherent in the analysands at the time, a form of destructive or destabilizing intervention in which we can see something of the elucidation of the subjectivity inherent in the cases—a point which I will modify later. This is, of course, most frequently understood in the terms of the means by which this rectification brings out the ways in which the subjectivity of the analysands is implicated—we might even say in a causal sense—in the very situations that were initially presented as external to them. The standard reference here is to Schema L, in which we might say the analytic discourse breaks out of a certain Imaginary frame of reference, with its focus on ego and object, to the broader Symbolic frame of reference, with a redirected emphasis on the unconscious desire in play in the Subject and that desire's reference point, the grand Other—the Symbolic framework in which the Subject is caught up. Of course, Lacan is quite explicit in this theorization with reference to the Rat Man case, in which his reading of the case demonstrates how the Rat Man's unconscious desire—read: Subjectivity—is linked very carefully to a series of events relating to his parents' lives, courtship, marriage decisions, and professional decisions—all of which formed the Symbolic backdrop, the Other, against which his life was consciously and unconsciously articulated (Lacan, 2006a, pp. 489–542; 1979a).

Note here that an interesting aspect of this, from a technical perspective, is Lacan's valorization of more explicit interventions—which he describes as "mantic" in impact—very early in the treatment, in contrast to the more traditional and austere interventions of scansion and punctuation advanced as critical in the preliminary sessions, those early sessions in which the analyst and potential analysand are exploring the possibility of engaging in an analysis (Fink, 1997). Are these mantic rectifications valuable in establishing the analysis, reconfiguring the social bond between the analysand and analyst as analytic discourse? I argue that they are, in many cases, and in fact, we have some evidence that Lacan himself employed such precise interventions at times. In Stijn Vanheule's discussion of clinical work with analysands with neurotic depressive complaints, he discusses several autobiographical accounts of analysands of Lacan's (2004). In addition to emphasizing the attentive listening of Lacan, the analysands emphasize interventions on Lacan's part—these mantic utterances—which, like Freud's, do not represent interpretations as such, but rather an intervention—what I believe we ought to name, theorize, and properly emphasize as rectification—that leads to a shift of these cases out of vague, poorly defined depressive complaints—the facile, naïve, and now ubiquitous depression of the *DSM*—towards what Vanheule describes as a structuring relationship of the Subject to the Other. I will wish to come back to Vanheule's paper again.

This theorization of rectification against an Imaginary and Symbolic backdrop—bringing out the Symbolic dimension of Subject and Other beyond the Imaginary ego and object representations (both with regard to the complaints themselves and with regard to the treatment relationship of analysand to analyst)—is indeed valuable in our clinical work, but Lacan adds another dimension to this. In *Direction of the Treatment*, he states, in reference to rectification, that "Freud begins by introducing the patient to an initial situating of his position in reality, even if this situating leads to a precipitation—I would even go so far as to say a systematization—of symptoms" (Lacan, 2006a, p. 498). Thus, here we see, even back in 1958, a relationship—here more in terms of clinical phenomenology—between rectification and symptoms, one that acknowledges the perhaps the oft-cited clinical experience of psychoanalysis or even sometimes psychotherapy that symptoms can often get "worse" in the establishment of the treatment. So, we see a link between rectification and the Symptom, which we can read against this opening of the Imaginary into the Symbolic. What I would like to do, however, is to further read in to this early observation the later developments of Lacan and Jacques-Alain Miller and state that rectification is not that of the subject's relationship with reality—*le réel*—as it has been translated into English in terms of the use Lacan made of *le réel* in the 1950s—but rather to state that rectification concerns the subject's relationship to the Real, that third order which comes to prominence in Lacan's later work in contrast to that of the Symbolic and the Imaginary. [So, if the Imaginary refers to these ego and object relations, and to the domain of meaning, and the Symbolic to—in part—the differentially defined structure of language which—as the Other, provides the signifying universe in which subjects speak, what is this Real? Well, for a first approach, one might start with *to apeiron*, the pre-Socratic term first used by Anaximander and defined variously as boundless, complex, that-which-can-not-be-handled, or un-measurable, with an emphasis more on the Nietzschean notion of an indefinite qualitative substance over the Aristotelian infinite (Freeman, 1995; Nietzsche, 2001; Wallace, 2003). Lacan glosses the Real variously as outside language and the Symbolic order, as "resist[ing] symbolization absolutely," and as "impossible" to know, to give meaning to, to reach; but, as something which nonetheless (perhaps in a curious tip of the hat to Anaximander) both ex-ists, as a kind of Kantian *noumenal* Thing that must be supposed to exist, and which is the ultimate object of anxiety and that which— through our missed encounters—is the very source of trauma, and thus also that which insists (Lacan, 1988; 1977a). Of particular relevance for us here is Lacan's great discovery, the object *a*. This Real—read: inscrutable—object differs from psychoanalytic partial objects in that it is not an object in that traditional sense—an Imaginary, discrete, know-able object—the breast, the turd, the gaze, the voice, but rather a Real object cause of desire, a Real remnant, a remainder left over when the subject, as speaking being, submits to, enters in, what Lacan defines as the "defiles of the signifier," the Symbolic order, a remnant of castration, we might say. It is a further elaboration of Freud's notion of the primor-dially lost object, which Lacan renders—and I apologize for compress-ing quite a bit here—in a series of moments: first and foremost, the loss of life "immortal" and "indestructible" and in no need of organs—the libido itself—that we as living beings lose in being submitted to sexed reproduction, we can't replicate ourselves indefinitely. Well, this is what Lacan evokes in a myth—replacing that of the split original being seeking to find its other half, the myth of Aristophanes in the *Sympo-sium*, still quite alive today—a myth of *la lamelle*, the lamella, something like a piece of thin membrane flicked off the egg, an attempt to portray this loss of pure life through a new myth (Lacan, 2006a, pp. 703–721). {Curiously, let me note, is this myth not given a grander melo-dramatic treatment by none other than J. R. R. Tolkien in his story, in the very pas-sage from the Age of (Immortal) Elves to the Age of Man, about which it is interesting to note the curiously lifeless and death-like character— and I am not sure how much this is intended—of the immortal Elves themselves, somehow capturing that relationship of libido to the death drive?} Well, in any case, this loss of the Real, this is reprised, as it were, in a whole series of other losses, less obscure moments, from birth itself, to the weaning complex (the loss of the breast so important to the Kleinians), to the loss of the turd, and the most critical loss, the loss assumed by the speaking being in taking on—as a kind of original sin—and assuming the mortification of the body resultant from the our entry into language and the Symbolic order. Well, this symbolization process is not complete—the mastery of the ego, language, the body, the Other—is always misrecognized—and the Symptom offers the particular psychoanalytic point of access to that object *a*, the remainder or failure of this process. Thus, rectification represents—to reread Lacan's statement above—the "situating of the analysand's position"—not in Reality, but—"in the Real" through the "precipitation of the symptom." This situating of the analysand's position in the Real is the very reason I chose a work of Francis Bacon for the poster for this Conference, for Bacon's portraits render nothing less than Symptomatic portraiture, portrayal, not of an individual in reference to his Symbolic backdrop or Other, but rather the subject—in the face of an Other, the backdrop, that scarcely exists—the subject as Real and as distorted through the Symptom, a subject in which the anamorphosis is no mere folderol in the portrait, as in "The Ambassadors" of Hans Holbein the Younger, but has been generalized to the subject itself.]

To draw a further logical conclusion here: without the precipitation or, perhaps, even the introduction of the Symptom, an analysis will not develop, and a transference will not be established, nor the possibility of interpretation. The Symptom is the Real and necessary condition for analysis to proceed, because without some approach to the Real through the treatment itself, it will only continue to appear in its very disguised forms—the analysis must touch on the Real.

This distinction here between rectification and other interventions—such as interpretation—thus reflects within technique an important logical or theoretical distinction explored by Miller, the distinction of the Symptom from the other unconscious formations (dreams, slips of the tongue, parapraxes, and so forth). In "Sigma(X)," Miller (2004a) hints at a valuable distinction breaking up the series of unconscious formations, which usually includes the Symptom. While the direction of the treatment towards unconscious formations allow us to approach the unconscious as a Symbolic Other—a locus to which the formations are addressed, as a site of guarantee of their meaning: the very process we see articulated in interpretation in our clinical work—the Symptom—in contrast—does not allow that. With the Symptom, that Other is called into question—as perhaps an Imaginary structure—and the subject is left only with the existence, not of the Other, but of the Symptom itself. This, we see frequently in clinical work: a patient—in reference to dreams or to slips of the tongue—will associate and interpret and elaborate some meaning or another, some reference to the past, to his history, and to the various Symbolic determinants of his reality, often putting together some formulation which seems to support some supposition of the world out there, past or present, in which he finds himself. This is the interpretive work in play establishing Imaginary meaning against a Symbolic Other, often a fairly stable structure. But, with the Symptom, this kind of associative and interpretive work of the analysand is much more hesitant, uncertain, stop and go. Some formulation may be reached, only to be discarded and replaced with another. No meaning of the Symptom ever seems stable, and that Other out there is indeed called into question, often to that very point where the Subject feels that his Symptom is indeed the only "real" thing out there or that very thing which defines his existence, the kinds of statement often articulated while the analysand is on the couch. And this Symptomatic sensation—meaning established, then broken and reformulated, a kind of limitless (to recapitulate Anaximander) return to some enigmatic Thing—this is not solely limited to the consulting room or to elaboration within the clinical context, witness Freud's own repetitively Symptomatic fascination with and repeated examination of Hamlet and, especially, the Moses of Michelangelo, indicative—in his case—of a failed mastery of the application of his Oedipalizing template to these pieces of artwork (Freud failing to heed the warning that it is the artwork that interprets, not Freud himself: another example of what I have elsewhere termed Freud's slippage from psychoanalysis to Freudianism [Svolos, 2001; Chapter Seventeen in this volume]). Luke Thurston (2004) describes this relationship of Freud to art with great elegance in the second chapter of his monograph, *James Joyce and the Problem of Psychoanalysis*.

Not only is the Symptom, then, to be distinguished from the other unconscious formations, but the technical issue relative to the Symptom—rectification—must too be distinguished from that relative to the other unconscious formations, which necessitates, I believe, the abandonment of a certain kind of "initial timidity" that Lacan stated often characterized the early stages of treatment for many analysts, and which we can see today—another point to which I want to return. Thus, we can see that the way in which we can situate the Symptom against the Real—the object *a*—in contrast to the situation of the other unconscious formations situated against the big Other is linked to a certain kind of technical issue.

I want to turn now to another way of situating the Symptom, another way of bringing out its psychoanalytic relevance and its centrality in the Direction of the Treatment. I will reference here the well known matrix that Lacan creates in *Seminar 10* to clarify the relationship among what we may initially describe as forms of psychological suffering—inhibition, symptom, and anxiety, famously linked by Freud in an eponymous work notable among his works for its rather scattered presentation (Lacan, 2014). In an attempt to delineate the three forms, Lacan introduces a matrix—a grid—with two vectors evolving from the upper-left hand corner. Lacan designates the x-axis (from left to right) as indicative of increasing difficulty, and the y-axis (from top down) as indicative of increasing movement. He will then go on to eventually situate nine forms of suffering as indicated below:

	Difficulty	>	>
Movement	Inhibition	Impediment	Embarrassment
V	Emotion	Symptom	*Passage à l'acte*
V	Turmoil	Acting out	Anxiety

Now certainly, we might muse over these various forms of psychic suffering and get a sense of how they do indeed have a certain phenomenological relationship as they shade or merge from one to the other, in spite of the rather vague notion of movement and difficulty on first hearing. Lacan's own elaboration of these forms is, in fact, based on interesting etymological relationships of them. It is, however, much more useful in theory and in the clinic to give a certain specification to the diffuse designations given to the axes—movement and difficulty. For if we rename, and here I will follow Lacan and the reading of *Seminar 10* of Vanheule cited above, if we rename—as it were, based on a certain reading of Freud's original Drive theory—movement in the terms of the Drive itself, we might reformulate that as the axis of the Real, of the extent to which the Real is present—in a form of psychic tension—within the particular form of suffering. Thus, in the first column we see the disengaged, seemingly lost suffering of inhibition evolve with a greater tension of the Real—affect, in a sense—into the agitation of Turmoil. Or, in the far right column, we see the embarrassed person who feels constrained and seems about to burst, evolve—again with increasing tension—into flat out anxiety. On the x-axis, we will similarly rewrite Difficulty as the extent of the subject's integration into the Other, and here again the nuances and shifts in these various forms of suffering take on a new clarity. For, while inhibition and embarrassement, say, may represent equally passive states, in the former there is no context or structure for the suffering, while in the other, the analysand might articulate in great details the ways in which he is situated in relationship with an Other.

With this theoretical backdrop in place, we can then reformulate these seemingly phenomenological distinctions into the more precise way in which each of these forms of suffering articulates a relationship of the subject to the object a, the Real, and the Other. They relate as different gradations, as it were, of presence of the Real and the Symbolic Other. This distinction then has immense clinical consequences. As Lacan makes reference to in the final sessions of *Seminar 10* and as further elaborated by Stijn Vanheule, these certain positions of suffering are valuable in allowing us to conceptualize certain technical issues of the preliminary sessions of an analytic treatment. For example, Vanheule comments in particular upon the importance of the three positions of inhibition, emotion, and turmoil in the complaints of those seeking help today for what is most often identified as depression. Vanheule then notes that with this group of patients (who he refers to as the neurotically depressed in contrast to the psychotic depressed, or melancholics), our most critical task is to revitalize not just the depressed Subject, but also the depressed Other. This disengagement of the Subject and Symbolic Other—characterized on the grid by the low degree of Difficulty, or integration of Subject and Other—requires certain interventions to increase—as it were—the level of difficulty, interventions such as careful and attentive listening to the signifiers of the analysand's discourse and interventions such as certain—what I think are worth continuing to identify as—mantic interventions that name, that signify, the suffering and are able to raise it to the status of a Symptom—move the suffering to the center of the grid. And it is this critical move—which I have above termed rectification, and not interpretation (Vanheule uses the latter term, not identifying a distinction here that I think is most critical)—that sets the analysis in motion.

Now, it is important to note that Lacan himself gives this very technique, rectification, a different term later in his work—hystericization, with particular reference to the work with obsessional neurotics (who are often particularly prone, among neurotics, to a phenomenological situating of their suffering in inhibition)—and hystericization is then promulgated as the key part of establishing the analytic discourse (Lacan, 2007). I think that this is incomplete, for it fails to properly register the fact that the suffering of hysterics is all too often not aligned along the terms of the Symptom (Freud's Dora case exemplifies well the fact that a certain technical positioning is often necessary in the case of Hysteria itself). In other words, going back to the matrix, a patient with a hysterical neurotic structure may also present with a form of suffering other than the Symptom. In fact, is it not acting out and anxiety and even embarrassement that are more often the form in which suffering is defined by the hysteric, which leads the analyst to a different set of imperatives early in the treatment—the use of less symbolization, or other interventions—even a bolstering of Imaginary structures and establishment of some meaning (is this not the very move of Freud's in the Dora case?)—to temper an overwhelming Real, or to disengage from the Symbolic Other.

Further, I want to hypothesize that it is this very issue of rectification and the progression to analysis in the early sessions that might form another backdrop with which to formulate all the issues associated with the management of what are now referred to as Contemporary Symptoms: the eating disorders, addiction, tattooing, drug use, depression, and other phenomena we see more frequently. Much has been made about the challenges of patients with these forms of suffering to psychoanalysis—post-Freudians looking upon this as a need for a turn away from "classical" psychoanalysis—as with Kernberg and his borderlines (1986), or to the curious work of Fonagy and his colleagues on affect (2002)—and within the Lacanian psychoanalysis, we, of course, have the work of the World Association of Psychoanalysis, much of which is addressed most directly in the later chapters on addiction (see especially Chapter Ten).

But, regarding this issue of Contemporary Symptoms, one interesting thing to note is the evocation in some of these theoretical discussions of a kind of earlier world of psychoanalysis in which these problems did not exist, in which psychoanalysts were confronted with Hysterics and their Symptoms, or the occasionally challenging Obsessional. And this very—what I think we may name nostalgic—image further brings to mind other times when psychoanalysis seemed to fail, such as the debates of the 1920s and 1930s about the inadequacies of psychoanalysis (say, in terms of Negative Therapeutic Reaction in contrast to the Golden Age); or, the debates in the 1960s within the IPA about the end of Hysteria, because there were no longer patients with conversion symptoms. This nostalgia, I would argue, is hardly an accurate reflection of the past, for Freud struggled—as is so easily forgotten in such arguments—to get his analysands into analysis, witness his comments in *Analysis Terminable and Interminable* and his letters about the difficulty he faced in getting patients to stay in analysis early in his career (and even the veritable proliferation of seemingly "contemporary" symptoms in some of his early case reports) (Freud, 1937c, p. 209). What he was struggling with was in fact what I call rectification. And, while the classical Hysterical conversion phenomenology has indeed become much less prominent (as Gérard Wajcman has so elegantly argued, largely because those with Hysteria no longer present to Neurologists, but to Psychiatrists; Wajcman, 1982), the fact is that the presence of the Symptom—this elusive form of suffering—is not a Thing inherent to the suffering subject itself, but something created, in a sense, through the analytic process by the contribution of the analyst. And, if our Contemporary analysands no longer present with Symptoms, or desire for analysis, we need to look to the preliminary sessions with such patients to rectify the problem.

CHAPTER SEVEN

The supposed-to know-to read-otherwise*

"The Supposed-To Know-To Read-Otherwise." This signifier that I have chosen for this title is a translation of a word Lacan uttered on December, 20, 1977. Elaborating on the *sujet-supposé-savoir*, he tweaked the word a bit to come up with *le supposé-savoir-lire-autrement*. Allow me to offer my translation of the passage where this occurs, in *Seminar 25*:

> There is surely writing in the unconscious, even if only because the dream, the principle of the unconscious—it is what Freud said—the *lapsus* and even the *Witz* are defined by being readable. A dream, it happens, one doesn't know why, and then, *apres-coup,* it reads itself; a *lapsus* also and everything that Freud said about *Witz* are truly notorious for being linked to this economy that is writing, an economy different from speech. The readable, it is in that that knowledge consists. And in the end, it's not much. That which I said about the transference I timidly advanced as being the subject—a

---

*"The supposed-to know-to read-otherwise" was presented at Clinical Study Days 5 of Lacanian Compass on the theme "The unconscious in the contemporary world" held in Miami Beach, Florida, on January 16, 2011.

subject is always supposed, it is not of the subject, as expected, it is only the supposed—the supposed to know. And what does that mean? The supposed-to know-to read-otherwise. The otherwise in question, it is truly that which I write, even myself, in the following way: S(λ). Otherwise, what does that mean? (Lacan, 1977b)

I would like to address this question of how to read the unconscious in the twenty-first century from the point that Lacan makes here about the transference: of the supposition, of a subject, who is supposed to know how to read something otherwise, to read it differently. Lacan asks: what does it mean to read something otherwise, to read it differently? Well, then, how do we suppose to read something, the unconscious, more specifically, otherwise in the contemporary world?

Let's look first at Freud, who is not of the contemporary world. What was the Freudian act of reading? Freud's patients presented themselves to him with their symptoms, their conversion reactions, their obsessions, their phobias, and so forth. And, through the act of listening to these patients, Freud discovered, he created the notion of the unconscious, the Other Scene, and he, in the most classical phase of his work, worked through an act of reading these symptoms and dreams and *Witz* and *lapsus* differently. Whereas his patients perhaps believed that there was nothing to be read there, no meaning to be obtained from what we now call these unconscious formations, Freud believed otherwise, believed that they represented an unconscious that could be read. And, Freud's reading was a rigorous one, one in which he found not only meaning, but a very particular meaning, in all his cases—the Oedipus complex.

Freud's first published comments on the Oedipus complex appear in *The Interpretation of Dreams*, and I would like to quote here from the translation by Joyce Crick:

> In my experience, which is already very extensive, parents play the main parts in the inner life of all children who later become psychoneurotics. Being in love with the one parent and hating the other belong to the indispensable stock of psychical impulses being formed at that time which are so important for the later neurosis. But I do not believe that in this respect psychoneurotics are to be sharply distinguished from other children of Adam with a normal development in their capacity to create something absolutely new and theirs alone. It is far more likely—and this is supported by occasional observations of normal children—that with these loving

and hostile wishes towards their parents too, psychoneurotics are only revealing to us, by magnifying it, what goes on less clearly and less intensely in the inner life of most children. In support of this insight, the ancient world has provided us with a legend whose far-reaching and universal power can only be understood if we grant a similar universality to the assumption from child-psychology we have just been discussing. (Freud, 1999, p. 201)

From that point in 1900 to the end of his career, Freud retained a belief in the Oedipus complex, which he found at the heart of all his clinical work. Examine the Rat Man and even the Schreber case, and you can see it in the anticipatory function of this complex in schematizing the material he encountered in his clinical work. It can be granted that later in his work, such as in the third chapter of *The Ego and the Id*, Freud modified this complex with the so-called negative Oedipus complex, but the critical emphasis persisted: the relative positions of rivalry and antagonism with one parent and love for the other, a configuration of positions of Imaginary relations.

For Freud, this complex is universal: to be found in all social and cultural discursive formations. And, in fact, we can look at his great later speculations such as *Totem and Taboo* and *Moses and Monotheism* as further attempts on his part to delineate this complex by establishing its origins. In this regard, the myth of the primal father is merely an extension of the myth of the Oedipus complex: a desire for knowledge of it in the first moment of properly human history. The critical discontinuity of human from primate—this unknowable moment of our history—is explained by Freud not through science, for which the task is impossible, but through the generation of a myth, myth here serving the function it always does, according to Lévi-Strauss.

Thus, for Freud, the Oedipus complex is the key to how to read the unconscious. But, this is not the only dimension of the Freudian act of reading. In her presentation on this theme of "Reading the unconscious," Elisa Alvarenga (2011) offered a very nuanced presentation on the interpretation of dreams in psychoanalysis today. She started with a close reading of the foundational dream of psychoanalysis, the dream of Irma's injection. In her presentation, Alvarenga stated that this dream retains its importance because:

> [...] it's a dream where we already have two aspects of the unconscious: on the one hand, its connection to the signifier, to the

signifier chain, which connects to the experiences of the subject Freud, his history and his suffering, and so, his truth, and on the other hand, its connection to the letter, something that creates a hole in the meaning constructed by language, and then connects to what Freud has called the navel of the dream, the *Unerkannt*, which Lacan calls the impossible to recognize. This non-recognized is of the order of something that cannot be said, and belongs to what Freud called the *Urverdrängung*, the original repression, the proper hole of the symbolic, which represents its closing. It establishes the limit of the readable, on the one hand, and also it's the index of what doesn't cease to not write itself. (Alvarenga, 2011, p. 2)

I agree with Alvarenga's formulation here, but I would like to note that the emphasis in Freud has always seemed to me to be on this first aspect of the unconscious, that of meaning, with special privilege to the Oedipal meaning. This second aspect, which really is nothing other than what Lacan mathematizes as the signifier of the lack in the Other, is present, but in Freud marks only a limit, a point of impossibility with regard to interpretation and the psychoanalytic act of reading. Indeed, in the dream of Irma's injection, it appears only as a footnote. And, one might say, it appears only in footnotes or metaphorical references, such as to the rock of castration that the interpretive waves of meaning only crash themselves on. I think it is with Lacan and with our current, what I will call Millerian reading of Lacan, that we have come to fully develop this last aspect, that of a reading, a "reading otherwise" oriented around a signifier not of the Other, but of the lack in the Other.

But: to return to Freud, thus, in my reading, for Freud, to read otherwise, was fundamentally to offer a universal reading, to read the unconscious through the lens of the Oedipus complex. This was indeed a large part of the scandal of psychoanalysis, subverting many ideals or notions held dearly at that moment in the history of civilization. But, at a certain point, the Freudian message was disseminated through society and culture. One might interpret the crisis in psychoanalysis in the 1920s as a function of the very success of psychoanalysis itself. Psychoanalytic interpretation seemed to lose its efficacy at this moment, and I think we might understand that from within the very context of this notion of "reading otherwise:" reading unconscious formations through the lens of the Oedipus complex no longer worked at the very moment analysands were themselves reading it in those terms. It no longer functioned as an other, or a different, reading. In other words, when a patient arrives complaining of an Oedipal wish of some sort, the Oedipal template of interpretation is meaningless, in that it does not read this otherwise.

I want to jump ahead, now, to the work of Lacan. But, here, I would like to quickly make a different kind of remark—elaborate a different point. When I think of the notion of "reading otherwise" with regard to Lacan, I think it is possible to look at the trajectory of his work as various attempts to do just that, to read the unconscious differently. Of course, first, there is the formulation of the unconscious structured like a language, and the concomitant linguistic reading of the unconscious. With the mathemes, there is a formalized and logifying reading of the unconscious. And, with his interest in geometry, the Moebius band, and the torus and later in knots, we have a topological reading of the unconscious. Jacques-Alain Miller has noted at many points in his teaching the way that Lacan works against Lacan—he constantly reformulates, shifts positions, modifies his approach. I think we can understand that as the way in which Lacan never ceases to read otherwise.

But, what about today? What about the twenty-first century? In his presentation at Commandatuba, Jacques-Alain Miller (2005) provided a stunning description, "A fantasy" he titles it, of our contemporary world—postmodernity. In his presentation, which I will try to summarize quickly here, he noted that now society is no longer organized around a master signifier, an S_1, but that our compass—the term he uses—the "dominant place" in our civilization is that of the object a, here no longer the part object of the body, a residue of nature, but industrially produced surplus jouissance, the *plus-de-jouir*. This *plus-de-jouir* acts on subjects, which are disoriented, producing an S_1, a One of evaluation, the incessant evaluation we find in self-assessment, in the workplace, in contemporary trends in the clinic, and—well, why not—in the explosion of signifiers we find now in the new social media, the constant evaluation in tweets and Facebook wall postings, of every aspect and thought and impulse of our lives. And, for Miller, knowledge, S_2, then is in the position of the hidden truth (or lie), knowledge now is nothing but a semblant. Well, as you see, this description of the contemporary world is indeed nothing other than the discourse of the analyst. Society today, Miller proposes, in what he calls his fantasy, is structured as the discourse of the analyst. (See Chapter Ten for a greater discussion of this vantage point on postmodernity.)

Well, this is indeed a striking concept, but, as Miller notes, this immediately creates a problem. If the discourse of the analyst previously worked by acting on the unconscious, which was previously organized as the discourse of the master (which, indeed, is what we saw with Freud—an unconscious reigned over by Oedipus, the master of the unconscious), well, what now? If psychoanalysis is no longer the other side of civilization, as Lacan formulated it in *Seminar 17*, and if psychoanalysis is now the same structure as civilization, then what? How then do we "read otherwise" in the twenty-first century?

I think we must start with a simple point. If we are going to speak about reading the unconscious, we must first have something to read, keeping in mind Lacan's remarks quoted at the beginning of the chapter on writing in the unconscious. In other words, if we are to emphasize that our act as psychoanalysts may not be one of listening, listening to speech, but that of reading, of reading a text, the first imperative is that of creating the text of the unconscious. And, how do we do that, but by taking the words of the analysand and adding punctuation. In several places in their work, Miller and Éric Laurent as well comment on the value of interpretation as punctuation. Of course, Lacan emphasized this first, even in the first phase of his teaching, in his elaboration of the short session, he emphasized that "It is therefore, a propitious punctuation that gives meaning to the subject's discourse" (2006a, p. 209). The act of the analyst in interpretation is the act of punctuation. An exclamation point might highlight a word or phrase. A question mark introduces equivocation. An ellipsis erases a long stretch of blah blah blah to bring two important words or phrases of the analysand together. The combination of ellipses and commas may create a series, highlighting a repetition. The combination of an ellipsis and a colon may introduce some causality in the relation of two words or phrases. The combination of an ellipsis and a question mark allows the analysands own discourse to answer the question raised elsewhere in the discourse. Spaces allow us to separate words into constituent phonemes that will resonate through the discourse. Quotation marks highlight the fact that in the analysand's discourse, he may be quoting an other. And, of course, can we not represent the very end of the session as nothing other than a page break? Our use of punctuation in interpretation should be as extensive as the exhaustive rhetorical tropes that, echoing Quintilian, Lacan, in "The instance of the letter," cites as constituting the defense mechanisms of the unconscious: periphrasis, hyperbaton, ellipsis, suspension, litotes, and so forth. And, indeed, we might even say that it is only with punctuation that the rhetorical character of the unconscious is fully elucidated. For, in the end, this very act of punctuation serves one very clear purpose—it takes the discourse of the analysand, a spoken discourse, and transforms it into a text. To read the unconscious, the unconscious first must be a text. We cannot read the unconscious unless the unconscious is a text, and we provide, as analysts, the punctuation that makes that possible. A subject as a text, indeed, is the very formulation Lacan makes in 1976 in his Preface to the English Language Edition of *Seminar 11*: "I am not a poet, but a poem. A poem that is being written, even if it looks like a subject" (1977a, p. viii).

I want to draw your attention again to Miller's text "A fantasy." Towards the end of the talk, in a place where Miller is emphasizing the jouissance value of the symptom, namely the symptom as a place where jouissance appears, instead of where it should appear, so to speak, he emphasizes what we can provide in our interpretations as a certain quilting point on this. He makes some comments about the importance not of the words of the interpretation, but of the tone of voice of the interpretation, noting that when people repeat an interpretation of Lacan's, they always repeat it in his tone. He states that "one must bring one's body into play in order for the interpretation to be raised to the power of the symptom." This resonates well with me, in that in my own practice I have found that the most effective interpretations, or the interpretations most commented on by analysands, take that place not as a function of their meaning content, but something else—yes, it may be the tone of the voice, or some grunt or other vocalization, which might be nothing other than the voice object, the voice as object *a*; or, perhaps some way of looking at an analysand that is noted, the object *a* as gaze; or, some other body gesture, say slapping my hand on a table. If the object *a* is the agent of psychoanalytic discourse, as Lacan formulates this in *Seminar 17*, one aspect of reading the unconscious is the extent to which we might make the object *a* operative in a psychoanalytic session. Indeed, when I look back at those moments now, I wonder if the very thing that is operative in the sessions is the way in which the analyst might be, in fact, assuming the position of the object *a*, the object *a* as Lacan formulates it in the final stage of his teaching, as a semblant, a semblant of being (1998a). In this regard, if we think of the analyst as a *parlêtre*, a speaking being—why not? This is a possibility—perhaps we ought to place as much care into our act as "being" as our act as "speaking." Why can't we literally accept this aspect of our interpretation—the body act of interpretation—as a form of reading otherwise, bringing the body, as Other, into play in a psychoanalysis?

To take "reading otherwise today" from a different approach, it is worth noting that in "A fantasy," Miller addresses this question of interpretation in the contemporary world more directly at one point in his text. He states that each of the four terms (or elements, of discourse—a, S_1, S_2, and $) are:

> […] disjointed from the others within civilization. On the one hand, the surplus-jouissance commands; on the other, the subject works; and on again another, identifications fall and are replaced by the homogeneous evaluation of capacities, and this while knowledge of different sorts is actively telling lies and nevertheless progressing. We might say that, in civilization, these different elements are scattered and that it is only in psychoanalysis, in pure psychoanalysis, that these terms are organized into a discourse. (Miller, 2005, p. 8)

We might say, then, that a psychoanalysis, taken to its conclusion, is a kind of articulation of the discourse itself, and the act of reading here is perhaps akin to the function of highlighters that I see students using now when they read, the analyst highlighting these four terms or elements within the discourse of the analysand.

I want to conclude this inquiry with a reference to a type of work particular to us Lacanians, a Testimony of the Pass, given by one of those psychoanalysts who have taken their analysis as far as it could go and have given testimony to this experience. In particular, I want to take up a point that Leonardo Gorostiza made in one of his Testimonies (Gorostiza, 2010). Gorostiza describes a consulting room dream when he was abruptly seen by a helicopter while watching a woman who allowed herself to be seen by him. The dream led to a shift, which had various repercussions, including a significant shift in his practice. Gorostiza said it marked a significant conclusion with therapeutic effects, which he theorized along the lines of Lacan's statements that at the end of analysis, the analysand may recognize that he is pure lack, or pure object a. But, Gorostiza pushed further, and he did not end his analysis at what seemed a reasonable end. In what became the final moment of his analysis, he emphasizes a neologistic phrase that he elaborated and with which he identified, that he was the "shoehorn-without-measure." This new signifier, which led to what he defined as his identification with the symptom, is described as coming out of a void, a void that was uncovered when "lying truth" vanished. Gorostiza highlights in the Testimony at this point—echoing a short theoretical text prepared for a Congress of the WAP on this theme—the incommensurability between the Truth and the Real, which, for him, came to light in another dream—rather amusing, with a colleague of the WAP yelling "I am the Truth" at him, and he replying "I am the Real!" I think that we must further draw the conclusion that this new signifier "shoehorn-without-measure" is nothing other than the Signifier of the lack in the Other, a signifier of the "void" or of the incommensurability of the Truth and the Real, to emphasize the two readings that Gorostiza makes. I wish to quote Gorostiza here:

> This creation is not of the "Ego," but of the subject, who arrived at confronting himself with his absolute difference. A subject who is no longer "poem," that is to say, he is no longer represented by a signifier—the signifier "shoehorn"—before the signifying Other. It is a new subject, "poet," having invented a new signifier which, like the real, does not have any sort of meaning. (Gorostiza, 2010, p. 48)

At the beginning of this chapter, I offered a quote from Lacan relating to reading, a definition of the transference as a supposed-to know-to read-otherwise. At that moment, Lacan stated that the Otherwise in question is that of the Signifier of the lack in the Other, which is also named by Alvarenga as that second aspect of the unconscious. Well, I think that that is precisely what Gorostiza achieved at this moment, the moment of the passage of analysand to analyst, in the elaboration of this "shoehorn-without-measure," which indeed is a Signifier of a lack, a void, an incommensurability, in the Other. But, surely we must note that this elaboration is not really a Reading of the unconscious. Indeed, Gorostiza notes that a new subject, a poet—a psychoanalyst, we might say—is born at this point. Perhaps, at the very end of analysis, it is less a question, then, of Reading the unconscious, but rather of writing the unconscious.

CHAPTER EIGHT

The body politic*

I want to start with the Imaginary, with some words about the body as Imaginary. This is the point of departure of Lacan regarding the body. The body, in Lacan's well known paper on the "Mirror stage," is the body of the toddler, who has not yet walked on its own, but who, catching site of its image in a mirror, is able to take account of its body for the first time, as its own entity, assuming the image it sees of itself, and, in doing so, throws off any support and walks forward on its own for the first time (2006a, pp. 75–81). The toddler, though, is born in a state of dependence and impotence—without the motor powers necessary to walk—and assumes it has powers at this moment that it does not have, and this discordance between the image of the body of the toddler and what the toddler is actually able to do with its body destroys the jubilation of the toddler, and this mis-recognition by the toddler results in the subsequent fall to the floor after a few steps.

This is one of the first bodies described by Lacan—an Imaginary body, a body that is an imagined body, an *imago* to use the old term

---

*"The body politic" was presented at Columbia University on November 22, 2014, as part of a seminar delivered on "The real politics of the body" at the invitation of the New York Freud Lacan Analytic Group.

here. This Imaginary body is the very basis for the precise, clear, and clean way that Lacan will cut through all the various concepts of the ego at that moment in the history of psychoanalysis. The ego is based on an image of the body, an image that is the same time a recognition of the body and also a mis-recognition. This body is, in a sense, a deceptive body—no truth is to be found in this body. The power and mastery that Lacan will associate at this moment to the ego are called into question by the mis-recognition or even misrepresentation that are to be found at the Imaginary level and further by the unconscious itself, and its manifestations in symptoms and dreams and so forth, which are a sign, or better yet a site, of the truth for the subject, which is found elsewhere, in the Other.

Where did this discord come from—this fundamental mis-recognition regarding the body and our relationship to the body? For Lacan, I would say that it is structural for the speaking being. Yet, this is not always as apparent in human history. Lacan addresses this issue, I would say perhaps in an oblique way, in his *Seminar 20, Encore*. In speaking about Aristotle, Lacan talks about a different relationship in antiquity between the Soul and Being—or between what thinks and what is thought of. We could say a different relationship between thinking and the body. He talks about there being a reciprocity here, a concordance, rather than a discordance, with regard to the body. We might even say that there was less of a problem with the body itself in antiquity, extrapolating here from Lacan's comments. When I read volumes two and three of Foucault's work on the History of Sexuality that discussed antiquity—*The Use of Pleasure* on the Greeks, and the *Care of the Self* on the Romans—that is indeed a conclusion I drew—that the power and mastery (the very attributes Lacan linked to the ego) associated with the body in antiquity was not a "problem" for subjects in the ancient world. Foucault might not express it this way, perhaps, but I read that he felt the ancients had a more coherent and less discordant knowledge of or representation of the body. When I read Foucault on this, many years ago, I wondered whether this was somehow a fact of antiquity, something different in their society, or something that Foucault was reading into it, a function of historiography. Lacan, also in *Seminar 20*, gave a very precise answer to this question—namely, that in antiquity and indeed all of pre-scientific discourse, a fantasy of what he called *le rapport sexuel* (the usual translation of "sexual relationship" misses it, what I get out of the French—namely, the notion of harmonious sexual relation) is inscribed within knowledge. Thus, when we talk about antiquity's knowledge of or representation of the body, there is a fantasy notion of harmony and relation that has not yet been broken by the advent of modern Science—which has cut through this fantasy, unmasked the fundamental a-harmonious and discordant relationship between men and women, shaken up the very concepts of male and female, but also of the relationship of a subject with the body.

This fantasy of harmony and proportion and relation is not unrelated to what Jacques-Alain Miller, in "The Real in the 21st century" refers to as nature—a figure of the Real before any disorder of the Real (2014a). Developing on Lacan's notion of the Real as that which returns to the same place, Miller makes an argument that nature provided this function as a type of Real—he spoke of a Real that disguised itself with nature, in the sense that the rhythms of the days, the cycles of the moon and movements of the stars, and the flow of the seasons provided a sense of order and rhythm and harmony in the way in which, in pre-modern society, they came back to the same place.

This version of a Real, of a nature that functions like a Real, is clearly a fantasy, in the sense in which Lacan develops in *Seminar 20* the notion of a fantasy of sexual rapport, or what I think we can call an Imaginarized or pre-modern Real. If we move forward two seminars in Lacan's work to *RSI*: we find that Lacan will make some specifications about the domains of the Imaginary, the Symbolic, and the Real—introducing the concept of consistency with regard to the Imaginary, the hole with regard to the Symbolic, and exsistence with regard to the Real. The Imaginary domain is that which creates consistency. Thus, antiquity's notion of nature is certainly a consistent nature—the sun of the ancient world always rises; but that is certainly not the case of the Sun of our world today (indeed, what analyst has not heard worries associated with the so-called natural world—the sun losing energy, or asteroids flying into the earth—our nature is not the consistent nature of the ancient world).

This is no less true when we think of the body itself. The body of antiquity is not only less discordant, but closer to some version of what we would previously refer to as a more consistent and "natural" state. This is certainly part of the argument that Foucault makes—the ancients were much more natural in their approach to their bodies and sexuality. To take a political issue important to Foucault, homosexuality was a more natural or accepted practice in the ancient world.

When we talk about consistency and the Imaginary body, though, there are a whole series of ways in which this concept resonates in the

Imaginary bodies of the twenty-first century. Take, first, though, the notion of the Imaginary as mis-recognition. This concept certainly has its utility in the clinic—say, for example, in the ways in which the body is mis-recognized at the Imaginary level in some cases of anorexia. But, in our time, in our clinic, I find the issue of the consistency of the body very much in question. There is, to take the most obvious example of this, the matter of what in the psychiatric discourse is named dissociation, depersonalization, and derealization—most dramatically found in what used to be referred to as multiple personality disorder. These types of subjective phenomena were scarcely reported in the literature (psychiatric or psychoanalytic) of a century ago, but are relatively common in the clinic today. I believe all of these phenomena are disturbances in part of the specular image of the body, of the representation of the body, but also of the consistency of that image and the place of that image in the world itself—a consistency that would hold a representation of the body in the world through time. One of the interesting things about this is that the Imaginary here thus relates not only to the very particular and precise notion of the ego as *imago* that Lacan developed in the 1930s, but also harkens back to another psychoanalytic concept of the ego of that era—the ego as perception-consciousness system. In these subjective phenomena, we see a loss of consistency of the perception-consciousness system, one that leads to sometime profound disturbance in the relationship of the subject to its body and the world itself. Now, of course, continuity and consistency in consciousness and ego and object representations is illusory, and I think all of us have experienced the effect of the lifting or unveiling of that illusion. For example, driving down a street only to find oneself a few blocks further down the road than one recalls, with no clear memory of driving that distance, but the obvious evidence that one negotiated that stretch of road without any problems—a micro-fugue, we could say. The point I want to make is that I find this consistency is missing today in certain cases—certainly especially in cases of psychosis, where this is sometimes the elementary phenomenon most evident. The case of Joyce, for Lacan, referencing the incident when Stephen Hero is pushed down and feels that he sheds his body like the skin off a piece of fruit, would be an example of this (Lacan, 2005).

The notion of the Imaginary is the very basis for the definition of politics as described by Carl Schmitt in *The Concept of the Political*. For the conservative Nazi jurist Schmitt, harmony and positive relations in the political realm are not a past fantasy (clearly the past had political conflict and violence), but a fantasy of the future political realm held by socialists and communists and other utopians who deny the conflict and potential for violence that are fundamental to human existence. Schmitt will define politics as essentially linked to identity. Humans are political not to the extent that we accept certain social, moral, or economic identities, but humans are political in as much as they take a shared identity with others that they are willing to fight for. The content of the identity is, for Schmitt, in essence, irrelevant. It is only the fact of a shared identity, and the willingness to join with friends, and fight enemies, that define politics. It is very easy to see how the body could fit within the Imaginary politics of Carl Schmitt—in the sense that the very point of identity could be a representation of the body itself, in the case of Nazi politics, the Aryan body, as the point of identity.

While the notion of the body as Imaginary is easy to grasp, what about the notion of the body as Symbolic? In the first letter to the Corinthians, Paul wrote: "Do you not know that your body is a temple of the Holy Spirit within you, whom you have from God, and that you are not your own?" I don't think that there is a sentence that better captures the advent of the Symbolic on the body than this. Your body is not your own, in the Christian tradition. The harmonious relation with the body is disturbed by the fact that your body is an Other's, God's, the Father's—who will name your body as His. The natural harmony and the consistency guaranteed by antiquity's society are dissolved at the moment of the eruption of Christianity in the Western world. You can read in the texts of the early Christian fathers the eminently political dimension of this. For, prior to the establishment of the Catholic dogma of the Church of the middle ages, we have a fractious collection of communities in the East and West with a striking array of diversity of practices regarding the body—a range of practices and notions regarding the body, sexuality, marriage, celibacy, virginity, the body in the priesthood, pleasure, the veiling or clothing of the body, fasting. Foucault's fourth volume on the *History of Sexuality* that was to deal with sexuality in early Christendom was never finished nor published—apparently the notes sit in his archives. But, we are lucky to have the extraordinary work of Peter Brown titled *The Body and Society* to describe how those in the Church dealt with questions of the body from the time of Christ through Augustine (1988). This book, which was first issued by Columbia Press in New York, was republished in 2008—an amazing fact in the United States for a book on such a specialized topic to be reissued in this way. You can read of the austerity of Tertullian—limiting sexual activity to a bare minimum in marriage; *enkrateia*, the sexual abstinence of all Christians demanded by the Syrians Marconian and Tatian, known as the Enkratites—advocating God's break with nature; the *didaskaleion*, Gnostic in spirit, small study groups organized around a guru, a spiritual guide, such as we see with Valentinus; Clement's cosmopolitanism—drawing on the Roman and Greek traditions to enrich his Christianity (Brown emphasizes the fussiness of the *Paidogôgos*—almost like a Christian parody of a Roman text on the body—a life guide on how to master the body, something quite at home today in the Western world); the shift in Origen, to a view of the body as an act of divine mercy, necessary for the healing of the soul, but a body with none of the natural characteristics of the ancient world, a body whose forms are all provisional—another approach that resonates with today; the separation from the city—severing the social bond—of Anthony and the Egyptian monks, the Desert Fathers, and the concomitant privation that came with it; the virgin girls and women linked to the Church; Gregory of Nyssa's view of sexuality as a sign of God's abiding care for humans after the Fall; John Christostom—preaching a separation of the body not from nature, but from Society, attempting to erase the link with the Roman notion of the body and the end of the ancient duty of reproduction; the noble and educated Ambrose of Milan, where we first find the Church as that point of identity in the sense of Carl Schmitt, a defining point of identity in the fights, with Arianism in the Empire, non-Christians, and pagans—but with a shift from the concept of spirit and flesh to more classical themes of the mind and the body, the latter as a mud-slick on which the soul might slip; the rigidity of the sexual differentiation in the body held by Jerome—one otherwise motivated by Origen; Augustine, the first to write so openly of his own sexual experiences, who went on to grasp all the social bonds of Roman society as a means to further the Church, the social body—for whom sexuality was no longer a way to fight death, but rather a "miniature shadow of death" (Brown, 1988, p. 408)—for Augustine, sexuality was linked to death in that it both mocked the will and demonstrated a *discordiosum malum*—"an abiding principle of discord lodged in the human person since the Fall." What struck me the most in Brown's work—and which I have tried to quickly survey here for you—is the rupture Christianity brought onto the notion of the body. But note that, while this will in the West eventually settle in the Middle Ages into a universal, stable, and dogmatic set of beliefs organized and promulgated through a Church unified by Rome, we can read of a very different history in the Early

Christian Church—disparate voices and beliefs captured in texts that articulate some radically different and opposing concepts regarding the body—drawing more or less from antiquity; linked or separated from the State with a body mostly viewed negatively, but at times in a favorable light. This is an eminently Symbolic discourse on the body, attempts by these authors to read and write what they view as the word of God and what that has to say about the body—the centrality of the Word—the Word of God—in these elaborations separates them so much from that of antiquity. I would also note, though, the importance of the Augustinian formulation regarding the *discordiosum malum*, a kind of prefiguration of the Lacanian concept of the sexual non-rapport.

The body as Symbolic is well known in our field and I do not want to say much about it here—just indicate a notion such as symbolization of the body as the mortification of the body, and remind you of that classical notion of the hysterical symptom of the body as something to be interpreted symbolically—a bizarre phenomenon which is seemingly without meaning, a discord in the Imaginary consistency of the body, but whose meaning and truth might be found elsewhere, in the unconscious, in the Other, the Other as reigned over by the Name of the Father. I will note here that we have moved from the small a of the ego, say of Schema L, to the big A of the Other, the Symbolic Other as the treasure trove of signifiers.

What is the politics of the Symbolic? It is, I believe, a politics for all, one organized around the relationship not of egos to alter egos, as in Schmitt, but a subjectification to the master, the master signifier, in the case of Christianity the Word, the Name of the Father, to the law. This is a politics of universalism, a universal law, and a transcendence of particular interests. For Alain Badiou in his reading of St. Paul, who Badiou states, first brings universalism into the political realm, it is thus a politics that goes beyond the particularism, say, of the morality of the Jews and their faith, linked to a people and a particular identity, and at the same time goes beyond the Greeks and their reliance on reason—the kingdom of God is open to all, whatever your identity—your ethnic background—and regardless of your intelligence—it is a faith open to all, who submit to the Word of God (2003). For Badiou, this is event that opens revolutionary possibilities.

But, I believe that Lacan reads this quite differently—it is Kant who most clearly articulates the Symbolic politics of the body. And, not in his most overt work on politics—"Perpetual peace," in which he proposed political conditions that could lead to the abolition of war through republican political organization, the rule of law and international political and legal organizations, the very utopian dream (peace and harmony) that Schmitt was to critique—and here I think that we can say that while the Imaginary never goes away, of course, and I will have more to say about that, Schmitt's turn to the Imaginary is surely a nostalgia of sorts, a looking backward. Lacan—in "Kant with Sade" and the *Ethics* seminar—develops a very different point—namely that in the very effort to eliminate the ego, the "pathological interests" as Kant will put it, in the establishment of the law that the subject submits to— a Universal law, not a particular law—we end up with the possibility of subjects for whom desire cannot satisfy any pathological interest, such as pleasure, but only desire linked to a duty to follow the law, and a concomitant, almost necessity, of pain in doing so (as opposed to antiquity—with a link between one's sense of the greater Good and one's personal sense of good) (2006a, pp. 645–670; 1992).

There are consequences of this for the body—a kind of alienation with regard to the body, which as we saw with regard to the Christian literature, we might concisely describe as the Other's body—consequences that extend even outside of Christianity proper from the well known Kantian definition of marriage as "the contract between two adults of the opposite sex about the mutual use of each other's sexual organs" to the body in Sade, as an instrument for the very jouissance of the Other. But, indeed, even there, at this endpoint, does not the seemingly endless pain caused to the bodies in Sade inflicted by others not bring to mind some of the very self-inflicted pain brought onto one's own body, such as Brown reported in some practices in early Christianity.

And, finally, I want to develop the concept of the body as Real, not the Imaginarized Real, but the Real Real. We find this body first described by Lacan in *Seminar 10* and *Seminar 11*—this is the body as object *a*, as part object, or a partial drive. The process of the symbolization of the body is not complete, there are exceptions, remainders, points on the body not symbolized, Freud's erogenous zones, which Lacan will rework in *Seminar 10* into the notion of the object *a*. We have gone from the dead body, the mortified body—to a body largely dead, with one exception— one body part invested with libidinal energy. This body, the body of the object *a*, can be found so much in the clinical work of the WAP and is, I think, an especially valuable formulation in the clinic of neurosis, in a clinic where the Name of the Father still has power. But, then, as is often the case with Lacan as he reworked his formulas, there is a dramatic shift. In the last Lacan, we have a different relationship of language and the body. This is the body linked with the creation of the concept of *lalangue* and elaborations of *Seminar 20, RSI,* and the *Joyce* seminar. This is a clinic where the Name of the Father is weak. The Name of the Father is no longer Universal and powerful, exerting an influence on all, with the rare exceptions of the extraordinary psychoses. The Name of the Father is merely one way to organize the psychic structure of the speaking being, one of many possible forms of the Symptom. In this clinic, we also see a new place for the body. The symptom as a formation of the unconscious is reworked in 1975 to the *sinthome* as a body event. The Real has the possibility to reverberate in the body itself.

There are very clear consequences of this for our clinical practice. If, in the Freudian clinic or the clinic of the first Lacan, we read the symptom from the perspective of the Other, as organized by the Name of the Father, in today's clinic, we are tasked—for example, by Jacques-Alain Miller in "Reading a symptom"—to read the symptom on the basis of the unique and particular encounter of the signifier on the body (Miller, 2011). This is not a universal clinic, but a clinic of singularity. Lacan described this in *Seminar 20* with his concept of *l'Un.* Unfortunately, this is translated into English most often as the One—unfortunate because the numerical resonance of the term evokes a very different notion of quantification. *l'Un* in French means not only One but is also the indefinite pronoun A. I believe that this is a much finer translation—a Clinic of the A. For one, it captures the notion of the singular, but it also provides us in English an interesting progression—from the small a of the ego, to the big A of the *Autre,* to the A of the singular.

If there is a politics here, it is not the politics of the ego, of Schmitt, of the small a; nor the politics of the Other, of the big A, of Kant and his flip side Sade; rather, it is a politics of the indefinite article, A, a politics of singularity. We see this developed in many ways in our field. For example, in politics associated with feminism—a shift from a hysterical politics, organized around the discourse of the master, to a feminine politics, in the sense of the work of Lacan in *Seminar 20,* organized around not the Other secured by the Name of the Father, but a signifier of the lack of the Other. In the psychoanalytic field, we find this the most in the notion of the symptom, the *sinthome,* as the singular way in which a subject may find his or her way in the world—no longer organized around a universal Oedipal complex, or the Name of the Father, which is relegated to a position now of one among an infinite possible symptoms. This privileging of singularity aligns well with a shift from society organized around a universal discourse with exceptions (the masculine logic as articulated in Seminar 20) to a greater place for the logic of the *not-all*, the feminine logic, which highlights singularity versus the particular example of the universal (aspects of which are developed in Chapter 16, below). And, for psychoanalysts, it is this politics that will define our engagement in the mental health field of this moment, where instead of the *l'Un* as A, we are contending with the *l'Un* as One—a calculating take on the subject that imports the number into our field. Outside of psychoanalysis and the matter of subjectivity, Fred Jameson has noted the centrality of singularity as a critical feature of postmodernity itself, identifying it in aesthetics, economics, politics, and even postmodern cuisine (Jameson, 2015).

As for the body, here, in the Real, we can certainly draw attention to the body as object *a*, as part object, a piece of the Real. Certainly, for the more classical neurotic, this is the body that counts. But, I think we might also take up again a new place for the Imaginary in the Borromean clinic of the *sinthome* and wonder if there is a different place for the body in this clinic. For, while we might stress the aspect of the fragility of the Imaginary consistency of the body, as I did above, I think we might also emphasize the aspect of creativity associated with the consistency of the body. In *RSI*, Lacan spoke of the imagination present in the consistency: "Consistency for the speaking being is what is fabricated and what is invented." I find this very much present in the bodies of the twenty-first century—in the unique way in which speaking beings will fabricate or invent a body for themselves, something that can be of immense importance in the clinic today. We certainly could read the contemporary body—piercings, tattoos, coloring of hair or skin, and all the various body practices of today as the means by which speaking beings invent or fabricate bodies. Indeed, is this not the message of Gilles Lipovetsky's book on *The Empire of Fashion*—the development of modern fashion not, say, as a function of the subjectivation of the contemporary body to corporate greed and relentless advertising, but rather an opportunity for the contemporary subject to fabricate and invent for itself a body, no longer tied to the some fantasy of a natural body (1994). And, in this new clinic of Lacan, this can touch on the Real in some way—in as much as through the *sinthomes*, these new ways of giving consistency to the body may be able to grasp something of the Real, or reverberate in some way with the Real. The Real is not only completely separated off, or present only in the part object, but can be touched upon in speech or in the body. I believe that we can go even further here, with a more specific notion of a Real politics of the body.

CHAPTER NINE

The psychoanalytic soapbox*

W hat is Jacques Lacan's "real" contribution to psychoanalysis? The first answer, the common answer, would be a reworking of Freud's psychoanalysis with linguistics. "The unconscious is structured like a language" is the first of his formulations that most people would quote. I am not so sure about this response to the question. This is not to deny the importance of the entire first phase of the Lacan's work. His reading, his rereading, of Freud, in the light of linguistics and anthropology, brought a precision to psychoanalysis that distinguished the work of Jacques Lacan from many of the other paths, divergences that others were taking within the field. However, while Jacques Lacan brought us in the early phase of his work a renewed vantage point from which to read Freud, and certainly provided some particular creations of his own, I believe that it is really only in the final phase of his work that Jacques Lacan created something new in psychoanalysis.

The creation of something new invariably involves a shock. We see this in the fine arts and in literature. It is no less true for psychoanalysis.

---

* "The psychoanalytic soapbox" was presented at Columbia University on November 22, 2014, as part of a seminar delivered on "The real politics of the body" at the invitation of the New York Freud Lacan Analytic Group.

Freud's work was a shock in his time. And, I believe we first have that effect with Jacques Lacan's final work.

My focus right now will be on *Seminar 23*, the Joyce seminar, *le Sinthome* (Lacan, 2005). When we work on that Seminar now, here, in the United States individually, or in groups, it is a struggle. It is very difficult work. We are confused. The formulations are shocking. There is all the work of Lacan, but also Joyce to tackle. For those of us here, now, I have felt and I have heard others speak of or fantasize about, how different perhaps it was in France, to have been present at the time of the seminar.

But, that apparently was not the case. Éric Laurent gave a talk at the moment of the publication of the seminar in France and spoke about its reception. I will quote him here:

> [...] one can scarcely imagine our dread back then as we sat in the audience of Jacques Lacan's seminar. In November 1975, we could but take measure of our unfathomable ignorance. First of all, there was Joyce, who we thought we had read when we were younger. We knew that this was just a first entry into reading Joyce, but we did think we had crossed the threshold. Now all of a sudden we found ourselves back on the outside. We simply weren't on the right page. We would have to start from scratch [...]. Our first impression was that this was a vast undertaking. And what about the knots! And the diagrams! How would we ever make heads or tails of it? We formed workgroups, cartels. The blind leading the paralytic. (Laurent, 2014, p. 4)

I smiled as I read that passage from Laurent, for it is certainly captured much of my own reaction and the reaction of those with whom I have studied this text.

We are lucky, however, in that we work in a community with others. In "The unconscious and the speaking body," Jacques-Alain Miller (2015) refers to his role in our community as a guide. I like that description very much, for what Miller has done in his work, with his reading of Lacan, is precisely that. He is able to extract points that allow us to orient ourselves in our approach to the work of Lacan.

Let us take the issue of what in France is referred to as *la clinique*, the clinic would be the literal translation, but we really don't have a good translation for this in English. We could perhaps call it clinical praxis to use an older term. I think of it as the clinical practice and concepts associated with something—an orientation, an ideology, or even a particular group of people (one might read about the clinic of autism, for example). One of the great benefits of Miller's work is the way in which he has been able to extract and identify stages or moments in Lacan's work—to identify the continuities and discontinuities in Lacan. There is for example a well-known paper that Jacques-Alain Miller delivered actually in the United States, in Los Angeles, on six different moments—paradigms was the word he used—in the way in which Lacan used the concept of Jouissance in his work (Miller, 2000). With regard to the clinic, we can start with a simpler distinction, into two phases: Miller has identified two clinics, two separate stages, in Lacan's work. First, there is a clinic defined by what psychiatrists would call a differential diagnosis of neurosis and psychosis, a clinic centered around the presence or absence of foreclosure. In this clinic, the responsibility of the psychoanalyst is first to make a diagnosis, one based on the identification of foreclosure versus repression; the presence of elementary phenomena; the presence or absence of a Symbolic transference; and so forth. The diagnosis then informs the direction that the analyst will take in the treatment. This is the clinic of Lacan that most are familiar with. Then, there is a second clinic, one in which the diagnostic distinctions are not present. In this second clinic, we speaking beings are all mad. There is a generalized foreclosure of the Real, in contrast to the previous clinic of localized foreclosure or repression. The Oedipus complex that played the central role for the Freudian clinic, the universal point of psychic organization, and that was retained, rewritten, in Lacan's first clinic, is no longer in that place, but it is only one form of psychic organization among many (for more on this historical change, see Chapters Twelve and Thirteen). This second clinic is Lacan's true creation and what he has left to psychoanalysis. And, I agree with Miller that we are just beginning to tease out how we might use this clinic in our work. We are just beginning to see how prescient Lacan was in leaving us a clinical praxis that is useful in our work now, with people in the twenty-first century, decades after Lacan's death.

What is particularly interesting to me is the central importance of psychosis now in Lacanian psychoanalysis. If one reads widely beyond psychoanalysis to include psychiatry, clearly there is a recognition that something is changing in the way people are presenting for help. See, for example, all the debates on the proliferation of bipolar disorder and autism and even attention deficit disorder—people working outside of psychoanalysis are struggling to respond to what they see in the clinics and hospitals, a struggle characterized by taking new forms of so-called psychopathology and attempting to fit them into old psychiatric diagnostic categories. In contrast, if we look back over the work of the École in France for the twenty-five years around the turn of the century, is not the work organized around the creation of the signifier "Ordinary Psychosis" perhaps the most clinically important work we have seen? This response strikes me as far more useful than what the psychiatrists have come up with. And, it is clear that *Seminar 23* was decisive in providing a backdrop with which to think through this new concept today.

I would like to spend some time now with Miller's text on "The unconscious and the speaking body" that I cited above. I would like to focus on four or five paragraphs in the middle of Miller's talk. In this section Miller discusses three words, three concepts from Lacan's work on Joyce, concepts introduced by Lacan in three places. The first is *Seminar 23* (2005), the seminar called *le Sinthome* and dedicated to Joyce and knots. The other two sources are Lacan's papers delivered at an international symposium on Joyce held in June, before the academic year during which he gave his seminar. These papers were published in a book some of you may have, *Joyce avec Lacan* (Lacan, J., Aubert, J., Godin, J.-G., Millot, C., Rabatt, J.-M., & Tardis, A., 1997). They have been also republished recently, one in the *Autres Écrits* (2001) and the other in an appendix in *Seminar 23*. The first word is *parlêtre*, in French, a neologism that is translated as "speaking being." This is the concept Lacan used to replace that of the unconscious. What is important in psychoanalysis is no longer so much the notion of an unconscious structured like a language, with a symptom or the other formations of the unconscious there to be deciphered. Rather we are now looking at speaking beings with their *sinthomes*, which Lacan re-defines as an "event of the body," some moment in which jouissance emerges in the body, with some reverberation in the body of the Real. So we see here two of the conceptual shifts, namely that of the speaking being replacing the unconscious and that of the *sinthome* replacing the symptom.

What I would like to focus on now, however, is the third concept that Miller discusses, namely *escabeau*. This word appears in one of Lacan's written lectures from the Joyce symposium held in Paris.

Before going forward, I would like to suggest a translation for *escabeau*. Literally, this is usually translated as stepladder or stool or wooden steps that one might stand on to be taller or reach something. When Miller gave the talk in Buenos Aires, he stated that the platform he stood on in front of the podium was a kind of *escabeau*. What both Lacan and Miller will emphasize is that this is the thing one stands on when one wants to say something, give a speech, and which carries an inflection of narcissism. Miller writes: "with his *escabeau*, to this he adds the fact that he believes himself to be a *maître beau*, a fine master. What we call culture is nothing but the *escabeaus* 'in reserve' that one can draw on to brag and flout one's vanity" (Miller, 2015, p. 37). Well, we have a very similar word in English that captures this perfectly, soapbox. Indeed, I believe that to say that someone is "up on his soapbox" is precisely what both Lacan and Miller are intending with this concept of *escabeau*. Here is what Wikipedia has to say about soapbox:

> A soapbox is a raised platform on which one stands to make an impromptu speech, often about a political subject. The term originates from the days when speakers would elevate themselves by standing on a wooden crate originally used for shipment of soap or other dry goods from a manufacturer to a retail store.
>
> The term is also used metaphorically to describe a person engaging in often flamboyant impromptu or unofficial public speaking, as in the phrases "He's on his soapbox", or "Get off your soapbox." Hyde Park, London is known for its Sunday soapbox orators, who have assembled at Speakers' Corner since 1872 to discuss religion, politics, and other topics. A modern form of the soapbox is a blog: a website on which a user publishes their thoughts to whomever they are read by. (Wikipedia, 2016)

Sometimes *escabeau* is described also as a stepladder, and in Lacan's text part of the Joycean play on words associated with *escabeau* is the way in which the word *escabeau* includes the word *beau*, which means "good" in French. In the text on Joyce the *sinthome*, Lacan talks about the *escabeau* and how this *escabeau* is first and foremost for the speaking being, even over the production of the sphere, which I interpret as the ego, the body. Rather than making the soapbox subservient to the sphere, the soapbox is first. Or, to put this different, people tend to look at their sphere, their ego, their body, as the primary fact of their existence, but for Lacan, primacy should be given to the *escabeau*. Lacan talked about how Joyce wanted to hoist himself up on the *escabeau* and how he wanted nothing more than the *escabeau* of the magistral saying. He talks about how Joyce knew how to *escabeau* himself more than anyone. Lacan also referred to himself as a master of the *escabeau* of *lalangue* under the spell of the jouissance of the symptom.

How do we make sense of this? Miller talks about the soapbox as being in a place where the speaking being believes he is a master, a master of his being. He then goes on to approach both the *escabeau* and the *sinthome* from the perspective of jouissance, stating that there are two jouissances for the speaking being. I will quote Miller here:

> What is it that foments the *escabeau*? It is the *parlêtre* from its angle of the jouissance of speech. It is this jouissance of speech that gives rise to the grand ideals of the Good, the True and the Beautiful. The *sinthome*, on the other hand, as the *parlêtre*'s *sinthome*, holds to the body of the *parlêtre*. The symptom arises from the mark that speech hollows out when it takes the figure of saying and it forms an event in the body. The *escabeau* stands on the side of the jouissance of speech that includes meaning. On the other hand, the specific jouissance of the *sinthome* "excludes meaning." (Miller, 2015, p. 37)

I want to make some comments about this set of formulations. The first is to note that this notion of soapbox, in as much as Miller assigns to it a value of phallic jouissance, is an extension of the concept that Lacan developed in *Seminar 20*, namely *lalangue*. If the first clinic of Lacan is characterized in part by the way in which the Symbolic order, the way in which speech and language, are dead and mortifying for the speaking being and distinct from the libido or the drives, Lacan, in *Seminar 20*, introduced a radical re-formulation of the relationship between the Symbolic and the Real. In this new formulation, there is a jouissance value within the Symbolic itself. Indeed, in the paper "Joyce the sinthome," Lacan explicitly used his old concept. He referred to himself as a master of *lalangue*. Miller, in this reading, offers a greater specificity to the way in we might think of how jouissance can be caught up within the Symbolic.

He refers to this soapbox as phallic jouissance, as a jouissance linked to speech, but also with the modifying adjective phallic. How are we to think of this attribution? The starting point here is Saussure, and in particular Lacan's appropriation of Saussure, in which the linguistic sign is built of signifiers and signifieds, but in a chain in which there is no necessary connection between the two, the signifiers and signifieds incessantly slide across one another, except where something allows an anchoring point. The signifiers themselves have no anchor, no point of stability to give them meaning—there is no Other of the Other. But, something can come in that place, a signifier, which can serve as the anchoring point and allow signifiers to produce a signified, to produce meaning. It is the Symbolic phallus that is that signifier that is "destined to designate meaning effects as a whole" (Lacan, 2006a, p. 579). Put in that context, then, this notion of the soapbox makes logical sense, in that, when the speaking being is on his soapbox, his signifiers pass immediately into his signified. On the soapbox, the speaking being creates meaning for himself. Furthermore, we might even say, perhaps meaning is created without mediation through the Other. This is the idiotic jouissance that Lacan alluded to in *Seminar 20*. The production of meaning, under these conditions, is not through the return of one's message from the Other but is directly delivered in a phallic fashion, inasmuch as the speaking being himself provides the linkage between the signifier and the signified. This brings a certain jouissance value for the speaking being. And, does this not capture the very implicit meaning when one throws the insult—"he is up on his soapbox." The insulted one is in public, out there in the open, speaking something important to him but oblivious to those around him, caught up in his idiotic, narcissistic words.

In his text, Miller makes another point about this concept of the soapbox. Namely, that this is a different way of working Freud's notion of sublimation. I will again quote Miller, where he notes:

> [...] *escabeau* provides a colourful translation for Freudian sublimation, but in its intersection with narcissism. And this is a connection that is specific to the era of the *parlêtre*. The *escabeau* is sublimation, but in so far as it is grounded on the first *I'm not thinking* of the *parlêtre*. What is this, *I'm not thinking*? It is the negation of the unconscious by which the *parlêtre* believes he is the master of his Being. (Miller, 2015, p. 37)

Miller then goes on to more substantively rethink psychoanalysis and the Pass itself within the concepts of the soapbox and the *sinthome*. He states: "To do an analysis is to practice 'the castration of the *escabeau*'"—one unmasks the Imaginary self mis-recognitions and the jouissance associated with them—"in order to bring to light the opaque jouissance of the symptom, but to do the Pass is to play on the symptom that has been uncluttered so at to turn it into an *escabeau*, to the applause of the analytic group." Could there be a more radical redefinition of psychoanalysis? One that is in fact based upon Joyce himself, who rejected psychoanalysis? For, if the brilliance of Joyce was the way in which he was able to make his *sinthome* into his soapbox, which is Lacan's formulation, do we not see that this here is the model that Miller proposes for taking an experience of psychoanalysis to its ultimate conclusion in the Pass, namely, that after an analyst destroys his own soapboxes, he would turn his *sinthome* itself into a soapbox in giving a testimony of what transpired for him in the psychoanalytic experience. This is indeed a new way to conceptualize how to say something about the Real of the body: to take the body event experienced as suffering and to turn it into something good, true, and beautiful in public, for the psychoanalytic group, for the polis. This is a very different sublimation— we don't put ideals on the soapbox but rather the *sinthome* itself. This is the Real politics of the body.

PART IV

ADDICTION

CHAPTER TEN

Introducing the new symptoms*

To attach to or detach from the Phallus

There is a very curious relationship between what Freud and what Lacan had to say about addictions. Freud makes a few comments on addictions in his work, most of them a gloss in one form or another of his comments to Wilhelm Fliess in a letter of December 22, 1897, in which he states that "masturbation is the one major habit, the 'primary addiction,' and it is only as a substitute and replacement for it that the other addictions—to alcohol, morphine and tobacco, and the like—come into existence" (1985, p. 287). Lacan had fewer things to say about addictions, but perhaps his most well known comment was delivered in 1975, as an aside, at a meeting of the École, when Lacan noted that there is no other definition of drugs than that which allows one to break the marriage, the relationship, with the Phallus (1976). With Freud, addictions are a means of maintaining a relationship with the Phallus—in this masturbatory sense, without the connection to the Other, a short

---

*"Introducing the new symptoms" was presented at the Seventh Annual Conference of Affiliated Psychoanalytic Workgroups on the theme of "Addictions," in Carrolton, Georgia, on March 10, 2006.

circuit to jouissance—with Lacan, addictions are a way of obtaining jouissance, but, instead of obtaining this through the Phallus, he speaks of obtaining it by breaking a connection with the Phallus.

My first thesis is that this divergence indicates a different place for the Phallus with regard to castration and its relationship to jouissance. For Freud, castration (of the mother or the child) for the male is linked to a perceived threat of the loss of one's Phallus, further linked to a perceived paternal injunction. Integration into the social bond is further, for Freud, linked to a certain perceived renunciation of enjoyment achieved through the mechanism of paternal identification and the pursuit of a jouissance regulated, in a sense, through that identification. Addictions, in this model, short-circuit the path to satisfaction, taking the subject out of the social bond in a mode of direct satisfaction, akin to masturbation. Now, Lacan does—for example, in *Seminar 5*—rework this Freudian proposition, rewrite it, importing linguistics and partially reformulating this structure of castration and Oedipus with his notion of the Name of the Father. And, in that sense, one can certainly easily read Lacan's comments in 1975 about breaking the relation with the Phallus in addictions as breaking the relation with the social order, disconnecting from the Other—as regulated by the Symbolic Phallus.

I would suggest, though, that we read this comment of Lacan's in the light of his later comments on the Phallus, in particular those which Jacques-Alain Miller has drawn our attention to within *Seminar 10*. Miller notes that in this seminar, we see the return of the Phallus, not only as Symbolic, but as organ. In this context, Miller notes that "The negative minus phi is, in fact, no longer a symbol of castration, but designates an anatomical property of the male organ which is completely the opposite of its Imaginarization as power, since it is a matter of the detumescence which strikes this organ at the moment of its jouissance" (2004b). This formulation on the Phallus, which Miller notes is not at all present in Freud, puts Lacan's comments into a completely different perspective, one in which as a body part, the Phallus does not represent an auto-erotic jouissance, as with Freud, but rather a body part which contains the death of jouissance at the very moment of its achievement as the very principle of the Phallus itself. This change in perspective on the Phallus from Freud reprises Lacan's general rejection of Freud's auto-erotic Phallus and a replacement of it with the allo-erotic Phallus Lacan identifies in the Little Hans case, where the boy is confronted not with the Phallus as a source of satisfaction, but as a parasitic foreign object affecting him in ways that he does not understand, sexuality appearing here in its traumatic character, fundamentally disruptive, and opaque to Hans' understanding.

We see here, then, a divergence—for Freud, addiction is an attachment to the Phallus as a means to obtain satisfaction by somehow avoiding the law or the passage through the social bond. For Lacan, however, addiction correlates with an escape from the Phallus in this other sense, addiction as a jouissance correlated with an escape from what Lacan calls the affliction of the speaking being with sexuality itself. In one case, the speaking being avoids the law, in the other case, he avoids the affliction of sexuality.

From malaise to addiction

With regard to history, however, it's easy enough to note that—the few comments such as I noted above notwithstanding—Freud and Lacan had relatively little to say about addictions, and they were hardly alone within the greater psy field. Amidst all the psy literature on neurosis and psychosis and the suffering of the time—say a half-century or century ago—all the discontent or malaise, to adopt the French translation, that Freud alludes to, addiction does not figure prominently. Which is somewhat surprising given the veritable ubiquity of addictions today. This is not only in the terms of the public debate on the various epidemics of drugs; not only in the proliferation of the new addiction diagnoses—such as alcoholism and drugs, but also, say, pathological gambling, or self-cutting, or anorexia and bulimia; and not only in the very ways in which patients frame their treatment demands today; but, it has even reached the level of political discourse. In 1979, our last period of soaring energy prices, President Jimmy Carter delivered a now-infamous speech in which he enumerated the psychic, spiritual, and social suffering of the American people and their relation to the energy crisis—the "Malaise" speech, which ruined his political fortunes. In contrast, in the energy crisis of the first decade of the twenty-first century—also a time of some discontent in the American political arena—we heard President George Bush declare that America is "addicted to oil" and that: "The best way to break this addiction is through technology." Addiction now is a political and social signifier.

In addition to its ubiquity, however, I think it is important to recognize that—in the broader psy field beyond psychoanalysis—addiction is the new template for diagnosis itself. Diagnosis in psychiatry and psychology has gone from the Realist diagnosis of classical psychiatry from Pinel through Kraepelin; through a phase of Modernist diagnosis, in which psychic structure and psychopathology were singularly redefined by Behaviorists such as Skinner (with Stimulus-Response and Operant Conditioning) and Wolpe (the generalization of phobia for all diagnosis itself); to a period of Postmodernism, in which we have the *DSM*—a heterogeneous, superficial, sprawling system—that includes everything from the Realist diagnostic categories to a whole series of new monosymptomatic diagnoses, all of which are fundamentally structured as addictions. These diagnoses—referred to as the "new symptoms" or "contemporary symptoms" in the Lacanian literature—are often configured as addictions elsewhere (see Chapters Twenty-two and especially Twenty-three below for further development).

Not every addiction is a new symptom

While addiction may be a new phenomenon, a new social construct, we might say, it is certainly clear that drugs and alcohol have been around a long, long time. What has changed, however, is how they are often configured in psychic structure. As Fabián Naparstek has pointed out, the use can vary quite dramatically as a function of social organization, varied social structures in different historical settings (2002). Thus, in aboriginal cultures of the past and of today, people will take drugs and experience much of the same physiological impact as anyone else using the drug, but the drug use in such cultures is often quite ritualized and, even more importantly, serves a function to support the social structure, bolster the Other or support the function of the Name of the Father in that social structure. This stands in contrast to some typical forms of drug use in our time, in the era of the new symptoms, in which no such support of the Name of the Father is in play and in which the relationship of the drug use to forms of jouissance must be articulated. Here, Naparstek describes various patterns of drug use—a drug use through which a jouissance is obtained, but within a Phallic limit, under some sort of Phallic control; also, a drug use which enables subjects to break from the Phallus, in the sense of the Lacan quote from 1975, and avoid the Phallus or the issue of sexuality; or, a drug use that enables one to confront the Other sex, such as performance enhancing drugs; and, a form of drug use in the psychotic in which the drug is used to limit an excessive jouissance.

This is not to say, however, that dimensions of this aboriginal use of drugs and alcohol are not present today. As Naparstek rightly emphasizes, each subject must be approached in his singularity. I will give a brief clinical vignette. A successful female professional sees me for help with addictions, an addiction to benzodiazepine drugs and alcohol, for which she had received some treatment through a drug treatment program using a twelve-step approach, which left her unsatisfied that anything had been resolved (but which had also led to the development of another so-called addiction to shopping, less harmful to her, but no less troubling). It quickly became apparent that she was not using drugs to escape or avoid sexuality or to exit the Symbolic order or the social bond. Rather, she was using drugs to prop up the Other, to enable her to participate in various social and professional functions, and to enable her to live up to a certain paternal semblant that she admired. In this sense, her use of drugs enabled her continued participation in her social milieu and supported both her identification (a vertical identification) with that milieu and with her father, who she also modeled herself after in this regard. Now, this drug use was at times ritualized (in the very socially validated consumption of alcohol), but was—with regard to the drugs themselves—also private. I think that such formulations of drug and alcohol use—as a support of the Other and the Name of the Father, evoking the observations of Naparstek on ritual drug use in aboriginal culture—are not necessarily rare, that we must be careful to not necessarily assume, in this sense, that every addiction is a New Symptom.

The New Sinthomes

That said, I do believe that this phenomenon of the new symptoms or the contemporary symptoms exists, and I think that it might be useful to try to trace out some reference points about this from the work of psychoanalysts of the World Association of Psychoanalysis in their elaboration of these concepts. First, I would draw attention to the collaborative work of Jacques-Alain Miller and Éric Laurent in the seminar on "The Other who doesn't exist and his ethical committees" (Laurent & Miller, 1997). There are two points I want to extract from this seminar. The first is that eponymous thesis regarding the Other. If there was an Other that existed, we can say that this is the Other of Freud and of the early Lacan: an Other marked by completeness and by consistency, this secured in an operation of *capitonage* by the Name of the Father. A key demarcation point in Lacan is in the late 1950s and early 1960s when, roughly corollary with his pluralization of the Names-of-the-Father in the incomplete seminar—the decentering of a single *point de caption* to secure the Other—Lacan introduces a barred and lacking Other. The consequences of this for the clinic are immense, with a bearing on the notion of the symptom and on our technique relative to the symptom. With a consistent and complete Other—Symbolic Other—we have a practice of interpretation, of Symbolic interpretation, and the symptom as unconscious formation can be decoded against this backdrop. The symptom's status is thus largely Symbolic. However, with an incomplete Other of this era, Lacan takes a step in the direction of what he will elaborate in *Seminar 23* on Joyce, in which the symptom is reconstituted as a *sinthome*, and we move from a focus on the interpretation of the truth of the symptom on the basis of a language secured by this intact Other to a reduction or distillation of the jouissance of the *sinthome* through *lalangue*, as Jacques-Alain Miller developed in his seminar *Pièces detachées*. It is this *sinthomatic* dimension that makes the new symptoms the new symptoms, which we certainly see in the clinic, in the way in which these symptoms are resistant—in many ways—to interpretation: a point to which I will return, but which is important as a way of defining the logic of what makes the new symptoms.

There is a second point that I want to extract from "The Other who doesn't exist"—the shift that Laurent and Miller observe from vertical identification—the identification with the paternal imago in its varied forms as enumerated by Freud in *Group Psychology and the Analysis of the Ego* that forms the basis for primary identifications—to horizontal identifications, identifications of members of a group with one another, as opposed to with a leader. In *Civilization and Its Discontents*, Freud identifies this horizontal identification as a specific feature of American civilization (Freud, 1930a, pp. 15–16). This sharp observation has many ramifications, including its impact on the very formation of Lacanian psychoanalysis and its institutions in the United States, where the leveling aspect of American equality identified by de Tocqueville—with its horizontal identifications—is a more challenging terrain to the development of psychoanalysis with its focus on singularity—in contrast to any identification—than the hierarchical, vertically identified, social structures of Europe, more conducive to the establishment of the psychoanalytic transference (Svolos, 2005, April 12). But, more important in the context of this issue of the new symptoms is the way in which we can see horizontal identifications in play. At one level, this is evident at the level of the symptoms themselves—where it is not at all unusual to see analysands adopting symptoms that they hear about from friends, or from internet searches. This phenomenon, especially true in adolescents and young adults, is based on a willful, conscious modeling, very different from the unconscious hysterical identifications identified by Freud, such as in the passage in the *Interpretation of Dreams* where he gives the vignette of the hospitalized woman with spasms whose symptom will be copied by other women in the same hospital ward (Freud, 1900a, pp. 148–150). That mechanism of hysterical identification passes through an unconscious process in which an Other is invoked, often with some figure securing the Other, as the very backdrop for the process—the doctor himself, we might hypothesize, in Freud's vignette. These new horizontal identifications, in contrast, have no such backdrop—the Other doesn't exist, as has been posited. Thus, we see the very phenomenological presentations of the symptoms themselves organized via a mechanism of horizontal identification, which is itself responsible for the very mono-symptomaticity of the treatment demands that we see addressed to us. But, there is yet another dimension to this, in that the response of the greater psy field to these demands itself replicates this structure, delivering treatments themselves that further solidify the Imaginary identifications in play. The most obvious examples of this are the varied twelve-step treatment programs such as Alcoholics Anonymous—all organized around the fundamental assertion of the participant that "I am an addict"— an alcoholic, a drug addict, a gambler, whatever. The whole logic of the treatment is based on that fundamental identification and a kind of management of that identification based on one's lateral, horizontal bonds with others—such as sponsors—with the precise same identification: a form of generalized pseudo-nomination. Everything about the structure of the twelve-step programs, from the system of sponsorship, to the organization of meetings, to the institutional framework of the groups themselves, is notable as well for an anti-hierarchical, anti-vertical, organization, and associated polemics.

From the discourse of the master to the discourse of the capitalist ...

Now, a second point in the work of the WAP: Domenico Cosenza formulates the symptom as the juncture between the clinic and politics (Cosenza, 2005), where the psychoanalytic symptom is—here he quotes Miller (Miller in: l'Instance de réflexion sur le mathème analytique, 1997,

p. 193)—the very definition of the social bond. Cosenza continues with a periodization, a shift from the Freudian orientation to the Lacanian orientation that can be read within the form of the symptom itself. The Freudian politics of the symptom is organized around the Name of the Father—a unique, universal politics, which defines the social bond for all subjects and is at the heart of the clinic. The subject's entry in society—into the field of the Other—is linked to an irrecoupable loss of jouissance that forms the basis for symptom formation. For Cosenza, the key to the politics of the new symptoms can be found in a reworking of symptomatic politics to be found in Lacan's rewriting of the social bond in our current era of advanced capitalism, or postmodernity. In particular, he draws upon a fifth discourse, first elaborated by Lacan in Milan in 1972 (1978a)—the discourse of the Capitalist—which appears only about a dozen times in Lacan's work, from 1972–1975, as best as I can tell. Lacan himself—who had little to say about it—indicates that this discourse is a variant of the discourse of the master, formed through the inversion of the master Signifier and the Subject in the discourse of the master, putting the Subject in the position of agent and the S_1 in the position of truth. The other salient feature in the representation of it is that the vectors—the arrows—shift as well, the vector at the top, labeled impossibility, is not present, and the arrow from Subject to S_1 in the Milan representation is reversed, giving a set of four arrows: from Subject to S_1 to S_2 to object a back to Subject. Cosenza highlights this last, emphasizing the effacement of the dimension of the impossible and—given the revised vector schematic—a permanent recycling of the object. He notes the precariousness of the limit-setting function of the Symbolic and the amplification of the *pousse au jouir*, which he links in the new symptoms to a fetishistic attachment to some objects—the so-called substances of addiction—based on unconscious partial drive functions.

I find this reading of relation of the so-called addictive substances to new symptoms to political formations compelling and want to elaborate on it with attention to a different aspect of this fifth discourse—the inversion of places that puts the Subject in the position of agency—that captures an important dimension of addictions, namely that the very name addict or alcoholic or gambler somehow as a secondary label misses a subjective dimension in play in its emphasis on the object itself (here, Imaginary object and not the object a), rather than on the Subject, Subject as consumer of objects. This subjective dimension is certainly rightly recognized in the political domain—say in the society of consumerism; in economics—where consumption drives the economy; and even in the ideological shifts in health care, the shift from the authoritarian doctor as master to patient-driven health care. Well, let us ourselves observe the fact that the Subject—as a lacking being—is in the position of agent here as well, a fact clearly recognized in the clinical domain by those—psychoanalysts or not—who treat so-called addicts, where frequently different drugs or alcohol will succeed one another as the object of addiction, or, where—even outside of psychoanalytic discourse completely—adherents to Alcoholics Anonymous will describe the "dry drunk"—where the object of addiction is not pursued, but the subjective structure remains intact. In the clinical vignette I gave earlier, when the woman discards the use of substances, she replaced it with shopping—preserving a type of subject position, with interchangeable objects.

But, unlike the discourse of the Hysteric—in the Freudian formulation, say, where beneath the layers of Symbolic interpretation one finds some irreducible partial drive element—where the object a is below the bar in the position of a truth separated from the Subject, the genius of Lacan's manipulation here is that, in the discourse of the Capitalist, beneath the bar, the truth of the Subject is the master signifier itself— here not the Name of the Father—but the signifier putting discourse to work, as a demand, to enjoy, to consume. Not the master Signifier as a master in the Hegelian sense, but in an unconscious, superegoic dimension. We might say here we have a master Signifier without a Name of the Father, which, coming from a different theoretical elaboration, is also precisely the point Marie-Hélène Brousse arrived at (2005), where she draws the further conclusion that without the Name of the Father to organize the fiction, the fantasy, of sexual relations, it is the objects of the Market—supported by this Father-less master signifier—that structures jouissance today.

… to the discourse of the analyst

As a final reference to the work of the WAP in this direction, I want to return to Jacques-Alain Miller, to a talk he gave in Comandatuba (2005). In response to a series of presentations asserting the disinhibited and rudderless status of contemporary subjects, Millers asserts that, in fact, it is the object a that represents the *boussole*, the compass, or point of orientation for postmodern discourse—imposing itself on the Subject, lifting inhibitions, giving the matheme a, vector, then Subject. This leads the Subject to produce some evaluation, an S_1, the countable One of evaluation, which—in the discourse structure of Lacan—is thus placed under the bar of the Subject. The fourth place is occupied by knowledge itself, as perspectival semblant in the place of truth—giving postmodern discourse precisely the structure of the discourse of the analyst. This radical hypothesis, interestingly, is not without support in Lacan's work itself: in 1973, at another conference in Milan, Lacan remarked (1978b) that there is a correlation in style between capitalist civilization and the extension of the discourse of the analyst. Miller supports this stunning proposition with the observation that Lacan designated the Unconscious and Society from Antiquity to today with the structure of the discourse of the master—against which psychoanalysis' efficacy in interpretation correlated with the fact that it was the opposite, the flip side of the master's Discourse. But, what now, if contemporary discourse has the structure of the discourse of the analyst?

Let's work this proposition further. First, it certainly allows us to account for a type of loss of efficacy in psychoanalysis, or at least in classic psychoanalytic interpretation. The practice of the golden age of Freudian interpretation—bringing light to an unconscious of which subjects were blindly unaware—just doesn't work now, in a setting in which, we could say, capitalism has—with the acceptance of subjects—reached into the unconscious, what Fred Jameson refers to, along with nature, as one of the final precapitalist enclaves, now colonized by global capital in postmodernity (1991, p. 49). Or, put differently, without the strong repressive apparatus, with the waning of the paternal imago that Lacan noted as far back as 1938 (Lacan, 2001), the unconscious itself—organized on the structure of the discourse of the master—may not even be a useful way of figuring psychic structure. Without an unconscious, or at least the Freudian one, the loss of interpretive efficacy makes sense, in that the discourse of the analyst works on the discourse of the master and, without an unconscious structured in such a way, perhaps Analytic Discourse is in a more precarious situation.

Miller notes, however, in this text that there is a difference between postmodern civilization and analytic discourse, in that the various elements are separated in postmodern discourse—not articulated with one another—as they are in the discourse of the analyst proper.

These two points—first, the loss, in a sense, or the transfiguration, of the discourse of the master in the formation of an unconscious against which to work; and, second, the fragmented, disconnected character of postmodern discourse lead themselves to the basis for a clinical approach to the new symptoms.

Rectification

I think that it's important to specify the nature of the challenge to psychoanalysis of the new symptoms. One of these is certainly related to a loss of efficacy in interpretation. The shift from the symptom to the *sinthome* conveys some of the dimensions of a theorization of this shift and an outline of a response to it—the move from interpretation of truth to a distillation of jouissance. One dimension sometimes evoked in this regard is the opaque character of the jouissance inherent in the symptoms, named autistic in some settings. I agree wholeheartedly with Fabián Naparstek that we do not want to limit the forms in which we conceptualize the jouissance manifested in the new symptoms. It may be an autistic jouissance to be obtained without reference to the Other or to the Lacanian phallus, a type of non-sexualized jouissance; or, a jouissance linked to the Phallus, the masturbatory jouissance of the male position; or, a jouissance articulated with the Other in the mode of feminine jouissance—and the varied presentations of drug use as acting out often can be articulated in such a way; or, again not to be forgotten, a drug use linked to the Other in support of the Name of the Father. Finally, there is the place of drugs in psychosis, where addictions may well serve as a means of containing jouissance, and the occasionally seen phenomenon of the eruption of an overt psychosis after a person stops using drugs or alcohol certainly indicates the importance of precision in diagnosis and prudence in the pursuit of treatment for addictions.

All that said, I want to give a vignette to illustrate some ways of responding to these challenges. A woman comes to my office with the common complaint regarding her addiction to some serious drugs. However, it becomes clear in our preliminary sessions that her use of drugs is not so monolithic, but instead takes on three forms. In the first, she uses very modest doses of different drugs to help her get through the day—not, say, to prop up the Name of the Father, or to integrate her socially, but rather to negate or efface her moods—the small ups and downs of daily life—especially the sense of lack of control or of stable identity, which Miller labels as essential elements of the feminine clinic of non-identity, or the being of nothing (1999). This is a very interesting use of drugs—one that many people search for in prescription pharmaceuticals that they get from psychiatrists. Her second use of drugs is to give her access to men, to enable her sexuality, which—drawing on the table of sexuation in *Seminar 20*, we could call her phallic vector, jouissance directed to the Phallus. The third use is a use of drugs she described as leading to a kind of pleasurably painful immobility—depression she initially labeled it—but really a certain type of, for lack of a better way of putting it, lounging around the house. This third use is—again with Lacan—the vector leading to the signifier of the lack in the Other, which only becomes clear through a series of connections, junctions, made that linked this behavior to a similar behavior on the part of her mother—a real Millerian *femme à postiche*—a dominant Other for this analysand—who only demonstrated her lack in a similar lounging behavior. This final articulation was especially fruitful in the case—shaking up ready-made horizontal identifications with her substance, fortified by Alcoholics Anonymous treatment—through a series of links that brought this into play. This operation is similar to what Lacan named—in a session of *Seminar 23* (Lacan, 2005) brought to my attention in a text of Mauricio Tarrab's (Tarrab, 2005)—splicing. I brought together disparate, fragmented, separate elements of this analysand's discourse and called into question her solid, objective identification. This operation is not effected through the introduction of a new word, an interpretation, a suturing that requires the addition of a stitch, but by pulling pieces together, a procedure whose efficacy may be formulated in the context of the fragmentation that Miller proposes in postmodern discourse. In the face of the fragmentation, splicing serves the purpose, not of solidifying knowledge, but of introducing an enigma. This notion of enigma—which Marie-Hélène Brousse highlights in the paper cited above as an especially important task with regard to the new symptoms—has, of course, always been a critical task in preliminary sessions—a calling into question of identifications. It is especially important in the context of today, where these identifications are held onto quite strongly—supported by the various groups such as Alcoholics Anonymous—the ethical committees that stand in for the weakened Other.

A final vignette details another response to the challenge. Again, a woman presents with troubles with a drug, again mediated through Alcoholics Anonymous treatment with significant emphasis on an inability to control the drug use. Here, again, I intervened, but in a different way, relatively quickly naming the use of the drug as a device, a device that enabled her to do things. This intervention, a nomination, had an effect, inducing an enigma by turning upside-down her formulation about her use—from a use of drugs out of control to a use of drugs as a device to control—leading to a sense of curiosity about why she chose to do that, introducing the subjective dimension. In the text cited above, Mauricio Tarrab talks about this type of intervention as a cutting up of a certain functioning of jouissance, not through deciphering—interpretation—but by nomination, a nomination he identifies as closer to the traumatic Father than the Symbolic Father. Here, I venture that this naming, we might say, not only introduces an enigma, but, through a kind of Symbolic mandate, reorders psychic structure in a way to set the analytic process in motion, introducing a bit of the discourse of the master against which the discourse of the analyst can play.

In both of these interventions—splicing and nomination—we are looking at two forms of rectification, of the establishment of the properly psychoanalytic symptom, and the shift from preliminary sessions to psychoanalysis. All of which makes sense, for with analysands and patients with addictions or any of these new symptoms, the challenge is not the end of the treatment but beginning the treatment.

CHAPTER ELEVEN

More, more, more addiction*

There is something paradoxical about the place of addictions in psychoanalysis today. In the Freudian moment of psychoanalysis, a person would approach the analyst because he was suffering in some way or another, a suffering that was senseless to the person— we see that in the cases that Freud has left us. Through the process of the psychoanalysis, some meaning would be elaborated. But, often, in the end, even when all the meaning had been properly elucidated in the treatment—and I think Freud really saw it in this way—something would remain of the suffering of the patient—a symptomatic remainder that would not go away even with the right interpretation. This is present at the very beginning of his work, with his notion of the kernel of the dream resistant to all interpretive efforts, found in *The Interpretation of Dreams* from 1900. But, Freud grappled with this especially in the final decades of his work, from the point of *Beyond the Pleasure Principle*, with his elaboration of the negative therapeutic reaction (the fact that a symptom persists even after a so-called proper interpretation),

---

*"More, more, more addiction" was first presented at Duke University's Center for Critical Theory on November 17, 2011.

repetition, the effects of trauma, eventually all brought together under the rubric of the death drive—a concept Freud elaborated to describe an essentially destructive dimension at the heart of the subjective experience, that can be found in fact in the symptom itself. At the moment of Freudian psychoanalysis, this is a point reached at the end of an analysis—a person will come in with sometimes vague or ill-defined suffering, searching for an elaboration of meaning, and will end an analysis left with the elaboration of a symptom, some piece of which remains, resistant, repetitive. The paradox of addictions today, in our current world—our postmodern world—the paradox of addictions— addiction as a form of suffering that is repetitive and destructive—is that they appear not at the end of an analysis, not as a residue of the analytic experience, but before an analysis—that they even might constitute the reason why a person would seek an analysis. I think this is clearly a contemporary phenomenon, one we do not see at all in the psychoanalytic literature of a century ago, and is indicative of a change in the world.

I think it worthwhile to begin with a few observations on the very words we use to describe this phenomenon of so-called addictions. In the psychiatric field, they are not called addictions, but rather substance use disorders. Here, in the psychiatric world, the emphasis is placed on the concept of the substance, which substantializes the drug as an object. And, which leads the psychiatric researchers to explorations of the effects of the substantial object—the drug—and its impact on the brain and body of the person. This scientific program forecloses both the subject and the unconscious, which are radically excluded from such a program and the associated medical treatments. My clinical experience is that this concept does not hold up in any way. This is not to deny that there are physiological effects of the chemical substance in drugs on the brain and body, but rather that individuals may use the same chemical compound, but obtain very different effects from their use of the same so-called substance. A substance that inhibits one individual may stimulate another. One person may get happy and another sad from the same substance. And, furthermore, the effect obtained from the drug may vary for a particular person depending on the context of the use of the drug—alone, or with one or another group of people. I believe that there are two flawed assumptions to this scientific paradigm. One problem is the reliance of this scientific model on a Pavlovian stimulus-response model. The drug represents the stimulus, which leads to a response on the part of the user. A more serious problem is the way in which this approach relies on the affect as some supposedly Real or objective gauge to the subjective state. For the psychoanalyst, the Lacanian at least, affects—with the exception of profound anxiety, *l'angoisse*—are deceiving. They are not natural manifestations of the body that can be directly interpreted. A smile does not necessarily indicate happiness, but it can mean many different things. Affects implicate the relationship of the subject to the Other, which must be elucidated through language—the meaning cannot be identified through observation alone, this being the foreclosure of the subject of the scientist in this research paradigm.

Psychoanalysis, in contrast, in its approach to the issue of addictions, can only proceed with the establishment of certain suppositions, related to the unconscious and to the subject of the unconscious, an unconscious subject that is elaborated in a kind of fragmentary or incomplete way over the course of the treatment. I think it may be worth pausing to say a bit about the notion of the unconscious subject, something missed in some presentations of Lacan. Here I will follow some points developed by Jacques-Alain Miller. The work of Jacques-Alain Miller—a reading of the work of Lacan that he has carried out for many years in his course titled "The Lacanian orientation"—and punctuated by many texts, Miller's "Reading a symptom" (Miller, 2011) plays an important role in this argument—is a key reference point for what I am developing. The Lacanian subject is the subject of the unconscious and, in this regard, is different from any substantial or pseudo-substantial entity, such as the ego—an Imaginary representation of the speaking being—or the soul or any thing along those lines. It is also not really the speaking subject, but rather the subject that is elaborated through speech. Lacan works the Saussurian linguistics—that language is based on the differential and diacritical relationship of signifiers with one another—and describes, in this sense, the subject as an effect of the signifying chain. But, it does not have a substantial existence in the signifying chain, but rather is supposed to exist in it, without being directly represented there. There is no essence to it. One cannot say of the Lacanian subject—"there it is!"—with any kind of certainty. Rather, this subject—an unconscious one—is supposed to exist there, and, in the course of an analysis, we make an effort to say something about it. Take the example of a dream, which Éric Laurent has discussed. The subject, the dreamer of the dream, is never definitively identified in the dream. A dream happens—a signifying chain—with all its meaning and senselessness. Nowhere, however, in the dream does the dreamer represent himself. There is no "I am this or that" within the dream. But, however, and this is what Freud taught us about dreams and which the practice of psychoanalysis continues to confirm to this day—there is a subject effect, I would say, in the dream. And, as Laurent points out, the subject can be found both nowhere and everywhere in the dream. Often, in a session involving a dream, an analysand will identify himself in several different places in the dream, none definitively, but each supposed in the elaboration of the dream. And, further, the subject can be supposed in what Freud termed the wish fulfillment staged by the dream, or, as we say now, the unconscious desire of the dream. This, I say, is a fundamental dimension of both Freudian and Lacanian psychoanalysis: namely, an analysand will have a dream, a slip of the tongue, some parapraxis (bungled action, forgetting of a name), or indeed some symptom. And, in talking about this in a session, the analysand will come to interpret these phenomena as what Lacan calls formations of the unconscious, and the analysand will develop a belief in—a supposition of—to use a more philosophical phrase, these phenomena as unconscious. And, through the analysis, an unconscious subject, which is never fully identified as such, will be supposed through these phenomena. To say that the subject has no existence as such, however, is not to eliminate the possibility of a Lacanian ontology. As our French colleague Clotilde Leguil has demonstrated, Lacan is distinguished from the Structuralists by virtue of an ontology that has some similarities with the Sartrean project (2011). While Lacan will reject existentialism for its refusal of the unconscious, he nonetheless will adopt part of the project of *Being and Nothingness* in his very definition of the subject. Unlike the ego, which has some Imaginary existence, but one that is always misrecognized and whose very existence, while Imaginary, covers over the lack that defines castration, through the entry of the subject into language, the subject, the unconscious subject, is defined by this very lack (the link with Sartre). It does not have existence, but, for the Lacan of the 1950s and early 1960s, is defined as a lack in being. Through speech, we might say that the subject attempts to bring being into the world. Lacan will ultimately resolve this issue in a different way, in his final years, with his assertion of the substance of jouissance, that jouissance has an existence, albeit in the Real.

These beliefs in the unconscious and the corollary unconscious subject are one of the foundations of psychoanalysis. That said, some psychoanalysts of the International Psychoanalytic Association have lost this belief in the unconscious. And, we see these analysts search elsewhere for support for their practice. The drive of some of these analysts towards neuropsychoanalysis—a somewhat bizarre collaboration between psychoanalysts and neuroscientists—can be understood in this context. The two different groups approach this for very different reasons. The neuroscientists are mining the work of Freud and other psychoanalysts to look for models that might offer more richness for their scientific endeavors, as they find that the reflex arc or stimulus-response paradigm of behaviorism is not so useful in the study of the brain. Thus, we can read of the Nobel laureate neuroscientist Eric Kandel (1999) declaring that Freud had proposed the single most valuable model for the function of the brain. For their part, the psychoanalysts of the IPA—having lost faith in the unconscious—turn to neuroscience to prop up their practice, finding some so-called proof to validate their work in this or that study.

For Lacan, the subjective dimension is fundamental in psychoanalysis. Indeed, the belief or the supposition regarding a subject becomes the basis of his very reformulation of the transference, the motor force behind the psychoanalytic treatment. Recall that for Freud, initially, the transference—defined as the way in which a patient might misperceive his analyst as an important figure from his childhood, a parent often—was initially described as an impediment to interpretation, and later seen, in its mildly positive form (a positive, but not passionate, disposition to the analyst) as a necessary condition for the treatment. Indeed, for Freud, the very possibility of developing a transference became the key to the Freudian differential diagnosis. Those patients capable of investing psychic energy, libido, in another person, in the analyst, were suitable for psychoanalysis, according to Freud. Those who invested all their psychic energy on themselves, narcissistically, in general to be understood as within the clinical structure of the psychoses, were not suitable for psychoanalysis. Lacan, in a reformulation of key psychoanalytic concepts in *Seminar 11*, separated out repetition from transference and also affects from transference, honing in on the key element of the transference as what he referred to as the *sujet supposé savoir*, which can be translated as both the "supposed subject of knowledge" and the "subject supposed to know." From the standpoint of the final work of Lacan, as elucidated by Jacques-Alain Miller, the knowledge that is supposed and elaborated over the course of an analysis is often structured around a symptom—not in the psychiatric or medical sense of some phenomenon of some noumenal disease or disorder; and, not in the earlier Freudian sense, as an unconscious formation, to be deciphered. This psychoanalytic symptom, rather, drawing from the work of Lacan on James Joyce, and the topological theory of knots—the Borromean clinic—is the symptom, or *sinthome*, in as much as it is what holds together the Imaginary, Symbolic, and Real for a subject. Over the course of an analysis, an analysand will identify his symptom, which has many facets—it is surely linked to his suffering, but also ego identifications and even what may call body images or other Imaginary phenomena; and, also the Symbolic identifications that might form the grounding of the unconscious, the master signifier or Unary Trait as identified in Freud; and, finally, also the Real, or what constitutes jouissance for the subject. This symptom is what holds it all together. For Freud, the Oedipal Complex, reformulated by Lacan as the Name of the Father, can be understood, in a sense, as a particular form of the symptom, but one which had a general function for a large group of people at a particular historical moment. If the symptom is that which structures the psyche for a subject, there was once a moment where the Oedipus played that role for a great number of people. I will come back to this. The key point I want to make here, however, is that this psychoanalytic symptom is something very singular to the analysand. So, in this regard, as a psychoanalyst, to speak about addiction as a symptom, within our psychoanalytic discourse, really does not make a lot of sense. We may use concepts such as discourse—discourse of the hysteric and discourse of the analyst, for example—and we also may use notions of structure—psychic structure of neurosis, hysteria, obsessional neurosis, psychosis, and so forth. But, addiction, in this sense, as a symptom in a very strictly psychoanalytic perspective—and our colleague Pierre-Gilles Guéguen elaborates this point in a paper (2009) with regard to other so-called new symptoms such as depression and anorexia—has no place in our psychoanalytic discourse.

But, certainly, if addiction does not exist as a proper concept of psychoanalysis itself, it exists in the world, and it is certainly now a signifier of the Other that we must contend with. And, finally, it is certainly a social phenomenon. So, then, the question shifts, perhaps, a bit. And, for me, as a psychoanalyst, I wonder—what might psychoanalysis have to say about this phenomenon?

I will want to approach this in several different ways. First, to adopt the discourse theory elaborated by Lacan around the period of *Seminar 17*. As you may know, Lacan was interested in ways in which he might be able to transmit something of the psychoanalytic experience outside of speech. To that end, we can certainly look at the Lacanian mathemes, his adoption of mathematical symbols, as one attempt. Let us look at the unconscious. I have already introduced some notions about the unconscious above. It is a hypothesized or supposed construct based on a relationship of signifiers. We need at least two, an S_1 and an S_2, that have some relation. One way to understand this is the action of one signifier on the group of signifiers, of the S_1 as a master signifier on the group of signifiers. In the case of the neurotic, as understood from the earlier moment in Lacan's work, this is the Name of the Father as a master signifier having a structuring function in the unconscious. The hidden truth, beneath the S_1, is the supposed subject of the unconscious. And, there is a product, or a leftover, or remainder elaborated at the moment of the establishment of the unconscious—which we can understand as the entry of the speaking being into language, with all that that entails—in the production of the object a, a part object, a drive object. In an earlier moment of Lacan's teaching, *Seminar 10*, this is a body object linked to a piece of the body found on the erogenous zones that is not fully symbolized, as it were, with the entry of the speaking being into language. At the point of *Seminar 17*, this exchange between language and jouissance is reformulated by Lacan as a *plus de jouir*, a surplus jouissance, a concept Lacan links to Marx's concept of surplus value. Put differently, initially, prior to the entry into language, the subject has some experience of a direct, or unmediated, or unregulated jouissance. Then, there is the point of the entry of the subject into language which leads to an exchange between language and jouissance. There is a loss of that jouissance. But, in the exchange, a surplus is created, as in the labor exchange described by Marx in *Capital*, which Lacan described as surplus jouissance. This is not the original jouissance, but one born of the exchange between language and jouissance. This discourse, based on the relation of these four elements in the four places I have identified on the board, is described by Lacan as the discourse of the master. It represented the dominant social discourse and was also the discourse of the unconscious itself, say, at the moment of Freud.

But, something happened between this moment of Freud's and our own. The Other today, the Symbolic order, is no longer what it used to be—to take the title of the 2012 Congress of the World Association of Psychoanalysis. This is registered by different disciplines in different ways, and I think one of the hallmarks of Fred Jameson's work regarding postmodernity is an attempt to specify this social and historical discontinuity within the Marxist framework. I would like to draw your attention to one aspect of Jameson's reading of postmodernity that is especially salient to the psychoanalyst, namely, his comment (1991) that it is in postmodernity that two of the last precapitalist enclaves are opened up to capitalism—nature and the unconscious. I think that it is with reference to this comment that we might specify something about the discontinuity that we might articulate in the Symbolic order—namely, between what transpired before our current moment and what constitutes our current moment. And, to get back to the theme of this argument, I think that this difference has a bearing on the social phenomena of addictions today—namely that they are a phenomena of the Symbolic order, the Other, today.

I would like to introduce several different approaches to this discontinuity, to explain this rupture within the Symbolic order. I developed these more fully in the previous chapter, but want to at least make reference to them again here. To set this up, let me go back to what I just described as the discourse of the master. I indicated that this discourse represented both a dominant social discourse prior to postmodernity and also the discourse of the unconscious. How can we understand this relationship between the psyche and the social? In the 1980s, Jacques-Alain Miller (1988), drawing from a single reference to it in the work of Lacan, developed the concept of *éxtimité*, or, extimacy. It is a concept that echoes some of Lacan's interest in topology, and which has numerous ramifications that we might develop. I want to highlight one point from this work, namely, for a speaking being, that that which is most intimate to us, in the very heart or kernel of our being, will often be that which seems most alien, foreign, or even external to us. This is a very different approach, drawn from topology, to a very classical philosophical issue of the relationship of the subject and the object. The notion of the Other itself has an aspect of this, being both the Symbolic order, the social world around us, and the unconscious. With the development of the hypothesis of the unconscious, the traditional divide between what we might call the innerworld and the outerworld is less interesting. What is outside can be what is within, we might say. And, in that regard, the discourse of the unconscious, the discourse of the master, was also, as

I indicated, from a certain perspective, the dominant social discourse of the era. Certain master signifiers—Name of the Father—functioned subjectively or psychically, because they functioned in the Other. How, then, do we describe a Symbolic order where these signifiers no longer function in the same way—the Symbolic order today?

Lacan offered one response to this, in a series of talks delivered in Italy in the early 1970s (Lacan, 1978a). He develops a fifth Discourse—one in addition to the discourse of the master, university, hysteric, and analyst—which he describes as the discourse of the Capitalist. In the discourse of the Capitalist, Lacan inverts the position of the S_1 and the Subject, putting the subject in the position of agent and the master signifier in the position of Truth. He also alters the vectors that define the relationship. The impossibility that reigned over the relation of the S_1 to the S_2 is not present and the vectors go in a kind of loop—from $ to S_1 to S_2 to a and back. Lacan, in the formulation, removes the dimension of impossibility, and the discourse is presented with an endless cycle of circulation. In this regard, in the discourse of the master, with an S_1 as an agent, the Name of the Father, there is both activity in the Name of the Father, but also a "No" of the Father. There, the master signifier distributes meaning, but also sets limits, and that limit-setting function is no longer in the position of agency in Capitalism, in Lacan's formulation. Indeed, is it not possible to look at the attacks on authority and structure—be they political or philosophical—as removing functions that set a limit to the flows of exchange (be it capital, labor, goods, information, and so forth) in capitalism? Then, there is the way in which Lacan moves the subject from a position of hidden truth to the position of agent, as developed in the preceding chapter.

A much more stunning proposition was elaborated by Jacques-Alain Miller in a talk at the Congress of the WAP in Commandatuba in 2004 (2005). There were a series of presentations by psychoanalysts attesting to the disoriented, disinhibited, and rudderless state of patients in their practice, something that had clearly changed in clinical experience from decades ago. Subjects were no longer in a situation in which their discourse was organized around some master signifier, around the Name of the Father, say, that structured their unconscious and provided primary identifications of a traditional nature. No, that era has largely passed, in spite of nostalgic efforts—politically and even among some groups of psychoanalysts, even Lacanians—to rejuvenate, to bring back the Name of the Father. Miller noted that Lacan once commented on the rise of the object a to the social zenith. This object a, something beyond the signifier, beyond measure, was originally, as I noted, the part object, that bodily erogenous zone not mortified with the entry of the speaking being into the Symbolic order. Well, as I noted, in the seven years from that formulation in *Seminar 10* to *Seminar 17*, Lacan expanded the concept of the object a into the *plus-de-jouir*, surplus jouissance, some thing resultant of the exchange between language and what we might call primary, unmediated, or natural jouissance. Among speaking beings, jouissance—in the encounter with language—is always dislodged from its natural place and appears in places that are unexpected. And, this is no longer necessarily tied to specific body parts or to the body, to an object extracted from the body in an encounter with language. In *Seminar 17*, Lacan noted the rise of the *lathouse*, a kind of false object a (as Pierre-Gilles Guéguen has proposed) that is scientifically constructed, as it were, and serves as a kind of stand in, a ready made object, to take the place of the object a for a subject. This includes all the products of our contemporary industry: everything from movies, to pop music, to images, to pornography to all the gadgets that we use today, and, of course, drugs. Miller noted that these objects a are now the agents driving people's lives, drive objects acting in the place of agent acting upon a desiring subject. We then end up with the matheme $a > \$$. The interesting thing is what results from this operation, namely, an S_1, with an emphasis here to be placed on the 1. This is no longer the master signifier, the Name of the Father, but the pure metric of One, the One of evaluation. This issue of evaluation reigns heavily in the psy field, the clinical field today. But, certainly not only there: in so many domains of our lives, it is necessary to produce measurable outcomes—the health field, economic field, education, and so forth. Everything must be quantified and evaluated, even down to basic acts of the everyday life of most people—eating and drinking, watching television, considering politicians, even intimate acts are all assessed and evaluated on websites, and through Facebook postings and tweets and so forth. Everything is inscribed and often quantified. And then, in the place of truth, we have knowledge, which is relegated to the status of a perspectival semblant. We see in this new formulation of Miller what Lacan referred to as the discourse of the analyst, a very radical statement that Lacan himself, in 1972, suggested (1978a), noting a correlation in style between capitalist civilization and the extension of the discourse of the analyst.

With this elaboration of Miller's, the seeming paradox of addiction that I began with is brought to the forefront. The drive object, the object of jouissance, which for Freud was something that was elucidated at the end of analysis, is now front and center in the world today. To explore this further, I would like to introduce yet another concept from Lacan that I find useful, namely that of the semblant. This French word, which is an archaic term in English as well, is somewhat difficult to translate. "Make believe" is a typical translation offered, though I think it more likely that we will just retain this word in French, like with jouissance. Our Australian colleague Russell Grigg has worked on this concept and described it well: a semblant is not an appearance (a representation of some essence), but rather a kind of pretense, rather than appearance, that does not fool anyone—everyone knows it is pretense—but which someone is happy to use (Grigg, 2007). We know that it is not something, but we get something, some jouissance, out of it, perhaps even more than we might out of the thing itself. Thus, there is a link between semblant and jouissance, as Russell puts it, the jouissance that one obtains from the semblant as make believe provides a surplus jouissance value to the semblant. Why is this concept important? Because, I think, it gave Lacan and psychoanalysis a better way to handle certain issues. Take the phallus. For Freud, the emphasis was on a certain biological dimension to the phallus as organ. In the 1950s, Lacan reworks the phallus as a signifier, a signifier of desire. But then, in *Seminar 10*, we find a reformulation that emphasizes a quality of the phallus as organ, but not in a way that Freud did, but rather, as Miller has put it as "an anatomic property of the male organ which is completely the opposite of its imaginarization as power, since it is a matter of the detumescence which strikes this organ at the moment of its jouissance" (2004b). Later, beginning with *Seminar 11*, Lacan will elaborate the notion of the semblant, and the phallus itself will be included as one of these semblants. I am often asked for some sort of example of the phallus as a semblant, and the simplest demonstration of this that I have yet found is the comedy (and with the phallus, it is often a matter of comedy) movies in the Austin Powers series. Is not the eponymous character's "mojo," as he puts it, a kind of pretense and make believe, for something he states he really doesn't have, but which nonetheless carries a great value of what Russell terms surplus jouissance for the character?

So, in the current work in the Lacanian Orientation, we talk of this moment as a moment of the shifting of the semblants—semblants such as the phallus and especially the Name of the Father, which, in this new formulation, is also no longer a signifier, a master signifier, but rather a semblant, no longer have the same value they had. These semblants provided the structure to society, but they have shifted, generally weakened, in our postmodern moment. One of the functions, to put it in a certain way, of these semblants—especially the Name of the Father and the Phallus—is to contain or handle or structure jouissance. With the weakening of these semblants in postmodernity (waning of authority, collapse of hierarchies, decline of the master narratives, and so forth), we then see a different phenomena of jouissance, a change in the means available to speaking beings today to handle jouissance. Éric Laurent, in a talk on addictions, describes this in a very stark way (2000). He speaks of how drugs represent the strongest sustained effort by the speaking being to incarnate the object of jouissance in the world. The object *a* is also now a semblant, not a substance, to recapitulate the point, and this drug use represents an attempt on the part of the subject to make jouissance exist. But, in as much as the true object of jouissance is, following Freud with his elaboration of the death drive alluded to above, death, we find this semblant, this use of drugs as an object *a*, especially destructive, leading its adherents to death. He elaborates this thesis in the context of certain types of drug cultures—say those associated with popular music—where the musician hero doesn't face the Father, but faces death, through his engagement with heroin or crack or meth or some other drug. Laurent references Lacan's *Seminar 17*: "exaltation of death as a mask of the ideal [...] is thus exalted the most is this thing that is proposed as fate, that is, the more or less rapid path towards death in the prime of youth, youth dying from overdose." Laurent remarks that in this exaltation of drugs, the strength of the ideal is preserved. Heroism, to use his term, among these celebrities is thus reconfigured, not as struggle with the Father, with the Symbolic order, but the struggle with death itself. What is the mask of the ideal here that Lacan alludes to? I am not sure. Perhaps this has to do with a notion that one might vanquish death, defeat death, surely an Imaginary concept, but not something unrelated to the experiences I have heard from many regarding the intoxication they experience with their use of drugs. Rather than confront the castration of the speaking being inherent in our entry into language—the loss of a primordial jouissance with the devitalization that words brings to the speaking being—a certain use of drugs, in this sense, attempts to return the subject to that state, in this regard a very Imaginary or ideal solution, but one that ultimately may well lead to death. This will give one clue, I think, to the difference between drugs as a semblant of the object *a*, in particular as a *lathouse* or false object *a*, and another use of the object *a* as cause of desire.

But, I want to extract one other point from the Laurent lecture. Following a reading of Lacan's comments at Vincennes, Laurent emphasizes that this semblant has a very particular function in a certain social group today, that of the *helot*. The term comes from Sparta: those with no rights in the polis, no rights for political existence who are able to dwell in jouissance. Lacan accused the student protestors in the 1960s of playing this role. For Laurent, this semblant provides a function of a guarantee for the Other, for the Symbolic order today. Within the Marxist paradigm, Fred Jameson has highlighted for us the central role of unemployment in Capitalism, in his book on Marx (2011). But, what of the drug cultures of today: and here I mean not the musician's use of drugs, the so-called heroic use of drugs noted above, but the hard-core crack and meth cultures of today. What we get with this is a new form for the organization of society. Society is no longer organized on the basis of name or family background; education or professional status; or even wealth. But, rather, this semblant of drug use organizes society based on what we term a mode of jouissance, based on consumption. This cuts across all traditional forms of social organization— I have worked with people who used crack and meth from all kinds of social backgrounds. I see a two-sided effect of this at the social level. On the one hand, a person might move from one group to another—these groups no longer provide the fixity of identifications of the previous world. But, on the other hand, there can be a strong segregating effect in these social groups. These groups, as forms of social idealism, as noted above, bring out all the aggression that Lacan identified with the Imaginary realm. This represents a way of conceptualizing a politics based on a notion of the Real. And, there is clearly a relationship between this drug culture and unemployment, in that the latter is most often the inevitable result of joining the cultural group.

To conclude, I would like to reference a well-known quote from Lacan, from the end of *The Subversion of the Subject*, where Lacan wrote: "Castration means that jouissance has to be refused in order to be attained on the inverse scale of the law of desire" (2006a, p. 700). I think that this sentence has a value in elucidating this issue of addictions. For if indeed, we do consider addictions as a form in which a speaking being attempts to bring the object of jouissance into the world, into the body even, as Laurent puts it, we can identify a conflict here between an attempt, perhaps Imaginary as we say, to bring jouissance into existence and the possibility of what Lacan calls attaining some jouissance through desire. In the former, the jouissance is not organized by the semblants of the phallus or the Name of the Father, but it is a homogenized jouissance, repeated over and over again, the *et cetera* that Miller has alluded to (2011)—a reiteration of the same One: "One more hit," "One more drink," more, more, more—in addiction, the person never says, I will have two today, or three drinks. It is a function of the One, in contrast to the Other, the Other which is always implicated in desire. I think that this gives one key to the approach of the psychoanalyst to addictions. Allow me to discuss a vignette: a patient is seen by a colleague. She had terrible problems with a particular drug (and acute psychosis) and was hospitalized for over a year. Sober, she is discharged to live in a group home. She remains sober for many months, then has a few days where she uses drugs again, not her drug of choice, but a different drug. In talking about it, she initially talks about how she was weak (yes, the contemporary subject does not have strong semblants now) and about how destructive this was for her, capturing the death drive or jouissance implicated in this recent use. This is what was reported to the person caring for her, but, to me, this is not enough. I ask for further details about exactly what happened. She was asked by some people who she knows from a program they all participate in to give them a ride. She did. They started using this new drug. She tried it, not sure why. She didn't like the feeling of the high on her body. But, she tried it again several times, still not liking it. I press her about why she did it repeatedly, when she did not like it, unlike the other drug. She reported that she admired the people in the car. They were the only ones in the program that seemed "together," she wanted to be part of this. I emphasize to her this point—using the drugs because she wanted to be looked upon favorably by this group. She immediately acknowledged the importance of this with a recollection of her first use of drugs, as a child: her older siblings, whom she admired, used drugs and wanted her to use them, which she did, for precisely the same reason. In this case, I think we can read the addiction in two ways. One is at the level only of the drug as a semblant of jouissance. But, from a different perspective, we can see in this vignette the outline of a possible relation of this subject to an Other, and the possibility of a desire that can be identified in the addiction, one linked to an experience from the childhood of this patient and an early experience with the drugs that she described as somewhat traumatic, an experience precisely repeated in her current use of this drug. I think this vignette gives one possible direction to our approach to subjects with addiction. There is a symptomatic repetitive jouissance, destructive, but senseless, and often linked to the drug as a *lathouse*. In the treatment, at least in the preliminary sessions, one direction that might be taken then is to articulate this jouissance with something, as the vignette demonstrates, to signify this act, put it into speech and words. And, in the process of that, the subject may enter into the analytic discourse, as indeed could be possible in the case I cite here, and a process I described in the previous chapter. And, at the end of that process, I believe, we will find another object *a*, some object much more particular to the subject. This leads me to the following hypothesis, with regard to addictions and this paradox. Namely: that the object quality, the symptomatic dimension of the addiction present on first presentation—that in which the object carries more the value of the *plus-du-jouir*, the *lathouse*, the surplus jouissance, is indeed a semblant of jouissance, an attempt by the subject, as Laurent put it, to incarnate jouissance in the world and in the body. But, I believe, that as with the semblants of today, that this is a weak semblant. Our role, in the treatment in addictions, as our Argentinian colleague Oscar Ventura wrote with regard to psychoanalysis in general, is twofold (Ventura, 2011). For the subject of today, for whom the loss of jouissance, the loss of the object, upon the entry into language—or castration, as we put it—for those subjects of today for whom that loss is unacceptable, and something to be immediately plugged up with some object, more and more a ready made object, a *lathouse*, scientifically constructed, for such subject, there is a need to mourn the loss of the object, with words. And with those words, I believe, we must work with them to find new semblants, or rework the semblants that they have, in order attain some jouissance through desire, through a desire oriented not around a ready made object, but an object cause of their desire. This is the formulation of psychoanalysis elaborated by Lacan at this point, in the early 1960s, and it defines the ultimate horizon of analysis as a process carried out through speech that, with a different signifying constellation, allows the subject a different point of access to desire.

In the final stages of his teaching, however, Lacan reconfigures the relationship of the Symbolic and Real in a way that has significant consequences for the psychoanalytic treatment and introduces, to me, a final question with regard to the issue of addictions. Beginning, say, with *Seminar 20* and the creation of the concept of *lalangue*, Lacan reconceptualizes the place of jouissance for the speaking being. In the 1960s, jouissance was localized in the object *a*, as I have described it above, and the remainder of the Symbolic order was itself dead. There is a clear barrier, as it were, between the Symbolic and the Real. This changes in *Seminar 20*. There is no longer a barrier between the two, but jouissance can be part and parcel of the Symbolic order. Language itself is described as an "apparatus of jouissance." In "Reading a Symptom," Miller emphasizes that the psychoanalytic act is one directed to:

> Interpretation as knowing how to read aims at reducing the symptom to its initial formula, i.e., the material encounter between a signifier and the body, the pure shock of language on the body. So, admittedly, to treat the symptom you have to pass through the shifting dialectic of desire, but you also have to rid yourself of the mirages of truth that this deciphering brings you and aim beyond, at the fixity of jouissance and the opacity of the real. (Miller, 2011, p. 152)

The question that I would pose to myself and my analyst colleagues is this: in what ways might the addiction complaints or addiction phenomena of today fall within this notion of a psychoanalytic symptom? Here, I think, there will be, of course, no rule, no general answer, each subject will need to be taken one by one. Does that addiction, as the subject goes through an analysis, as much suffering it may cause the subject, have the value of the "fixity of jouissance and opacity of the real" that Miller describes?

PART V

PSYCHOSIS

CHAPTER TWELVE

Ordinary psychosis*

I will now present a true twenty-first century concept, "Ordinary Psychosis," which—while a vital concept in the work of the Lacanian orientation now—cannot be found in Lacan's work itself. In fact, Ordinary Psychosis is a new concept, introduced publically by Jacques-Alain Miller on September 19, 1998. So, its general use is a phenomenon of the twenty-first century, but it is very important now in our clinic, especially in clinical practice in public settings, or institutional settings, with young people, and with those presenting with the newer forms of suffering. It is a description of what we might call a form of psychosis which is not at all uncommon today, one that might be distinguished by its very "ordinary" presentation, a psychosis in many ways different from the "extraordinary" psychoses we are familiar with from the psychiatric clinic: schizophrenia, mania, melancholia, paranoia. Ordinary psychosis was developed as a concept to describe psychoses that do not always present with a full elaboration of what we used to call typical, but what we might now think of as unusual, symptoms, as well

---

*"Ordinary psychosis" was presented at the Clinical Study Days 2 Workshop on "The Lacanian orientation in practice" on January 12, 2007, in Miami Beach, Florida.

as psychoses that do not manifest overtly the structure of psychosis. It is rather often a psychosis where the structure is subtle, a psychic structure that may resemble nothing other than a neurosis, but one in which the treatment may not go well should the psychosis be missed.

But, before presenting Ordinary Psychosis proper, I want to go back to Lacan, and to extract some points from Lacan, points where Lacan is addressing the issue of psychosis, especially some points where I think we might find something of what we will come to call ordinary psychosis at stake.

I want to begin this extraction by going way back into the 1930s, into Lacan's pre-psychoanalytic period. First, I want to point out something in Lacan's medical school thesis, *On Paranoid Psychosis and its Relationship with Personality* (1975a), a really remarkable book that would be very interesting to devote more time to in its own right, a work even recognized by the historian of psychiatry German E. Berrios in his encyclopedic *The History of Mental Symptoms* (1996) for Lacan's emphasis on the importance of the factor involved in the crystallization of psychosis and on the need to shift focus from personality to personalization. What I would like to emphasize, however, is something Lacan writes in defending his thesis—dedicated in large part to the extended presentation of a single case, that of Aimée and what he described as her delusion of self-punishment. Lacan writes about the "manifest value of a *particular solution*," that which we might understand as the very singular way in which a psychosis might develop, this process of what Berrios called personalization. It is this idea of a "particular solution" that I think is so important and which I think we will see return again, much later, in Lacan's final statement on psychosis.

We must note another point of Lacan's from the 1930s, however, a comment Lacan makes towards the end of "The family complexes in the formation of the individual." In this text (2001, pp. 23–84), Lacan draws attention to the importance of the paternal *imago* in the formation of the individual and the determination of what he calls pathology and notes that the specific forms of neurosis in Freud's time were linked to a specific social and family organization and use of the paternal *imago*. He also comments that what he identifies as a decline in the paternal *imago* will have consequences for the psyche. Thus, we see that in addition to his concerns with personalization and what we might call now subjectification conceptualized in this particular solution, Lacan is keenly interested in what will later be conceptualized as the Symbolic

Other and is working, even at this pre-formal stage of his work, on articulating a linkage here.

Lacan will not address psychosis so directly again, however, until the 1950s. Of course, it is at this point in his work that he wrote his paper "On a question preliminary to any possible treatment of psychosis" (2006a). Importing a formalization from linguistics into his clinical work, Lacan approaches the question of the structure of and crystallization of psychosis through the concept of foreclosure. The psychotic subject forecloses—rejects or refuses in a most radical way—the signifier of the Name of the Father. This lack of Name of the Father, under a certain condition that triggers a psychosis, correlates with a lack of paternal signification, whose consequences are most evident in the Symbolic language disturbances in psychosis, and a lack of Phallic signification, with consequences in the Imaginary on the representation of the body and also with regard to sexuality. Lacan's theory is that at the point of the triggering, the psychotic subject will encounter a Real Father in the Other, at the place where the Name of the Father is lacking. This is the One-Father, or A-Father, who will disturb a certain Imaginary configuration.

I want to highlight some points in this briefly presented resume. First, Lacan is here shifting from a theory of psychosis organized around a kind of proto-Imaginary figure such as the paternal *imago* to a theory in which the key conceptual figure is a signifier of the Name of the Father. Lacan has thus moved from a less formally defined concept to one in which Sausurrian linguistics (and Lévi-Straussian anthropology) will provide a formal logic for this function. And, in this second move of Lacan's, psychic structure is no longer metaphorically represented as in the texts from the 1930s, but more precisely defined with a formalized representation. However, what is interesting here as well is that Lacan does not write as much with the historical preoccupations that we saw in the *Family Complexes*, and it might be easy to infer (mistakenly, I might add) from this point of what we might call structuralism in his work that what Lacan theorizes is a psyche as an ahistorical structure.

But, I also want to draw attention to what Lacan did not theorize in the text "Preliminary question," what is absent in this presentation. Lacan does not address the question of the psychic structure before the triggering. What is the nature of the psychic structure of the untriggered psychosis or what was called the prepsychotic? Several years before the paper on a "Preliminary question," Lacan did approach this issue in his *Seminar 3* on psychosis, in a section in which he comments on a case of Maurits Katan of an adolescent who develops psychosis (Lacan, 1993). Lacan comments on how, prior to the triggering, this boy imitates an older friend and that this Imaginary identification—that has some relationship to Helene Deutsch's "as if" phenomena—forms an Imaginary compensation for what is lacking in the Symbolic. This early stage of psychosis—prior to the triggering—can be defined then in two ways: on a diachronic level, after the foreclosure of the Name of the Father and prior to the encounter with the One-Father; but also in a more synchronic way, by the foreclosure of the Name of the Father and an Imaginary compensation for such a foreclosure. Thus, in a sense, we have a diagnostic alternative to psychosis and neurosis, namely an untriggered psychosis. And, for Lacan, the clinical consequences of this diagnosis of a psychotic structure without a triggered psychosis are important, for an analysis—working with a non-triggered psychotic subject in the manner one would approach a person with neurosis— might certainly be a trigger an active psychosis in such a case, the very reason for Lacan's caution about the psychoanalytic approach to psychosis, in contrast to some psychoanalytic orientations in the 1950s. Indeed, the very title of the critical paper, "On a question preliminary to any possible treatment of psychosis," implies such a need to properly elucidate the nature of psychosis prior to any attempt at treatment. The analyst must be able to identify the psychotic structure in such a case, for such a patient should not be treated with the usual psychoanalysis. And, furthermore, we have an implied therapeutic imperative as well— work with the analysand towards the avoidance of an encounter with the One-Father.

Lacan left it at that, more or less, until the 1970s, after another break of two decades. It is at this point that Lacan will offer his final major statement on psychosis in his *Seminar* on Joyce, for which some of the groundwork was laid in place by the unpublished *Seminar 22, R.S.I.* This seminar explores what we could call the enigma of Joyce. Lacan's Joyce is a psychotic subject, but one who never has the symptoms of a full-blown psychosis, a psychotic subject whose psychosis is never triggered. To use the terminology of the 1950s, the Name of the Father is foreclosed, but there is no psychosis crystallized in an encounter with the One-Father. Though Lacan does not use these terms, it is as if Joyce is a permanently untriggered psychotic subject, and concepts that

Lacan will develop in this seminar can, in this context, be described as a rethinking of the concept of untriggered psychosis.

The issue of stabilization then becomes paramount—how does Joyce achieve this? It certainly is not because he avoided any One-Fathers. As Ellman's biography reveals (1982), Joyce had many, many encounters with editors, publishers, creditors, employers, and friends in his life, any one of which certainly could have triggered a psychosis. Lacan, rather, draws forth his old notion of Imaginary compensation from *Seminar 3* in the way in which he describes how Joyce's ego, as a writer, allowed him to make a name for himself, and compensates for the foreclosure of the Name of the Father, a veritable shift, we note, in the status of the Imaginary relative to the other registers.

But, Lacan will drop the terminology of the 1950s and reformulate psychic structure entirely in this last stage of his work. The context of this formalization is no longer linguistics, but knot theory. And, I will provide a quick resume of Lacan's work here, which I think has two logical stages to it. In the first, Lacan will argue that foreclosure is represented by a break in the three-ringed Borromean knot of the Imaginary, Symbolic, and Real—a failure in knotting. In the case of Joyce, Lacan identifies the failure of the knotting, a failure that leaves the Imaginary ring disconnected or unknotted: drawing on an episode of depersonalization from *A Portrait of an Artist as a Young Man*, when the hero (read: Joyce) is beaten up by some classmates and has a subtle disturbance in his sense of his body, Lacan hypothesizes an elementary phenomenon experience of Joyce at the level of the Imaginary (Lacan, 2005, pp. 143–155). Lacan adds that this failure of knotting was compensated for with a fourth, supplemental ring—in the case of Joyce, the ego, his writing—as a fourth ring that is woven in to hold the three rings intact, together. This knotting thus reprises earlier concept of Imaginary compensation (the ego, of course, is Imaginary) and will allow the structure to hold together, without falling apart. In the second stage, Lacan rewrites psychic structure more generally as a four-ringed Borromean knot, in which it is the *sinthome* that, as the fourth ring, holds the other three together. And, the *sinthome* is nothing other than a general form for what used to be the Name of the Father, which is now but one possibility as a type of *sinthome*, a possible fourth ring. Thus, here we see an extension—as it were—from the two registers of the Imaginary and Symbolic (as emphasized in the earliest Lacan) to the three registers of Imaginary, Symbolic, and Real to even yet four registers of the Imaginary, Symbolic, Real, and *Sinthome*.

And, of course, with this final shift, all of the earlier clinical formulations are recast. But, the key to this recasting, is to realize that Joyce's case—originally seen as exceptional, unusual, and very particular given his very singular place as a writer—is not the extraordinary one. We must invert this organization completely. Joyce's form of psychosis is rather the typical one, the ordinary one, the one encountered more often, the one perhaps resembling more a neurosis; and, that schizophrenia and paranoia and so forth are rather the extraordinary cases, remarkable for their florid symptoms. This is, I believe, a key to the approach to ordinary psychosis. In the cases that we now identify as ordinary psychosis, we do not find the symptomatology of classic forms of psychosis and the structure and even the typical sequences of the triggering (the encounter with the One-Father leading to the development of the failures in paternal and phallic signification). We may see cases of psychosis with only limited evidence of failure of paternal signification and Symbolic disturbances; we may see cases with only limited disturbances in phallic function; we may see cases of psychosis without a clear encounter with the One-Father at the triggering; and, we may see cases without any overt language disturbance or disturbance of the Imaginary, as documented so well in *La Psychose ordinaire* (l'Instance de réflexion sur le mathème analytique, 2005b), a transcription of the texts and discussion of the meeting of the Members of the École in which Miller introduced the concept of Ordinary Psychosis.

I will close by noting two important features of this work. The first is that the *sinthome* of Lacan in 1975 is, in some ways, only a more formal representation of this "particular solution" from 1932. The Name of the Father, as a fourth ring, certainly provides a very stable (and, in some ways, oft-described universal) form of knotting of the subject. It is difficult, however, to give any rules for the *sinthome*, however—it may work as a form of Imaginary compensation—some ideal ego or even body image; it may also draw more from the Symbolic—in the form of a certain nomination we may see in some stable psychoses; or, it may incorporate more of the Real, as we see in many cases of toxicomania or other so-called addictions. The *sinthome* may be more or less effective in knotting together the psychic structure. And we may handle the *sinthome* very differently from case to case, perhaps working with it directly, perhaps substituting one *sinthome* for another, or perhaps modifying its form, or perhaps not wanting to do anything with it—as in a case presented at the Congress of the WAP in Rome where an analysis was refused to a patient for whom the search for a scientific answer was the patient's *sinthome* itself. In each case, we must find—in this concept of Ordinary Psychosis—the way in which the *sinthome* functions or can function as a particular solution.

And, finally, let me close with an observation from part of my clinical work—from my institutional practice, at a public clinic. I interview many patients there in conjunction with psychiatric residents, and this Ordinary Psychosis is indeed rather ordinary and not at all uncommon. In fact, psychiatrists and other mental health workers are struggling now—with concepts such as the monosymptomatic diagnoses and with expanded use of diagnoses such as bipolar disorder or disruptive behavior disorders or developmental disorders or personality disorders—to come to terms, in very poor ways, with this. I do think, however, that ordinary psychosis is a very useful way to approach these phenomena of our times, that this form of psychosis has become ordinary over the last few decades (I see it more commonly in young people, I have noted), and that it correlates with postmodernity. This has been addressed in Lacanian work here in the United States and the WAP in general in many ways—the shift from the Ideal to the object *a* as the organizing point for identification; the rise of the discourse of the capitalist; and the shift from the discourse of the master to the discourse of the analyst itself as the key organizing discourse of society today. Lacan, again, provides early on—in his comments about the decline of the paternal *imago*—a first sketch for this. I think we must continue in this work as psychoanalysts should we wish to respond to the clinical demands of our times.

CHAPTER THIRTEEN

Ordinary psychosis in the era of *sinthome* and semblant*

We may first place Ordinary Psychosis in a diachronic sense within the work of Lacan. The signifier "Ordinary Psychosis" is not one of Lacan's, but of J.-A. Miller, but the signifier and its conceptualization are linked to the last teachings of Lacan. First, we find Ordinary Psychosis articulated with the *sinthome*, from *Seminar 23*. Some analysts use Ordinary Psychosis to designate a psychosis without evidence of an acute break, or the extraordinary symptoms of a classic psychosis, in the model of Schreber. In this context, analysts use Lacan's *sinthome* to articulate a psychic stabilization, that holds psychic structure together, as Lacan did with Joyce, where his ego, his writing, repaired a deficit in Joyce's Imaginary presumed from the bodily disturbance described in *A Portrait of the Artist as a Young Man*. This has led to a debate: is Joyce an Ordinary Psychotic? Joyce may have never presented with an acute psychosis, but his means of sinthomatic stabilization is not ordinary, but quite extraordinary. This

---

*"Ordinary psychosis in the era of *sinthome* and semblant" is a concise summary of a talk titled "A-topos rex" presented at the Paris English seminar on "Ordinary psychosis" in Paris, France, on July 11, 2008.

question of Joyce interrogates the way we use Ordinary Psychosis. Do we take "ordinary" to refer to all subjects with a psychotic structure for whom there is no evidence of extraordinary phenomena, or is it rather to be used in a circumscribed sense, in which the sinthomatic stabilization is what is ordinary, "banal" as M.-H. Brousse (2009) elaborates, one more like neurosis?

Ordinary Psychosis is also linked to what Miller (2008) has referred to as the semblantization we find in the last Lacan. One is that of the semblantization of the Name of the Father. No longer the crucial "Real" pivot point in psychic structure of "A question preliminary ...," Lacan first pluralizes the Name of the Father in the eponymous seminar and then makes it a function, or predicate. The object *a*, a residue of jouissance in *Seminar 10*, is reformulated in *Seminar 20* as a semblant of being. The same is true of the Other. This had substance, as the "treasure trove of signifiers" in "The subversion of the subject". Here too we find a shift in Lacan's teaching to an Other which is barred, which does not exist, but which still functions as a semblant. This semblantization generates a tension between a use of Ordinary Psychosis that preserves the distinction between neurosis and psychosis and a perspective in which we find a universal character to psychosis, which we find elaborated in a variety of ways, from Lacan's statement that "all the world is mad" (1979b) to Miller's (2001b) elaborations of a universal foreclosure (of jouissance itself, always excessive to the power of the Symbolic—language itself functioning as a delusion for all speaking beings).

The notions of *sinthome* and semblant also allow us to shift from a diachronic to a synchronic perspective about Ordinary Psychosis and psychic structure. Freud's clinic and Lacan's first clinic is a clinic of neurosis. There is a substantial quality to the Other and the Name of the Father (as the stabilizing point of the Other) which exist. In this clinic, psychosis is conceived with reference to neurosis, as an exception, based on foreclosure, the non-existence of this thing in that place. In the clinic of the last Lacan, however, the *sinthome* has a universal place as the way in which each subject may singularly knot his psychic structure, or form a social bond with the Other. In such a clinic, the Name of the Father is merely one form of the *sinthome*. The Name of the Father is merely an especially stable form of knotting. Lacan gave us an indication of this in the introduction of the four-ringed Borromean knot in *Seminar 22: R.S.I.*, where Lacan identifies the fourth ring as "psychic reality," which—for Freud—he identifies as the Oedipus complex. In the next seminar, this fourth ring is generalized to the *sinthome*, the Name of the Father one form of it. While this latter clinic supplants the clinic of foreclosure, it does not invalidate it. The stability of the Name of the Father as a *sinthome* is such that it seems to have substance, rather than semblance. In neurosis, the stability of the structure is such that the logic of the clinic of foreclosure applies. Indeed, this relationship of the clinic of foreclosure to the clinic of the *sinthome* is not unlike the relationship between Newton and Einstein. Newton's physics are valid within certain parameters of mass and velocity that are neither too great nor too small. Newton's physics is not useful in extreme values of those parameters, in the way that Einstein's physics proved useful. However, while Einstein's physics does thus supplant Newton's, Newton's physics is still valid in the limited parameters. In the same way, while the sinthomatic clinic covers a broader array of psychic structure with greater utility, the clinic of foreclosure is useful in certain parameters.

This clinic of the *sinthome* brings us a greater flexibility in our treatments with subjects with Ordinary Psychosis. In the clinic of foreclosure, the treatment is directed along the lines of signification, anchored in the Name of the Father. Jouissance in this clinic is the Imaginarized jouissance, as Miller (2000) has specified, a jouissance that is evacuated through the process of symbolization. In contrast, the clinic of the *sinthome* is organized along a direction indicated by Lacan's *lalangue*, based on a direct linkage between signifiers and jouissance. While the evacuation of jouissance may be an issue at play in treatment, the treatment is not oriented only towards signification and the elimination of jouissance, but towards a linking of signification and jouissance. As Laurent specifies (Laurent, n.d.), this shift from the relation of S_1 to S_2 to the relation between S_1 and object a is crucial in the clinic of Ordinary Psychosis. In many treatments, the quantity of jouissance remains intact (to use an old Freudian notion), but the psychotic finds new ways to manage his jouissance. A subject's *sinthome* links a significatory identification to that subject's object a, a piece of jouissance, his semblant of being. With the *sinthome*, the subject does not eliminate the jouissance as such (often so destructive for the psychotic), but rather finds a way to make do with it. The *sinthome* is in a way the *point de capiton* of *lalangue* for the psychotic.

The *sinthome* is nothing other than the social bond for the subject. In the case of neurosis, it is the *sinthome* as Name of the Father structuring the Other, or in its Freudian reading, Oedipus rex ruling over society and the unconscious like the Aristotelian *topos* over discourse. But, in its most general form, the *sinthome* establishes the social bond. While the Other doesn't exist, for each speaking being, there is a semblant of the Other. This is the Other the subject makes use of to engage the world, be it through the fantasies of neurosis or the most singular ways of the psychotic, those sinthomatic and semblantized structurations of the Other, so a-typical, reigning over the Other—the *A-topos rex*. In this situation, the analyst has considerable latitude to assist the psychotic subject to make use of an Other that will work for the subject, an Other specific for the subject's *sinthome*. This process of elaboration of a semblant of the Other for the psychotic subject constitutes the other level for the direction of the treatment. In some of the most striking cases presented in the Paris English seminar on "Ordinary Psychosis," we heard just this process described variously as "creating his own personal myth," "creating a bond with the Other," "creating a Symbolic matrix that gave him a possibility of negotiating in the world," "allowed her to enter into the discourse of the Other," and "built a family romance." Indeed, it is fully the desubstantialization of the Other into a semblant that has created not only the perspective of a new diagnosis for psychosis, but a new horizon of possibility in treatment.

PART VI

ENCORE, ENCORE: CONCEPTUAL
EXTRACTS FROM *SEMINAR 20*

CHAPTER FOURTEEN

Encore, encore: knowledge*

I want to offer a hypothesis that I will try to use to frame this presentation of *Seminar 20*. I want to present *Seminar 20* as an answer by Lacan to a question of Lacan from nine years before—from the end of his *Seminar 11*. In the concluding session of *Seminar 11*, "In you more than you," Lacan ends the session with a discussion of hypnotism. Following Freud, Lacan notes that in the structure of hypnotism, the patient's point of identification—the ideal signifier—and the object *a*—the libidinal object—are confused, in that the doctor or hypnotist—that Ideal—becomes the very object of the gaze of the patient in hypnotism—either directly or via the shiny object the patient is instructed to focus on. The "mainspring of the analytic operation," as Lacan refers to it, is the "maintenance of a distance between the I—identification—and the *a*" (1977a, p. 273). In contrast to ego psychology, which offers identification with the analyst (or, a part of the analyst) as a possible definition for the end of analysis, Lacan notes that: "It is from this idealization that the analyst has to fall [in other

---

*Chapters Fifteen–Seventeen in Part 6: Encore, encore were presented as a seminar in Miami Beach, Florida, on May 5, 2012, sponsored by the Nueva Escuela Lacaniana.

words, to fail to fill the place of the I], in order to be the support of the separating *a*, in so far as his desire allows him, in an upside-down hypnosis, to embody the hypnotized patient" (1977a, p. 273). Lacan continues to note that "after the mapping of the subject to the *a*, the experience of the fundamental fantasy becomes the drive." He follows this with two questions and an observation: "What, then, does he who has passed through the experience of this opaque relation to the origin, to the drive, become? How can a subject who has traversed the radical phantasy experience the drive? This is the beyond of analysis, and has never been approached" (1977a, p. 273). Thus, several questions: what can be said of the analysand who has finished an analysis about the relationship with the drive, the Real, and what might be said about the Real, about that which is resistant to speech, to meaning?

The mechanism of the Pass is certainly one answer that Lacan will give to these questions—the creation of an institutional device that allows analysands to give testimony to this "beyond of analysis." My proposal here is that we read *Seminar 20*, and indeed all the developments of the final Lacan that follow, also as an answer to these questions, and as Lacan's answer to the question of a "beyond of analysis." And, this is especially vital in the twenty-first century, where the issues associated with the drive, the object *a*, and the Real are front and center not only in the psychoanalytic experience, but in twenty-first century society.

I want to first explore this proposal with regard to knowledge. Let us begin with a quote from the third session of *Seminar 20* on "The function of the written." Lacan states that "What is at stake in analytic discourse is always the following—you give a different reading to the signifiers that are enunciated than what they signify," or in Bruce Fink's alternative translation, which I like more: "you give a different reading to what is enunciated as signifier than what it signifies" (1998a, p. 33). I want to offer a few comments on this sentence. I choose this sentence because, while it does not immediately address the question of knowledge as such, it introduces something important about what Lacan advances about knowledge, namely a shift from speech and listening to the written and reading. One dimension of the earliest work of Lacan is certainly the focus on speech—on the speech of the analysand—in which speech is the horizon—the process of analysis is described in terms of a shift brought about from empty speech to full speech.

With this quote, Lacan redefines analysis—not as a process that operates at the level of speech, but at the level of the written. We could certainly pursue this shift in various ways. One point relates to a set of technical imperatives associated with this shift—first and foremost that regarding the role of the analyst's interpretation as punctuation. Lacan himself, in the debates on his practice of variable length sessions, comments on the role of the end of the session as "punctuation," and Jacques-Alain Miller also consistently emphasize the analyst's interpretation as providing punctuation to the raw discourse of the analysand. It is this act of punctuation that turns speech into the written. There are a variety of ways in which we might explore this notion of punctuation (as developed more explicitly in Chapter Seven).

I want to develop this differently, however, here. I want to note that the shift from the speech to the written corresponds to a shift that Lacan makes with regard to the "material," we might call it, or, the "stuff" with which we work in psychoanalysis. In the earliest Lacan, it is the phoneme that is the basic element of speech and the stuff with which we work in analysis. With *Encore*, it is no longer the phoneme, but the letter with which we work. Lacan's use of the concept of the letter is very specific, and is made with a clear reference to modern science, science that can be described with a formula, such as in physics. In contrast with modern science, Lacan gives a very precise definition of what he calls pre-modern science, when he states that before scientific discourse as such, "no knowledge was conceived that did not participate in the fantasy of the inscription of the sexual link" (1998a, p. 76).

Lacan makes a reference here, for example, to Plato and Aristotle, in particular to their use of the terms "active" and "passive" with regard to the discussion of form and matter. Lacan describes this here as a fantasy. I would emphasize here that the Greek philosophers felt that they were describing knowledge, or creating a knowledge about the world, about reality. But, as Lacan will state later, "everything that we are allowed to approach by way of reality remains rooted in fantasy" (1998a, p. 87). What Lacan reads in the notions of pre-modern science is a fantasy—thus, the concepts of active and passive—about the sexual relationship, the sexual link, which does not exist. In contrast to these pre-modern fantasies about science, or knowledge, modern science is constructed of letters and formulae that have a different relationship to the Real. Lacan at one point in the seminar writes Newton's formula for gravity on a board: $F = gmm'/d^2$. This is a different kind of knowledge. There, letters are read in the Real, or extracted from the Real. So, there is pre-modern knowledge—which is a fantasy, a fantasy that tries to stand in for a sexual relationship that does not exist, and modern science. I would like to read this perspective on knowledge in the context of what Lacan will articulate a few paragraphs later:

> The aim of my thinking, in so far as it pursues what can be said and enunciated on the basis of analytic discourse, is to dissociate *a* and A by reducing the first to what is related to the imaginary and the other to what is related to the symbolic. It is indubitable that the symbolic is the basis of what was made into God. It is certain that imaginary is based on the reflection of one semblable in another. (1998a, p. 83)

Thus far, Lacan is presenting a very classic reading of his work. He continues: "And yet, *a* has lent itself to be confused with S(X), below which it is written on the blackboard, and it has done so by means of the function of being. It is here that a scission or detachment remains to be effected" (1998a, p. 83). I would like to read the second half of this passage in the context of Lacan's observation on science. In as much as the fantasies of the world take advantage of the function of Being—seem to describe existence (though they are only reflections of themselves—in that the Imaginary is built on the mirror)—they have a hold on the subject in that they make a claim to reality. This happens, according to Lacan, because of a confusion of the object *a*—the basis of fantasy—with the S(X),—a signifier of a sexual relationship that does not exist, of the jouissance of the Other, even, we might say, of a Truth that does not exist.

So, to return to my initial question, when Lacan asks about the "beyond of analysis" in *Seminar 11*, that question is linked by Lacan to the "beyond of fantasy," the traversal of fantasy. The work on science, I propose, offers some indications of how Lacan will answer that question. One relates to the role of fantasy in making up for a sexual relation that does not exist, an issue that we see is present both at the psychic level and at the social level itself. A second development will be that of the jouissance of the Other—Woman—as beyond the fantasy, which I will develop further in a later chapter on the feminine. And finally, Lacan's work on the letter and on the "One" represent, I propose, a different attempt at approaching the Real.

I would like to comment some on this concept of the One. As I noted before, in pre-scientific discourse, knowledge was knowledge of the

world—there was a connection to Being—for Lacan this is Imaginary—
a correspondence of the soul and Being (we might see this, for example,
in Aristotelean ethics in the correspondence of the good for an individual
and society's Good). Lacan puts it in the following terms:

> The nature of mathematical language, once it is sufficiently isolated
> in terms of its requirements of pure demonstration, is such that
> everything that is put forward there—not so much in spoken com-
> mentary as in the very handling of letters—assumes that if one of
> the letters doesn't stand up, all the others, due to their arrange-
> ment, not only constitute nothing of validity, but disperse. It is in
> that respect that the Borromean knot is the best metaphor of the fact
> that we proceed only on the basis of the One. (1998a, p. 128)

In other words, with mathematics, everything must fit, if something
doesn't hold, like a broken ring in the Borromean knot, the whole thing
collapses. Or, recall Newton's formula for gravity. If there is an error or
mistake—in one letter—the whole formula loses its validity. It is an ensem-
ble, held together in such a way that one mistake in the formula leads it
all to collapse. This is not the case, say, with Aristotelean philosophy.

Lacan continues: "The One engenders science. Not in the sense of the
one of measurement" (1998a, p. 128). I think that this is key—recall that
in French, *l'un* means both the number "one" and the indefinite article
"a." I think the number one of measurement is part of the One, but only
a part of it. The One is much more than the number One. I think it is
more useful, perhaps, to translate this term as the indefinite article "A."
This translation allows a more useful reading of the following passage:

> It is not what is measured in science that is important, contrary to
> what people think. What distinguishes modern science from the
> science of antiquity, which is based on the reciprocity between the
> *vous* and the world, between what thinks and what is thought of,
> is precisely the function of the One, the One in so far as it is only
> there, we can assume, to represent solitude—the fact that the One
> doesn't truly knot itself with anything that resembles the sexual
> Other. (1998a, p. 273)

In the clinic, in the psychoanalytic experience, it is the body and affects
that alert us to what Lacan calls the "meaning effects" of some letter.

The knowledge that is constructed in a psychoanalysis is present in the unconscious, in the Other. Lacan states that the "knowledge is in the Other and owes nothing to Being [recall that the unconscious does not exist as such] except the latter has born the letter thereof." The letter is in the unconscious, to put it more simply. The speaking being, however, is oblivious to the knowledge in the letter. Lacan states:

> The unconscious evinces knowledge that, for the most part, escapes the speaking being. That being provides the occasion to realize just how far the effects of *lalangue* go, in that it presents all sort of affects that remain enigmatic. Those affects are what results from the presence of *lalangue* insofar as it articulates things by way of knowledge that go much further than what the speaking being sustains by way of enunciated knowledge. (1998a, p. 139)

In other words, Lacan's fundamental thesis regarding the speaking being is that, in contrast to Freud and his *Wisssentrieb* [drive for knowledge], we *don't* want knowledge. Indeed, Lacan opens with "I don't want to know anything about it," or, as he presents it more elaborately in the beginning of the session "On the Baroque," "'The unconscious is not the fact that being thinks'—though that is implied by what is said thereof in traditional science—'the unconscious is the fact that being, by speaking, enjoys and' I will add 'wants to know nothing more about it at all'" (1998a, pp. 104–105).

But something happens in a psychoanalysis that will link the subject with knowledge and this notion of the letter. Lacan gives a concise formulation about this at the beginning of "Knowledge and truth," saying that in analytic discourse, "a is written in the upper left-hand corner, and is supported by S_2, in other words, by knowledge in so far as it is in the place of truth. It is from that point that it interrogates $\$$, which must lead the production of S_1, that is, of the signifier by which can be resolved what? Its [presumably S_1's] relation to truth" (1998a, p. 91). In other words, going back to the quote from *Seminar 11*, the analyst must allow the Ideal, the point of Identification, to fall, in order to occupy the place of the object a. And, in occupying the place of the object, or bringing out the object a in the psychoanalytic experience, the object a as agent in the psychoanalytic discourse—in querying the subject—the psychoanalytic discourse will produce the master signifier, the One (but, a One that first is not a number; a One that is not only a signifier; or, rather, more precisely, a One that is a signifier on the side of its dimension of the Real, of jouissance, *lalangue*, beyond meaning, the other side of the signifier; namely, a signifier S_1 linked to *a* and not to S_2)—that which is beyond the fantasy.

Now, we may not want to know anything, but, as Lacan states, "Analysis came to announce to us that there is knowledge that is not known, knowledge that is based on the signifier as such" (1998a, p. 96) (You may want to recall here the epistemology of Donald Rumsfeld regarding the weapons of mass destruction and the Iraq war. He elaborated three possibilities: known knowns, known unknowns, and unknown unknowns. Slavoj Žižek was quick to point out that he left out the fourth logical possibility—unknown knowns—a very Lacanian definition of the unconscious). Lacan continues:

> A dream does not introduce us into any kind of unfathomable experience or mystery—it is read in what is said about it, and one can go further by taking up the equivocations therein in the most anagrammatic sense of the world. [...] Do we need this whole detour to raise the question of knowledge in the form "What is it that knows?" Do we realize that it is the Other?—such as I posited at the outset, as a locus in which the signifier is posited, and without which nothing indicates to us that there is a dimension of truth anywhere, a *dit-mension*, the residence of what is said, of this said, whose knowledge posits the Other as locus. The status of knowledge implies as such that there already is knowledge, that it is in the letter, that it is to be acquired. (1998a, p. 96)

Thus, the letter, which is something of the One, is there—is there to be acquired. And, it contains knowledge. I want to mention here one final comment about the One from Lacan, which touches on how we might think of the One. In the final chapter on "The rat in the maze," Lacan notes that: "The One incarnated in *lalangue* is something that remains indeterminate between the phoeneme, the word, the sentence, and even the whole of thought. That is what is at stake in what I call the master signifier" (1998a, p. 143).

How do we see this in the experience of a psychoanalysis? I would like to review this in the context of the Testimony of the Pass that Mauricio Tarrab gave in New York, the Pass being the very mechanism created by Lacan to bear witness to this "beyond of analysis" (Tarrab, 2007).

Tarrab identified his suffering as involving a sensation of menace and exposure to fatality and inhibitions relating to his body and professional life. He identified the origins of the symptom in childhood, in particular in the signifier "paralysis" (2007, p. 29). A childhood neurosis led him to a psychologist at age five. This encounter with a psychologist occurred in an institution where children who were paralyzed were receiving rehabilitation and led to a phobia and set of obsessive symptoms relating to the fear of catching a debilitating disease and a belief that the mother "wants me sick." Tarrab also evokes a love for the Father and a way in which he took charge of the suffering and jouissance of the Other. He talks about the importance of "taking care of the Other" (2007, p. 29). This ideal of caring for the Other or love of the Other will, at the end of the analysis, find its reverse, he states, in the "most real of drives."

Tarrab then describes a session in which he comments the name of his father echoes the name of the analyst and the jouissance of the ripper. But, he comments on how his father was a fool, who ruined his life, who wasn't a ripper, but ripped. I interpret this as a kind of shift of love for the father to a hate of the father (or, in terms of an earlier Lacan, an approach to the father as the Imaginary Father who messed the kid up. Note also that the terms of love and hate are closely linked, as we will see when we take up the question of love in the next chapter). Tarrab then talks about wandering the streets of Rome after the session and ending up at a restaurant across from the Pantheon, which he interpreted as the "Pantheon of great dead men." This realization leads him to an episode of chest pain and suffocation—these affects he associates with an aggression against the father, presumably a reaction to what transpired in the session. Here, he describes a very particular affect that troubled him—associated with the heart and with breathing. As I stated earlier, Lacan notes that: "Those affects are what results from the presence of *lalangue* insofar as it articulates things by way of knowledge that go much further than what the speaking being sustains by way of enunciated knowledge." What Tarrab will then proceed to do in this Testimony is identify what in *lalangue*, we might say, is that letter, that One, associated with the affect that took charge of his body at that moment. My hypothesis is that the One, the letter, is the Spanish word *soplo*—murmur, blow, breath—that he will elaborate. To put this in a different language, that of psychiatry, Tarrab had something like a panic attack, but, in contrast with the psychiatric approach in which such attacks are "unprecipitated," or unlinked to something outside (the psychiatric refrain that anxiety is like fear but without an object) and thus without meaning, the Lacanian approach is that this panic attack, this moment of *angoisse*, is linked to something, but not an interpretable meaning (say, S_1 plus S_2), rather a singular signifier that grabs hold of the body (S_1 and object *a*).

This One—in my reading of the testimony—has two precise moments of elaboration in the analysis. In his testimony, Tarrab goes on to talk about a presumably earlier childhood memory. Something sexual happens that he cannot remember when he is very young. He runs up some stairs and collapses. His mother will state that he had a *soplo al corazon*. The meaning of the term in English is "heart murmur," but the importance here relates to the Spanish *soplo*, which has the different meanings of murmur, blow, and breath. These words of the mother regarding the body were very important—traumatic—as language can be for the subject: linking, as Tarrab notes, sexual arousal and the threat of death—this is a very precise example of the symptom as "body event" (Lacan, 2001, p. 569). My reading of this first description is that it describes a function of the One as signifier, but also at the same time at this moment of the analysis also a dimension of the object *a*. The object *a* in as much as *soplo* here is that which gives the subject a semblance of being—I am the child with a murmur—and also is linked to the fantasy of how the child is linked to the Other—to what Tarrab describes as the "mortifying desire of the Other" (2007, p. 31).

Next, there is a dream. In the dream, Tarrab "shows the analyst a written report of some medical tests I have taken. The report contains a terrible announcement. The analyst [in my dream] reads it and says: what's written there is not correct." In the session, the analyst states "It … is … not … yours" (2007, p. 31). Tarrab notes this as a comment on the way in which he had been engaged in "the reading that the subject continued in attributing a mortifying desire to the Other." Following the dream, there is a shift—Tarrab realizes that "what's written is not mine, however the reading is, and therefore I will have to take charge of this reading and of the jouissance drawn from it" (2007, p. 31). I find this passage an especially beautiful description of analysis. What is written in the unconscious is not mine, it is Other, but that the analysand can, as Tarrab puts it "take charge of the reading" and the jouissance drawn from it. I think that is what Lacan is getting at in "Knowledge and truth" when he writes:

> "What is it that knows?" Do we realize that it is the Other—such as I posited at the outset, as a locus in which the signifier is posited, and without which nothing indicates to us that there is a dimension of truth anywhere, a *dit-mension*, the residence of what is said, of this said whose knowledge posits the Other as locus. The status of knowledge implies as such that there already is knowledge, that it is in the Other, that it is to be acquired [...]. The subject results from the fact that this knowledge must be learned, and even have a price put on it [...] knowledge is worth just as much as it costs [...] less to acquire than to enjoy it. (1998a, p. 96)

I read Tarrab's comment as about that—the knowledge he obtained is only worth what jouissance can be obtained with it. He cited a striking relief at this moment of the analysis—much of his suffering is lifted, there was a change in jouissance.

But, Tarrab is uncertain how to end the analysis. He describes that the Other is a hole, or has a hole—the signifier of the lack in the Other— but he is not sure how to get out of it. He describes an act that he will interpret. He was attracted to Chinese calligraphy and unexpectedly purchases a book by François Cheng, who worked with Lacan on this subject. The title is in French, which Tarrab does not speak—*Et le souffle devient signe*. He looks this up in a dictionary—"And the Breath Become a Sign." *Souffle* in French is the same word as *sople* cited above.

Tarrab then goes on to recall a childhood memory—his Father almost dies from a lung disease. To recover his lung function, he has to blow to inflate a ball. Tarrab recalls that when his father took a nap, he would lie next to him, "attentive to his breathing, synchronizing it to that of his father, always vigilant that it did not stop." Tarrab talks about for him this was "to be the breath that the Father lacked" (2007, p. 32).

I want to quote Tarrab at length here:

> Illuminating the fantasy would then situate the "I am that" in a blunt manner. But it also showed that in addition to the determina- tion of this identification, there had been an unfathomable decision of the subject that became evident then. A decision: to be that breath, had given consistency to this identification of which meaning—all

the meaning possible—and satisfaction had been drawn. It became then completely evident how an entire existence had been plotted from this decision.

What I have just described is the logical moment of the pass. It is the moment when, in a flash you catch the fantasy framework that had until then sustained all the significations of one life. In that moment we perceive this construction of the fantasy and at the same time this fantasy solution is eclipsed, loses its value, falls. (2007, p. 32)

I think that this is precisely an aspect of the *soplo* as the One, the master signifier, that Lacan is talking about throughout this seminar. It is that which distributes meaning throughout the unconscious. And, as Tarrab notes, is linked with jouissance (through the body event), and in the way in which the jouissance of the breath is part of this, but not a jouissance linked to the Other, to woman.

CHAPTER FIFTEEN

Encore, encore: love

When it comes to love and hate—these two fundamental passions to which Lacan will add a third passion, that of ignorance—Lacan will first lean on the importance, not of love, but of hate, in the psychoanalytic experience. Recall here three fundamental texts from the 1930s and 1940s: the encyclopedia chapter on "The family complexes," the paper on "The mirror stage," and the paper on "Aggressiveness in psychoanalysis." We can say that at this stage in his work, Lacan elaborates a number of theories on the Imaginary—on Imaginary relations—on the relationship of the ego and the semblable, or, the child and its siblings. In contrast to the ego psychologists, whose ego had many functions, we might say, we might best understand Lacan's ego as an *imago*, as an image, constructed by the subject through its relations with others, and in particular in relation to some ideal ego. But, in contrast to the ego psychologists with their ideology of adaptation of the ego to reality, Lacan placed an emphasis on a different fact—namely a fundamental discordance between the subject's representation of itself to itself in the ego and the subject itself. The ego for Lacan represents the way in which a subject misrecognizes itself—a misrecognition with a series of consequences, including a failure of the subject, for example, to manage its own body, the body for

171

the speaking being is also experienced through a discordance mediated by the ego.

For the subject, for the child, others come into the world— semblables—or other egos—that the subject engages in relations with. One whole set of these relations are mediated on this Imaginary plane of ego to ego, but, as Lacan describes, mediated through the subject's ideal ego. Lacan will go forward to describe these Imaginary relations— the entry of the relation of ego to semblable—in various terms: the way in which the other will disrupt the relation of the ego to the ideal—the fact that an other person can bring about a recognition, as it were, of the misrecognition of the subject; or, he will describe this in terms of rivalry: the rivalry of different egos for identification with the ideal, for example, in the way in which siblings may rival to serve as the Imaginary phallus for the mother; or, he might describe this as jealousy—the other has something which the ego lacks, Lacan's classic example here being St. Augustine's description of the hatred he felt looking upon another nursing at the breast.

Of course, in the classic phase of Lacan's work, these various Imaginary passions—passions that incorporate the libido itself—are resolved with the passage of the Imaginary into the Symbolic.

But, let us pause for a minute, before Lacan fully elaborates the role of the Symbolic in his texts of the 1950s, to look again at the paper on "Aggressiveness" (Lacan, 2006a, pp. 82–101). After a few pages on aggressiveness as it manifests itself in relation to the body, Lacan describes some classic aspects of analytic technique—the analyst does not give advice; the analyst provides the dialog with a participant devoid of individual characteristics; and, the analyst does not take on the burden of suffering of the patient (which is linked to a certain self-love of the patient—Lacan quotes La Rouchefoucauld: "I can't bear the thought of being freed by anyone but myself"). Lacan then states:

"We must bring out the subject's aggressiveness toward us, because, as we know, aggressive intentions form the negative transference that is the inaugural knot of the analytic drama" (2006a, p. 87). I find this formulation striking. It seems to me to be completely against Freud, for whom if the transference is the motor force of the analysis, it is a gently positive, but not erotic, transference that drives the treatment, not a negative transference. For Lacan, though, it is hate, not love, that is the key passion here. How does Lacan describe it? He goes on to state that:

This phenomenon represents the patient's imaginary transference onto us of one of the more or less archaic images, which degrades, diverts, or inhibits the cycle of a certain behavior by an effect of symbolic subduction [subtraction], which has excluded a certain function or body part from the ego's control by an accident of repression, and which has given its form to this or that agency of the personality through an act of identification. (2006a, pp. 87–88)

How do we read this sentence? I think that we must read it by looking forward to later developments of Lacan. I believe that this "function or body part" excluded from the ego's control is a prefiguration of the object *a*, a part object that is a remainder, that is not subject to rule of the phallus, to castration, to the symbolization and mortification of the body. My hypothesis is this is the object given to the Other, "the archaic image transferred to us," Lacan states through an "accident of repression" as Lacan puts it here. If we jump forward to Lacan's discussion of the Real and Imaginary Father in *Seminar 7*, we see two losses that the subject must endure. In its confrontation with the Real Father, the subject endures castration (I do not have the organ to allow access to the jouissance of the Mother)—a loss associated with the passion of fear. But, as Éric Laurent (2006) explains in a reading of this, there is the second loss of privation. At a second moment, there is a loss that corresponds to our separation from the Other—an object is extracted from our body and is given to the Other, in the very act of separation from the Other. We hate the Imaginary Father for this. I think that we can read Lacan's sentence there through these later developments. I think the analyst here is an avatar for or is able to facilitate an articulation of what Lacan terms Imaginary Father. And, the hatred is linked to the separation of the subject from what Lacan will later describe as the object *a*, the part object—that remnant of jouissance. We can also read this in the context of Lacan's comments from *Seminar 11* quoted in the previous chapter, namely, that the analyst must fall from the position of the ideal—the analyst must fail to be the Ideal—the Imaginary Father—in order to be the support of the object *a*, in order to what he says "embody the hypnotized patient." I believe that we must take this concept of "embody" in a particular way and read it in the context of *Seminar 20*. In *Seminar 20*, Lacan will redefine the object *a* as the semblant of being. There is a motif running through the seminar about a disjunction between the letter or knowledge, and Being. As speaking Beings, because of the Other, in a sense, we do not have Being, or we have an eccentric relation to Being. However, I think the object a, as a semblant of being, is indicative of a fantasy of a relation of being—the very concept of how it is through the fantasy that the subject constructs the reality around him. We end up, in a sense, having to do that for ourselves, but at the moment of entry into analysis, as I think Lacan is alluding to here, we have hatred—at the Father or God for having failed to do it for us—and for ourselves as well for the messes we have constructed. For this operation to take place, however, the analysand must go beyond the realm of the Imaginary—the idealized—in order to confront not his Being directly, but the semblant of Being constructed through the fantasy by virtue of the possibility of the analyst's taking the place of or introducing the object a. Let me also add that in Tarrab's Testimony in the previous chapter, we saw the impact of this very precisely in the fall of the father from the father he loved to the hated father, who was ripped, who messed up his life and his child's, leading to the elaboration of the *soplo*.

But, again, let me point out that this perspective of Lacan's is a radical departure from Freud, who builds the transference on a different basis.

This is not to say, however, that while Lacan gives hate this central place as a passion within the psychoanalytic experience, that he will ignore love. Indeed, Lacan will, like Freud, emphasize the relationship of love to the transference. The transference love is indeed love. We will see this even within the context of Lacan's reformulation of the transference in *Seminar 11* as the *sujet suppposé savoir*. This is usually translated into English as the subject supposed to know. But, I think that the French is ambiguous enough as to the reference for the word "supposed," that we must also accept an equivocation in the translation as also the "supposed subject of knowledge." Thus, when the transference is in place, the analysand will suppose that there exists a subject who is supposed to have access to knowledge, presumably about the suffering of the analysand. This formulation, linking love and knowledge, is endorsed by Lacan in *Seminar 20*, where he states that: "I love the person I assume to have knowledge" (1998a, p. 67).

I think that, if we recognize the equivocal nature of the translation of the *sujet supposé savoir*, we can see various modalities under which transference, the so-called positive transference, may be negated. The first would be at the level of the Imaginary, or we could say, the person of the analyst. The analysand might believe that there is a knowledge somewhere about his suffering, and that some subject has that knowledge, but it is not the person that he is talking with. "I hate you because someone is out there who can help me, but not you!" This is the reproach to the Imaginary father—an Ideal is preserved, and because you, as an analyst, fail to live up to it—my life continues to suffer. I think that there is a second form of negation to the transference. In this, the existence of a knowledge is supposed, is accepted by the analysand, but it is a knowledge that cannot be subjectified. This position would be a kind of refusal of psychoanalysis (and perhaps also of science as well). Lacan states in *Encore*: "A dream does not introduce us into any kind of unfathomable experience or mystery—it is read in what is said about it" (1998a, p. 96). The final form of negation would be the failure to suppose the existence of a knowledge. I would suggest that this is the position that some people have now coming into analysis: they do not believe a knowledge is possible about their suffering: certain ideologies of our time having the effect of somehow foreclosing the possibility of knowledge about suffering—suffering merely a behavior to be retrained, a rather odd ricochet effect of science. I speculate here on this for a particular reason. It seems clear to me that while for Freud, the passion of love is the key to the transference and analytic experience, for Lacan it is a situation involving both love and hate, passions that he implies throughout *Seminar 20* must be taken together. Lacan even coins a term in *Encore* of *hainamoration*, which brings together *haine* [hate] and *énamoré* [enamored], to which he adds the following in addition: "It is here that analysis reminds us that one knows nothing of love without hate. Well, if the knowledge that has been fomented over the course of the centuries disappoints us, and if today we must overhaul the function of knowledge, it is perhaps because hatred has never been put in its proper place" (1998a, p. 91). I think it is clear to what extent the two passions are linked in the psychoanalytic experience, especially the beginning of analysis, as Lacan noted in the paper on "Aggressiveness". How does this play out at the end of his teaching, in *Seminar 20*?

I believe that we can first approach this question in part by looking at the status of the object *a* in the psychoanalytic experience. How does this function in the analytic experience? In *Seminar 11*, Lacan specifies this in an abbreviated way as follows:

> [...] the analysand says to his partner, to the analyst, what amounts to this—*I love you, but, because inexplicably I love in you something more than you—the* object *a—I mutilate you.*

> This is the meaning of that breast-complex, that *mammal-complex*,
> whose relation to the oral drive Bergler saw so clearly, except that
> the orality in question has nothing to do with food, and that the
> whole stress is placed on the effect of mutilation.
>
> *I give myself to you*, the patient says again, *but this gift of my
> person*—as they say—*Oh mystery! is changed inexplicably into a gift
> of shit*—a term that is also essential to our experience. (Lacan, 1977a,
> p. 268)

At this point in his work, it is the relation of the subject and object *a* that
defines the horizon of the analytic experience. There are the passions—
the passions of love and hate—and at a different level than those passions, we discover the relation of the subject to the object *a*, the object
cause of desire. I believe that we find the level of these passions of love
and hate distinct from the relation of the subject and the object *a*.

In *Encore*, Lacan makes the same formulation. In the very first session,
for example, he says that:

> Love constitutes a sign and is always mutual. Love is always
> mutual? yes—that is why the unconscious was invented—so
> that we would realize that man's desire is the Other's desire,
> and that love, which is a passion that involves ignorance of desire,
> nevertheless leaves desires its whole import. When we look closer,
> we see the ravages wrecked by this. [...] Love demands love. It
> never stops demanding it. It demands it [...] *encore*. "*Encore*" is the
> proper name of the gap in the Other from which the demand for
> love stems. [...] Is love about making one? (Lacan, 1998a, pp. 4–5)

I would like to inquire if we can read this well-known passage not in
terms of romantic love, but rather in terms of the psychoanalytic experience. In this passage, Lacan delineates love and desire, as separate,
but interlocked domains—something that is certainly true of a
psychoanalysis. There is an interesting logic that Lacan develops: love
is mutual. Because love is mutual, the unconscious was invented. Then,
Lacan states that the unconscious was invented—by the psychoanalyst,
I would add—so that we—and here, I would say that the "we" is the
analysand—would realize that man's desire is the Other's desire—a
restatement of a very classical formulation of Lacan. Then, he adds that
as a passion, love is the ignorance of desire. Love and desire are, here,

in this sense, disarticulated. He goes on to state that while love ignores desire, the full import—importance, I imagine—of desire remains intact, and that this disjunction—the ignorance of love and the disjunction with desire—causes ravages, presumably, in the sense in which these two different subjective vectors pull the subject in different directions, as it were, without the subject's awareness. Lacan continues with this enigmatic sentence about how encore—still, or again, in English—is the proper name of the gap in the Other—here, I imagine as well, this as a notion of the lack in the Other that will resonate though the seminar—from which the demand for love stems. And, here, I would read this phrase in the context of transference as love, as the supposition of a subject supposed to know. The gap in the Other—which is in part a failure of meaning in the Other—a lack of knowledge (in the case of an analysis—about one's own suffering) leads the subject to a demand for love, love as a supposition that someone somewhere knows, in other words, has that knowledge. And this person can be, in the transference, the analyst who, via the identification that plays a prominent role in the beginning of the analysis, the analysand wishes to become one with, share in the identification, the identification that must fall, for the analysis to shift from the level of the Imaginary to the object *a*.

I would suggest that we might even adopt Lacanian mathemes to indicate, then, these two vectors. There is love that is organized around a fusion to the One—an Imaginary One, or an Imaginarized level of the One—which we could otherwise write as a shared Identification: a link to the analyst at the level of I. This love is in contrast to desire which, to go back to the formulation presented above from *Seminar 11*, involves a bond of the subject with the object *a*. This is how I read this passage as a commentary on the psychoanalytic experience itself.

I think the following passage in the seminar, in a sense, confirms this reading—this is the famous passage about Picasso's parrot.

> I can tell you a little tale, that of a parakeet that was in love with Picasso. How could one tell? From, the way the parakeet nibbled the collar of his shirt and the flaps of his jacket. Indeed, the parakeet was in love with what is essential to man, namely, his attire. […] Clothes promise debauchery, when one takes them off. […] To enjoy a body when there are no more clothes leaves intact the question of what makes the One, that is, the question of identification. The parakeet identified with Picasso clothed.

The same goes for everything involving love. The habit loves the monk, as they are but one thereby. In other words, what lies under the habit, what we call the body, is perhaps but the remainder I call object *a*.

What holds the image together is a remainder. Analysis demonstrates that love, in its essence, is narcissistic, and reveals that the substance of what is supposedly object-like—what a bunch of bull—is in fact that which constitutes a remainder in desire, namely, its cause, and sustains desire through its lack of satisfaction, even its impossibility.

Love is impotent, though mutual, because it is not aware that it is but the desire to be One, which leads us to the impossibility of establishing the relationship between "them two" ... them two sexes. (Lacan, 1998a, p. 6)

The I and the *a* for Lacan, thus, are closely related. It is the object *a* that holds the image—the I—together. The first implication that I would draw from this is that love here, is in part, an impediment, in impediment to the avowal of desire. This is indeed also a very classic Lacanian motif, then, which goes back to the development of schema L, in which the Imaginary domain—with the interplay of ego and semblable—is developed in contrast to the Symbolic dimension, and the relation of the subject to the Other. But, I think that there is an additional dimension to this here, when one brings in the notion of the object *a*, in particular the object *a* in as much as it is the remainder which holds together the image.

CHAPTER SIXTEEN

Encore, encore: feminine

For Lacan, sexuation—of course, a term we do not have in English, as it is not really gender as such and has nothing to do with the body—is a matter above all of choice—the choice to "be"—and I say this with a certain trepidation, but then again does this not have to do with the semblant—to identify oneself as a man or to be a woman. We could even stretch this further and state that these represent two different logics, logics of an approach to the world, one identified as male, the other female.

Lacan states in beginning his presentation on what will be the graph of sexuation: "Let us approach things first from the pole at which every x is a function of Φx, that is, from the pole where man is situated. One ultimately situates oneself there by choice—women are free to situate themselves there if it gives them pleasure to do so. Everyone knows that there are phallic women" (Lacan, 1998a, p. 71). Then, a few pages later he states: "Any speaking being whatsoever, as is expressly formulated in Freudian theory, whether provided with the attributes of masculinity— attributes that remain to be determined—or not, is allowed to inscribe itself in this [feminine] part. If it inscribes itself there, it will not allow for any universality—it will be a not-whole, insofar as it has the choice of positing itself in the Φx or of not being there" (Lacan, 1998a, p. 80).

My proposition to start is thus that for Lacan, sexuation is not a function of genetics—with the speaking being's chromosomal configuration—nor with the body even—the presence or absence of the penis or any other of the so-called primary or secondary sexual characteristics, but is rather a kind of subjective choice. A speaking being might situate itself as a himself or a herself. This choice—or situation of the speaking being—is a choice related to how the speaking being confronts the phallic function, which Lacan also terms the father function.

Let us see how Lacan describes this in his discussion of the graphs of sexuation. Look at the formula at the top of the graph first on the male side—all of x are subject to the phallic function, but there exists an x that is an exception. Lacan states:

> On the left, the lower line $\forall x \Phi x$—indicates that it is through the phallic function that man as whole acquires his inscription, with the proviso that this function is limited due to the existence of an x by which the function Φx is negated: $\exists x \overline{\Phi x}$. That is what is known as the father function—whereby we find, via negation, the proposition $\overline{\Phi x}$, which grounds the operativity of what makes up for the sexual relationship with castration, insofar as that relationship is in no way inscribable. The whole here is thus based on the exception posited as the end-point, that is, on that which altogether negates Φx. (Lacan, 1998a, pp. 79–80)

I want to speak about this exception. If castration is the prohibition of access to the jouissance of the Other—of the Mother—the exception, the sole exception to that, is what Lacan identifies as the Real Father, the Father, as I indicated in earlier chapters, of castration. Everyone is subject to this castration—to the phallic function—which is universal for the male, except him. This is the father that Lacan will elsewhere associated with the Freudian myth—in *Totem and Taboo*—of the father of the primal horde, the father who had all the women, what we call the alpha male. For the woman, on the other hand, there is no exception—$\overline{\exists x \overline{\Phi x}}$—but at the same time, she is not entirely subject to the phallic function—this *pas-tout*—not whole, or not-all, is critical. What are some implications of these two different positions—which Lacan refers to as "inscriptions"—a word choice of Lacan's that indicates to me that this is something written—something to be read in the letters carried by the unconscious—again: what are the implications of these two different inscriptions? For the male, we might say—castration is more complete, more thorough—jouissance is more evacuated from the body and from language and speech. The Other—the Other as language, body, woman, unconscious—is more thoroughly symbolized, mortified. This is the universal dimension—the for-all—that Lacan described. And, I think that this is related to the One discussed two chapters above. But, at the same time, for the male, there is the exception. My proposal is that the object *a*—as the leftover, or remainder, of the father function, or phallic function, is an avatar of the Real Father, another manifestation of the exception to the prohibition against jouissance. Is this not the classic for-mulation of Lacan's in "The subversion of the subject" where he writes (2006a, p. 700)—"Castration means that jouissance has to be refused in order to be attained on the inverse scale of the law of desire"? Jou-issance is forbidden universally, with the exception of that jouissance associated with object *a* and the fantasy. The dimension of perversion for the male (Miller and Laurent both comment on how the male desire is fetishistic and a woman's is erotomanic) is linked in some sense to the concept of the Real Father.

The male jouissance, thus, is thoroughly phallic—masturbatory, Lacan will comment on a little later. The male holds onto this phallic jouissance, idiotic, the jouissance of the One, without an Other. Mascu-line jouissance is universally separate from the Other, except through the fantasy. Lacan states that the "$ never deals with anything by way of a partner but object *a* inscribed on the other side of the bar. He is unable to attain his sexual partner, who is the Other, except inasmuch as his partner is the cause of his desire" (1998a, p. 80). In other words, if phallic jouissance is the jouissance of the One, the only approach to the jouissance of the Other for the male is through the object *a*, this remain-der, the exception.

The inscription of a woman is different. The universality, the limit-ing function, of castration is less complete on a woman's side. There is a jouissance in speech, in language, for a woman that is different from that of men. I do not think it is an accident that Lacan will create the concept of *lalangue*—Lacan's notion that seems to me akin to the idea that signifiers themselves are not only mortifying—Symbolic—but also can have a *jouissance* value—I do not think it an accident that Lacan will present this thesis at the moment of his investigation into feminine sexuality. I would propose that *lalangue* is, in a sense, a function of the fact that the castration function is not complete (*pas-tout*) on the Other, on the Symbolic. This is one dimension to the erotomanic character of feminine desire (to be a little sloppy with the term desire here—as desire is masculine)—a woman can obtain a *jouissance* of the Other, through language. This partial foreclosure of the father function also can be connected to that dimension of "crazy" we find in the feminine position.

I want to add here a very important point. Woman, for Lacan in *Encore*, is a very different issue from what Lacan previously elaborated with regard to hysteria. And, hysteria and woman are not only different, but, in a sense, opposite. Lacan defines hysteria in *Encore* as "to play the part of a man" (1998a, p. 85). When a woman situates herself on the male side, it is in relation to the castrating father, to the phallic function as a universal—even if it may be often as a challenge to that father—to that authority—even to the point of wanting to occupy the place of exception, as object *a* in relation to the father. A woman, on the other hand, here represents a position where the father is not universal. It is not against the father, but beyond the father.

I would like to pause here and return to Lacan's earlier text on feminine sexuality, the "Guiding remarks for a congress on feminine sexuality" from 1958 in the *Écrits*, with the assistance of a sharp paper on that text prepared by our Belgian colleague Geert Hoornaert (2011), to approach this from a different angle. Lacan puts it this way in 1958: there is an adequate *Vorstellungrepasentanz* (signifier, say) of masculinity, which is the phallus. This says all that there is to say about masculine sexuality. The Phallus also says something about feminine sexuality, but not everything. There, representations come to flood the picture—*vortstellung* or representations, or, in Hoornaert's reading, semblants—come in to say something about what the phallus cannot say about feminine sexuality— Lacan will elaborate a whole series of these: feminine masochism, misrecognition of the vagina, penis envy, rectal dependence, and so on. In Hoornaert's reading, Lacan is trying to advance a very subtle argument in which, against Freud, he is arguing that the feminine position cannot be defined only with reference to the Phallus, but against the post-Freudians, trying to argue that these part objects or part drives cannot explain it either. And, on a different level, Lacan is arguing that while the masculine side of sexuality has a signifier that says it all, that signifier cannot say it all with regard to the woman—and semblants are evoked with regard to feminine sexuality. Thus, in contrast to man, where a signifier can prescribe the exercise of sexuality, for a woman there is a point of foreclosure. A semblant is necessary to mediate this relation with the Real.

Since femininity "in and of itself" is a real, the element foreclosed from the universe of discourse, *to be a woman*, subjectively, is always, *to be a woman in conjunction with an element of the Other*. Anything that a woman can say about her sexuality must necessarily pass via an element of semblance that misses its real. Wherever she appears as woman, she has, in this masquerade, passed via an element that makes her appear, that gives semblance to her real. Woman is thus a being both completely "relative" and completely "absolute." [...] *Relative woman* is a woman is so far as she positions herself in relation to her man, he who serves "as a relay so that [she] becomes this Other to herself, as she is to him." [...] Absolute woman is she of whom nothing can be said. Nothing will be said of her real, quite simply because the real cannot be said; something of it can be felt, and something of what can be felt thereof may well colour the semblance that a woman—one by one—will mobilize to put *in-form*. (Hoornaert, 2011, pp. 95–96)

This reading of Hoornaert works well when put in the context of Lacan's graph twelve years later. If we examine the bottom half of the graph, we see the classic formulation I have made with regarding the role of fantasy in the approach of the male to the Other: the vector $ > a. For the woman, the feminine sexual position has two vectors: one towards the phallus. This is that which corresponds to what Hoornaert calls the relative woman—the woman who positions herself using a man to become other to herself in the same way that she is to him. Then, there is the absolute woman, whose sexuality touches on something that is Other, that remains radically Other. Lacan states:

The Other is not simply the locus in which truth stammers. It deserves to represent that to which woman is fundamentally related. Assuredly, we have but sporadic testimonies of this, and that is why I took them up last time in their metaphorical function. Being the Other, in the most radical sense, in the sexual relationship, in relation to what can be said of the unconscious, woman is that which has a relationship to that Other. That is what I would like to articulate a little more precisely today.

Woman has a relation to the signifier of that Other, insofar as, qua Other, it can but remain forever Other. I can only assume here that you will recall my statement that there is no Other of the

Other. The Other, that is, the locus in which everything that can be articulated on the basis of the signifier comes to be inscribed, is, in its foundation, the Other in the most radical sense. That is why the signifier, with this open parentheses, marks the Other as barred: S(A). (1998a, p. 81)

To go back to my initial proposition regarding *Seminar 20*—if there is a "beyond of analysis," something "beyond the fantasy," my final proposition is that this is linked to the feminine position of sexuation. On the masculine side, because of castration, the Real is more completely foreclosed. On the feminine side, however, through the signifier of the lack in the Other, a woman has a greater access—as it were—to the Real, through the signifier—or, better, semblants—of the Real that she is able to elaborate. It is certain that this constitutes something of a beyond, even a feminization associated with psychoanalysis itself.

PART VII

REMARKS ON PSYCHOANALYSIS

CHAPTER SEVENTEEN

The specificity of psychoanalysis relative to psychotherapy*

O f course, both psychotherapy, in its psychodynamic orientation, and psychoanalysis work through the use of words and speech. Many have worked in different ways to define psychoanalysis and distinguish it from psychotherapy, in particular psychodynamic psychotherapy. In the United States, in the past, when psychoanalysis—in its typical American form—reigned supreme, this was an issue with great consequence. Psychoanalysts were held in high esteem and occupied all of the powerful positions in various clinical and educational institutions, and psychoanalysis was seen by many as the ultimate form of mental health care, the best treatment available for a range of psychological and even medical problems. With that authority taken on by the American psychoanalysts of that era came significant prestige and money, and the analysts who held the tiller of the analytic ship were very keen on maintaining control of the direction of this ship and access to the ship itself.

---

*"The specificity of psychoanalysis relative to psychotherapy" was delivered at the first Friday Conference of the Center for Psychotherapy and Psychoanalysis in Omaha, Nebraska, on September 7, 2001.

One of their particular approaches to this was the medicalization of psychoanalysis, and the position consistently taken by the American Psychoanalytic Association over many decades of requiring medical training as a prerequisite for psychoanalytic training. This position of the American was never given up, and it was only with the successful advancement of a civil lawsuit that non-physicians were allowed into the Institutes associated with the American. This position of the American went against the previous psychoanalytic traditions in Europe and even the explicit wishes of Freud, which were partly articulated in his essay *On the Question of Lay Analysis* (Freud, 1926e). This is, of course, a critical issue, that of the access of people to psychoanalysis.

There was, however, an equally significant, though perhaps less obvious stake in this issue, that of the status of psychoanalysis itself, of psychoanalysis as a practice. For, one additional consequence of these unfortunate years in the history of American psychoanalysis was that psychoanalysis ceased to be psychoanalysis as such, but was instead configured as a psychology—as one among many—to be articulated within the medical group of psychologies, and, as a treatment, it lost what I will call its psychoanalytic specificity. This was, of course, the effect of Ego Psychology, which dominated the American psychoanalytic scene for so long.

These historical facts—this story of American psychoanalysis in the middle of the last century—are important to us today, those who hold that the path laid out by Freud is of value and needs to be preserved, because they allow us to situate the precipitous decline of psychoanalysis in this country, which I would instead label as the decline of the mirage of psychoanalysis, for my assertion is that psychoanalysis was never established in this country in the institutions that claimed to have done so. What we saw in the 1960s and 1970s in the turn away from so-called psychoanalysis was the turn away from Ego Psychology, a turn that did not completely correspond with the rise of biological therapies, as many claim, but had its own independent and internally driven trajectory. And, equally important, those trying to forge a psychoanalytic path in this country, those working to explore other paths—the Kleinians, Object Relations therapists, relational psychoanalysts, and, separately, all who worked without medical licensure as the legal basis for their practice, were forced—in many cases—to found other organizations to proceed and called their work something other than analysis.

Allow me to point out that this particular American story of psychoanalysis is not the story elsewhere in the world. Many European and South American countries have long allowed non-physicians to practice psychoanalysis and, in fact, in many countries, the practice of therapy itself was not regulated by the State. This, I argue, is important for it is doubtful to me that psychiatric training is the privileged route to psychoanalysis, and it certainly shouldn't be the required one. On other issues, the differences are significant. The individual Associations of the International Psychoanalytic Association have a remarkable degree of variability in the regulation of analytic training and practice, and most fostered a variety of orientations, or, at the least, did not simply prescribe a limited Ego Psychology. Then, there is the issue of Lacan and those—such as myself—who follow in his orientation.

It is the Lacanian rejuvenation of psychoanalysis—and even return to psychoanalysis from various deviations away from it, as I will speak to below—that account for the different paths psychoanalysis has taken in different national settings. Psychoanalysts of the American Psychoanalytic Association have, until recently, largely ignored Lacan. And analysis, as I said above, has largely suffered in this country. In France, Europe, and South America, the situation is dramatically different. Psychoanalysis has prospered in these countries, and I largely credit that to their explicit or in some cases latent reception of Lacan.

Now—what is this "rejuvenation of psychoanalysis" that I speak of? Let us turn back to Freud and trace a history—perhaps more of a story—of psychoanalysis to bring light to this question. But, first, what is this psychoanalysis that I speak of? It is the theory of the unconscious and the practice that results from it. Freud's real genius—in as much as we may use such a term—was the discovery or the invention of the unconscious. This discovery largely resulted from a particular practice of listening, of listening to the hysteric patients who repeatedly turned to him for relief of their suffering. This discovery of his was a contingent one, for his practice of listening was based on his failures: his failures as a hypnotist and in the use of other therapies to address the sufferings of his patients. Failing to succeed with other techniques, he fell back upon listening.

From this listening, he took to directing his attention to the most peculiar aspects of his patients' discourse, of what they were telling him. His focus was directed increasingly not on the obvious utterances made by patients, their stories and explanations of their lives, but rather at a set of seemingly disparate phenomena—their dreams, their slips of the tongue, irrational obsessions or fantasies that overwhelmed them, failures of their memory, or desired actions that his patients would complain they would be unable to carry out for no clear reason. Freud paid special attention to these things, and he noticed something. This was that if he could get his patients to direct their attention to these bizarre things and speak about them, they could be deciphered—deciphered on the basis of that which was their cause. For, in fact, he quickly realized that these various phenomena were not random, were not without meaning, were not trivial in any way—but were in fact attributable to a cause, and pregnant with significance.

He named that cause of the symptoms the unconscious, a series of thoughts—representation of thoughts, to use his term—whose very representation is not conscious, is not part of the conscious memory of an individual, but whose representations must be supposed through the deciphering of the forms in which the unconscious exerts itself. These forms: dreams, slips of the tongues, and so forth, even the symptoms themselves—identified as unconscious formations by Lacan—are known by their irrational and bizarre character, and the key Freudian discovery relates to their deciphering and the supposition of the unconscious as the locus for their signification. Thus, for the neurotic, we see repression as—in a sense—the key mental operation. Thoughts which could not be symbolized or incorporated into consciousness—generally in infancy—are repressed, not forgotten, but deposited, as it were, into the unconscious, from which they return, in the disguised forms as noted above.

I emphasize the formal aspects of his work, for they are the key to psychoanalysis in theory, as well as in its clinical application. But Freud, of course, went on to formulate additional ideas about the unconscious. Once he began to accumulate clinical experience concerning the unconscious in his series of analyses, he began—in the manner I would say of a good scientist, but a bad analyst—to specify the content of the unconscious, of what is found there, and what is always found there. The most well known statements in this regard relate to the Oedipus complex. I have elsewhere termed this move away from interest in the forms to determination of content, as Freudianism, and it is Freudianism that we must separate from psychoanalysis to delineate the history of those who have followed Freud (Svolos, 2001).

I wish to make comments along different lines about this matter of the content of the unconscious, or the result of the process of formal deciphering known as psychoanalysis. The first of these is that even in his earliest work, Freud recognized a certain limit of meaning, a point at which supposed content could not be identified, a point of resistance to meaning, and here I of course refer to his two brief notes in *The Interpretation of Dreams* regarding the navel of a dream. In the *Standard Edition*, these can be found first in the striking footnote on page 111, and then again on page 525 (Freud, 1900a). Freud speaks there about a tangle of dream thoughts that cannot be unraveled, however great the effort of interpretation, a point where the dream reaches into the unknown. Thus, even Freud, in contrast to the Oedipalizing interpretive template that he promulgated so forcefully (witness his case histories), recognized—even early in his work—something else present.

The other observation I wish to make relates to one of Freud's most extended discussions of fantasy, the under-read "A child is being beaten." In this work, Freud writes on the occurrence of beating fantasies, which he had encountered on various occasions. In his discussion of such fantasies, of which he cites varied articulations from his clinical work, Freud theorizes three phases of the fantasy: first, "My father is beating the child;" second, "I am being beaten by my father;" third, "A figure of authority is beating some children." The key to this fantasy, and its various forms and transformations, all of which are evident in the text, lies for Freud in this second phase of the fantasy. What Freud says there is interesting, and I'll quote him: "This second phase is the most important and the most momentous of all. But we may say of it in a certain sense that it has never had a real existence. It is never remembered, it has never succeeded in becoming conscious. It is a construction of analysis, but it is no less a necessity on that account" (Freud, 1919e, p. 185).

I highlight this, because I think it brings out a critical issue in our clinical work—namely one related to the limitations of interpretation, and the role of logical or formal supposition in what Freud here terms construction, namely the construction of the unconscious. It also speaks to something special in the ontological status of the unconscious, that in addition to having something in its content of an unknowable limit—a navel, as noted above, the unconscious is also defined in terms of not having a Symbolic presence—Freud says it is neither remembered, nor conscious—but as something only known through its effects, as something necessary to explain something else. This will be what Lacan will late in his work term the Real—Real with a capital R—that domain put in contrast to the Symbolic—the realm of the signifiers, words or thoughts, to put it simply, language even—and the domain of the Imaginary, the ego and object representations, images, that subjects make.

Moving on—this distinction between the elucidation of the forms of the unconscious and the determination of the content of the unconscious can even be seen within Freud's own clinical work and the different ways in which it has been read. And, in this regard, we might say that Freud slips, at times, back and forth between psychoanalysis and that mirage of psychoanalysis that I have termed Freudianism. Take Freud's first major published case, that of Dora (Freud, 1905e). Go to this case and read it or re-read it, and you will see it begin with a highlighting of certain symptoms—a speech disturbance, some respiratory symptoms—(very typical of the hysteric patients Freud saw at the time) and also an series of dream interpretations (here note the light brought on different unconscious formations), only to collapse with Dora's abrupt departure from analysis in response to Freud's simple Oedipalizing interpretation of the object of Dora's desire—Freud having missed (and acknowledging himself the lapse) the homosexual interest of Dora in Frau K. That moment, the moment of failure (though I think we must commend Freud for his bravery in presenting these cases, especially the failures), is instructive for it demonstrates that slip, a slip from the therapeutic goal of bringing forth unconscious formations, to that of mastering the material delivered—in this case through his Oedipal template. It also shows the potentially damaging therapeutic consequences of such a slip.

Now I am tempted to think that Freud learned from his mistakes, and as evidence I wish to look at the Rat Man case (Freud, 1909d). Early in the case, as many have noted, including Lacan in his "The direction of the treatment and the principles of its power," Freud offers a rather brutal interpretation of the role of the Rat Man's father as the agent preventing his marriage to the poor girl he was interested in (Lacan, 2006a). This interpretation, in addition to its strikingly strong position so early in the analysis, was also likely untrue, false, in the sense that the father was probably dead at the time the marriage was considered. Freud also, during a session where the matter was first raised, offered a fairly lengthy theoretical exposition, display, so to speak, of his knowledge regarding the content of the unconscious and how it worked, this being the discussion of the transformations of love and hate in the sixth session of the analysis. Now, this move of Freud's was successful—the analysis continued, and in fact, a wealth of new material followed from here—and Lacan, in his statement on the case, defends Freud's maneuver, stating that though the interpretation was factually untrue, it was true to the unconscious desire of the Rat Man. Let us look at Freud's own comment here, a comment found, as with the signal observation of the navel of the dream, in a footnote, on page 181 of the *Standard Edition*. Freud states a position that we might say has been lost for many who have followed Freud, those who have taken display of mastery in interpretation or in matters of theory to be of value in and of itself. Freud's gloss on this, however, is quite different. He states, regarding his theoretical presentation to the Rat Man:

> It is never the aim of discussions like this to create conviction. They are only intended to bring the repressed complexes into consciousness, to set the conflict going in the field of conscious mental activity, and to facilitate the emergence of fresh material from the unconscious. A sense of conviction is only attained after the patient has himself worked over the reclaimed material, and so long as he is not fully convinced the material must be considered as unexhausted. (Freud, 1909d, p. 181)

Thus, Freud's own seeming slip from psychoanalysis into Freudianism here is merely a technical maneuver on his part to elicit additional unconscious formations, not an end in itself.

The subsequent history of psychoanalysis can be read as a series of variations on and responses to these various coordinates in Freud's work that I have articulated here. Ego Psychology, for example, must be understood as the substitution of Freudianism for psychoanalysis, leaving us with what I termed above the mirage of psychoanalysis. This theoretical shift has critical technical repercussions: namely, the substitution of the analyst as master, master of his ego and of reality, and of the unconscious of the patient—Freudianism's analyst—for the analyst as the enigmatic elicitor of unconscious formation. Successful analysis is then structured around a recognition of such mastery by the analysand (our term for the patient, or client, in analysis) and subsequent identification of the analysand with such a master, the analyst. The transference—that supposition of knowledge—given by the analysand is accepted by the Ego Psychologist as a just sense of mastery.

Kleinianism and Object Relations, in contrast, must be seen in great contrast to Ego Psychology in that, instead of endorsing Freudianism, both seek to repudiate Freudianism. This repudiation, however, is not only in the terms of a rehabilitation of psychoanalysis, as I defined it above—though I would say that both of these orientations remain truer to analysis than ego psychology—but rather a repudiation through substitution. In this sense, the critical move of these two theories has been to replace Freudianism's Oedipalization with a series of pre-Oedipalizations, a series of elaborations of theories of the unconscious based on a template of necessary pre-Oedipal configurations. This too is not without consequences, for I cannot help but wonder if the very interactive interpretive style characteristic, say, of the Kleinians is not derived from a need to verbalize or articulate a whole series of non-verbal phenomena—what Lacan would term Imaginary—whose basis in various archaic, or pre-linguistic, stages in development would thus lead to the necessity of their articulation on the part of the analyst—the analysand cannot speak of them at all: no words or memories. The move away from Freudianism, I endorse, but not to replace it with something else.

There is one final historical development I want to discuss—common in various contemporary therapies and that we might attribute to Carl Rogers, who certainly articulated its theory as much as anyone. I would describe this development—like Kleinianism—as the response of Rogers and others to Freudianism, and to a certain extent, to psycho-analysis itself. The key to understanding Rogers lies in the rejection by the analyst of the position of mastery. In terming his therapy as Client-Centered, Rodgers argued—and not without a significant validity that I will endorse—that the truth of the patient, if we can put it that way, is not to be found in the analyst—whose mastery will deliver the truth to the analysand, or client, to use his term—but in the client himself. The therapist simply reflects the thoughts and feelings of the client back onto the client and whatever is inhibiting the client from actualizing his self—his true self—will resolve itself.

Now, given my criticism here and elsewhere of what I term Freudianism, I might endorse this Rogerian criticism of Freudianism. After all, though I did not discuss this at length above, one of the key tenets of the Freudian discovery of the unconscious is that the unconscious is particular—particular to each individual, with a unique set of associations and meanings to be delivered to the symptom. That being the case, the Truth certainly is with the patient, with the patient in the form of unconscious truth. And this is certainly no news for those here engaged in clinical practice of analysis or therapy, for the clinic shows time and time again how erroneous our interpretations may be— whether voiced or not. However, the knowledge or assumption that the Truth is in or with the unconscious of the analysand does not make that Truth necessarily any more accessible to an analysand. The unconscious is, by definition, repressed and, as such, inaccessible to the analysand.

The real critical issue here is the transference. What is often empha- sized with regard to the transference is its emotional or affective charac- ter, the Transference Love. What Lacan brought to the discussion is the key relationship of love to knowledge. One of his formulations which came to represent a key definition of transference here is the notion of the *sujet supposé savoir*. This French phrase can be translated in vari- ous ways—the subject supposed to know, or the supposed subject of knowledge. Transference comes into play when someone supposes someone else to know something. Attribution of knowledge, at least within the clinical context—though the implications for other forms of social bonds are intriguing—is itself the transference.

It is this attribution of knowledge that can lead to a willingness to engage in the analytic process that in turn leads to the unconscious. Without the transference, there is no analysis, for the knowledge con- tained in the ego is itself seen as adequate by the patient. The Rogerians deny any benefit to the transference and refuse to allow themselves to be situated by the analysand within the transference in a position of mastery, thus recognizing the danger of assuming the position of mas- tery (such as the Ego Psychologists). In doing so, however, they close the path to analysis off in their work. Furthermore, as can be seen so eas- ily in the clinic, the transference is often only slowly modified, so that regardless of the particular position they want to be in, the Rogerian suffers the transference effects whether he likes it or not.

The answer to this dilemma—the presence of an at times intractable transference and a desire to refuse a position of mastery—is the subtle management of the transference that, to an extent, defines the particu- larity of psychoanalysis. That the transference will happen is not to be opposed, resisted, but in fact is somewhat welcome in that it is the motor force of the analysis itself. However, the analyst must never allow him- self to assume the status attributed to him within the transference. The analyst cannot accept the transference on its terms. Oh, how tempting it can be for many clinicians—to be the love object beyond all others of a patient; or, equally dangerous, to see oneself as the wise person who the analysand will look to for advice, for guidance, as a model of behavior; or, even—this more dangerous yet—to confirm a sense of reality or the world around. These positions, these identifications—whether true or not—must be refused, the analyst must forever situate himself eccentric to the identifications proposed for him within the transference.

This positioning or maneuvering I speak of is not to deny the transference, to evade its presence—in fact Lacanians are hesitant about any interpretation of the transference—but to use the transference—a belief about knowledge—to direct the analysand to the site of knowledge in the unconscious itself, through the display of its formations as we saw above, and even to its limits—to that navel where knowledge will never reach. In fact, it is that failure of knowledge—reaching the navel of which the analysand will forever know nothing—that leads to the end of analysis at the point of the disappearing of the transference—the end of a supposition of a subject of knowledge.

This is a point, perhaps, where we might mark one of the great distinctions between psychoanalysis and psychotherapy. Now, psychotherapy is something that Jacques-Alain Miller—in "Psychanalyse pure, psychanalyse appliquée, et psychothérapie"—has neatly pointed out to us does not exist (2001a). It does not exist in the sense that so many different clinical perspectives and theoretical orientations can be subsumed under its rubric. However, the fact it does not exist will not stop me from speaking about it. Speaking about it, specifically, in terms of those "talking therapies" that are not psychoanalysis, which is in contrast to the psychotherapies and which has a certain specificity to it.

This distinction between psychoanalysis and psychotherapy will not be based, as it should be clear from my first statements here today, on certain what Lacanians refer to as Imaginary self-representations of the analyst to himself of what he is doing that makes his work analytic—namely, the presence of a certain diploma certifying a course of study, or having certain medical background, or membership in an Institute, or even the use of a couch—our only tool, the only gizmo we have as analysts. This distinction will be based not even on frequency of sessions (though that can have a significant impact on progress of work), or the presence of face-to-face interactions, or even the use of free association or examination of childhood or sexuality. This distinction will be based on the discursive relationship of the analyst to the analysand, specifically how the treatment—and most specifically the transference, as well as interpretation—is directed by the analyst.

We have already looked at one distinction based on the focus of attention of the practitioner. The analyst is waiting for unconscious formations, for those rare moments of access into the signifying material that constitutes the unconscious. Therapists may work on—to use the common term—any material: current struggles, the patient's sense of self or others, representations of a situation, statements of one sort or another about the analyst. This is all conscious material and, to a certain extent, however gripping it might be, its value in analysis is less than those peculiar formations I developed earlier.

Another way of coming to terms with the difference between psychoanalysis and psychotherapy is through examining the nature of the efficacy of the psychotherapies and whether that is in any way related to psychoanalysis. Here, I follow the path laid out by Jacques-Alain Miller in the article cited above. In speaking of this difference, Miller introduces a reading of the famous graph of desire from Lacan's essay "The subversion of the subject and the dialectic of desire in the Freudian unconscious" to offer a theorization of the difference (2006a). In this reading, it is the shifting of identifications and the generation of meaning that defines the efficacy of psychotherapy. In other words, the representations that the patient makes of himself and of the world—these things we speak of in terms of ego and object representations—or that we alternatively see as identifications—are what is at stake in psychotherapy. For example, the patient presents to a therapist because he feels he is depressed. He identifies himself as depressed and has an outlook on the world that the therapist might define as unrealistically unhopeful. In psychotherapy, the critical issue would thus be to change that patient's outlook on the world—shift his object representations—as well as to cause a shift in the patient's self-representation as being depressed, and through this process of rectification effect the psychotherapeutic cure.

This is generally done in therapy through the assumption of the position of mastery—as we saw above—subsequently enabling the therapist to rectify—to refigure—the ego and object representations of the patient. Assuming and taking on the position of the master imparted onto the therapist in the transference, the therapist uses that power to effect these changes in ego and object representations. Are there beneficial effects from this? No doubt there are. For the patient, some relief from a state of suffering can result from these shifts, this process of rectification. So-called unhealthy behaviors can be modified with such a technique.

But notice here that the stakes are no longer necessarily those of the patient's. The benefits described—those of the reduction of unhealthy behaviors and a return to a so-called higher level of function—are not necessarily those the patient thought, but are, for the most part, the point of view from which the therapist operates. Taking on the position of mastery, the therapist uses that power to advance his agenda, which is most often those socially laudable goals I cited above. But note, not all therapists work from this perspective. We have all in our work encountered therapists who find child abuse, multiple personalities, and satanic rituals in case after case and the significant debates on this and the whole nature of recovered memories speak to the power of the therapist to rectify patients' ego and object representations in a totally different way.

This process is, in fact, all described by Freud himself, who articulated the difference between psychoanalysis and psychotherapy as that between psychoanalysis and suggestive therapies. This difference is first spoken of by Freud in his 1904 essay simply titled "On psychotherapy." In it he contrasts psychoanalysis with the suggestive therapies, of which hypnosis was the model. I wish to quote Freud here at some length:

> There is, actually, the greatest possible antithesis between suggestive and analytic technique—the same antithesis which, in regard to the fine arts, the great Leonardo da Vinci summed up in the formulas: *per via di porre* and *per via di levare*. Painting, says Leonardo, works *per via di porre*, for it applies a substance—particles of colour—where there was nothing before, on the colourless canvas; sculpture, however, proceeds *per via di levare*, since it takes away from the block of stone all that hides the surface of the statue contained in it. In a similar way, the technique of suggestions aims at proceeding *per via di porre*; it is not concerned with the origin, strength and meaning of morbid symptoms, but instead, it superimposes something—a suggestion—in the expectation that it will be strong enough to restrain the pathogenic idea from coming to expression. Analytic therapy, on the other hand, does not seek to add or to introduce anything new, but to take away something,

to bring out something; and to this end concerns itself with the genesis of the morbid symptoms and the psychical context of the pathogenic idea which it seeks to remove. It is by use of this mode of investigation that analytic therapy has increased our knowledge so notably. I gave up the suggestive technique, and with it hypnosis, so early in my practice because I despaired of making suggestion powerful and enduring enough to effect permanent cures. In every severe case I saw the suggestions which had been applied crumble away again; after which the disease or some substitute for it was back again once more. (Freud, 1905a, pp. 260–261)

Thus, we see Freud's reluctance to endorse psychotherapy, or what he terms suggestive therapy, is not due to any lack of efficacy, but rather to the lack of sustained efficacy. It is not that psychotherapy does not have effects, rather that they are not sustained, and the reason for that is the failure of psychotherapy to encounter the unconscious. This encounter with the unconscious that defines psychoanalysis is, in fact, what we might call the analytic wager—it is what is at stake in psychoanalysis, namely, that through the encounter with the unconscious that defines the work of analysis, a change will result, a change that—because of some modification of the position of the analysand relative to the unconscious—will have some more lasting effects.

In contrast to Freud, however, it is not clear to me that we ought to speak of this change in terms of efficacy, for this encounter with the unconscious can have a range of results. In spite of the frequent exacerbations of symptoms, shifts in mood, and increases in anxiety that occur in the course of an analysis, we often see—at the end of analysis— precisely a modification of self and other representations and, often, a reduction in suffering—the suffering of the symptom. With analysis, however, these are not necessarily given results or goals, and, in fact, as soon as they are made goals, one loses the possibility of psychoanalysis, because the focus is directed away from the unconscious to such Imaginary representations. It is this that is the component of analysis we can only speak of as a wager, a bet, on what might happen from such an encounter.

Now—I wish to go back to where I started and speak, to end here, of this psychoanalytic wager on a social level. Those who entrusted themselves—in this country and elsewhere—with the future of psychoanalysis bet badly. They bet on Freudianism, and not psychoanalysis.

They bet that by securing their guild like status as analysts, with their Institutes and couches and hierarchies and so forth, they would secure a future for psychoanalysis. It was a bad bet. Psychoanalysis is a form of discourse—a form of talking and listening—something that existed before Freud wrote about it, and that clinicians enter into, from time to time, without intending to or even without being aware of it. I wish to promote this discourse, this form of social relations, for the intrinsic value of its particular configuration, for the value that it can have for those of us who respond—as clinicians—to the suffering of others. And anyone can join in this—it requires neither a medical degree, nor the guarantee of some institute, nor a certain level of experience—simply desire itself.

This desire, however, is quite fragile, and, in its clinical guise—as the desire of the analyst (with a forsaking of mastery, refusal of ego identifications, and even renunciation of therapeutic goals), it is a difficult position to maintain. Those of us involved in this clinical work have help, a certain formation or training, which allows us to bear that desire: our own analyses, the closely supervised work of our first analyses, long study—not just of psychoanalytic theory—but psychiatry, philosophy, literature, linguistics, art. If there is a purpose in the psychoanalytic institution, it is surely to promote such pursuits. Why all this study and effort to maintain a position best defined, perhaps, by the sacrifices one must make to speak from it? Sometimes I define it strictly negatively— to understand all the positions one must avoid as an analyst—but other times I think it can be best understood as the groundwork necessary to maintain awareness of the impossibility of the act of psychoanalysis. This is Freud's term, from "Analysis terminable and interminable"— impossible—under which he grouped psychoanalysis with government and education, "professions in which one can be sure beforehand of achieving unsatisfactory results" (Freud, 1937c, p. 248). Lacan's take on this, however, hits the mark even closer: the analyst must be a saint (1990). This is the ethical attitude necessary to strive for the impossible, and those renunciations, refusals, and even abjection noted above are the proper guides for us in approaching the unconscious.

CHAPTER EIGHTEEN

Neurasthenic psychoanalysis and the Name of the Father

In the eleventh number of the *Papers of the School One Action Committee*, Rivka Warshawsky raises the specter of a neurasthenic practice of psychoanalysis. She asks:

> How can we estimate the possibility that the practice of psycho-analysis itself may become infected with this great weariness, with this "life as a result of the race toward progress?" The question should not be confined to non-Lacanian practitioners, but to the danger of a neurasthenic practice of analysis infecting the Lacanian practice, too. It is a serious question. (Warshawsky, 2005)

I want to say something about this question, because this use of the term neurasthenia I see as evoking a certain kind of style or affect.

Lacan himself raised such an issue, in the "Function and field of speech and language," where he uses the word "gloomy" and speaks of "reticence," (and the linkage of these two concepts is the key to what I want to develop here) to evoke something akin to Warshawsky's question. I will quote Lacan here:

Freud rose, however, to a position of total mastery regarding the dialectic of the work and the tradition of its meaning.

Does that mean that if the place of the master remains empty, it is not so much due to his disappearance as to an increasing obliteration of the meaning of his work? To convince ourselves of this, isn't it enough for us to note what is happening in that place?

A technique is being transmitted there, one that is gloomy in style [d'un style maussade]—indeed, it is reticent in its opacity—and that any attempt to let in critical fresh air seems to upset it. It has, in truth, assumed the appearance of a formalism that is taken to such ceremonial lengths that one might well suspect that it bears the same similarity to obsessive neurosis as Freud found so convincingly in the practice, if not the genesis, of religious rites. (Lacan, 2006a, p. 203)

My first observation here is that this issue of weariness, of gloominess, is a description of a type of style, a stance, in the way in which both Warshawsky and Lacan are describing the approaches of psychoanalysts to their analysands and also presumably to their Schools and other institutions and even to psychoanalysis itself.

This stance, then, of the gloomy analysts is one of "reticence" in Lacan's formulation of 1953. Lacan links this to a problem in clinical approach and training as well, which he attributes to an excessive rigidity, a formalization of training and practice which obliterates the true meaning of Freud's work—a reliance on Imaginary conceptualizations and technique, in contrast to the true, Symbolic, meaning of Freud's work. We might say that for Lacan, in 1953, he uses this notion of a neurasthenic practice as failure for the practice to be secured by a Symbolic Father. Thus, here I would say we have a contrast between a type of fidelity to the Father—in a return to Freud—and a type of neurasthenic style, linked to what we might call Imaginary fixations.

We can read this quite differently, though, if we go back to the idea of this weariness, or gloominess, as a style or affect. I think it's even quite plausible to go further and designate it as a kind of personality—using this work in a very precise Lacanian sense: of personality as "the manner in which someone subsists, survives, keeps moving, in the face of the object *a*" [*la façon dont quelqu'un subsiste face à cet objet petit a*] (Lacan, 1978a). This changes things quite a bit—for now this neurasthenia represents nothing less than a type of reticence in facing desire, or jouissance itself—a type of response to the Real. Now, to reformulate neurasthenia in this way as a type of response to or defense against the Real makes some sense, evoking Miller's comments about neurasthenia in Commandatuba (2005). Rereading Freud's 1908 paper on "Civilized sexual morality and modern nervous illness," Miller observes Freud's response to neurasthenia—described by Freud's contemporaries as a kind of symptomal response itself to the exigencies of modern life, its frenetic pace. It was the first New Symptom, akin to forms of depression ubiquitous today. Miller notes that, of course, Freud turns away from this explanation and identifies its logic as a neurotic response to a loss of jouissance demanded in conformity to a certain organization of sexual relations in monogamy.

This is a different point from before—before, in psychoanalysis, a certain type of return to a Symbolic Father allowed one to avoid neurasthenia. Here, adherence to the Name of the Father is the very agent—in a sense—of neurasthenia itself. But, there are two different ways of using the notion of Father in play here. In the first case, Lacan's quote, the Symbolic meaning, or value, the truth, of Freud's work is obliterated in an imaginarization of Freud as the Father of psychoanalysis, a process of imaginarization of his work in a set of rigid rules regarding practice and training. In the second approach to neurasthenia, a type of highly prescribed relation to the Real—a certain knotting of the Real and the Symbolic, we might say—is linked to neurasthenia. But, perhaps they are not as different as they seem and speak to a similar "use" of the Father.

Let me add that I think there are institutional ramifications to this—which was the original intent of Rivka's question.

With regard to our colleagues in the IPA, certainly Lacan's comments on the formalization of psychoanalytic formation and training from the "Function and field" are no less true today than in the 1950s. In fact, we could certainly argue that under the pressure of Evaluation and State intervention into psychoanalytic practice, the IPA's path of collaboration is very much along the lines of the formalization that Lacan evokes, and that—furthermore—it is not very hard to detect gloominess about the future of psychoanalysis in the meetings of the IPA groups in the United States, at least, where many IPA analysts no longer have analytic cases.

When I think about the AMP, however, I do not find such gloominess—the very vibrancy and vitality of the response of our

French colleagues to some serious challenges and attacks is, in fact, if anything, the very opposite of gloom or weariness.

Regarding the clinical exigencies of today, the work of the AMP is equally vibrant. In its evolution and invention of the concept of Ordinary Psychosis, we see a group of psychoanalysts engaging a challenge to psychoanalysis in a vital way. Similarly, in the work under development on the theme of the new symptoms, we see a group of psychoanalysts committed to responding to the demands of today.

In fact, it is these two dimensions—the international engagement of the psychoanalysts of the AMP in response to the political challenges to psychoanalysis and the recent developments of Ordinary Psychosis and the work on the new symptoms in the arena of applied psychoanalysis—that were decisive in my desire to join the School and the AMP.

And here, I think, this second issue of neurasthenia as a type of response to the Real can be brought to bear in a decisive way. We might even formulate Ordinary Psychosis and the new symptoms as new forms of returns of the Real or defenses against the Real in psychic structure and in the formation of the clinical demands today. And, faced with this Real, the psychoanalysts of the AMP engaged it, responded to it. They did not "turn their backs to it," evoking Lacan's comment on psychosis.

The important thing about this engagement is the very invention required of psychoanalysts in the response to it, an invention born of the very social and psychic forms of the twenty-first century, and which we see in the varied, yet related, responses of analysts throughout the world to these challenges, which brings to mind Lacan's comments in Baltimore on the role of invention in varied domains (1970). The thing about this invention is that in it, psychoanalysts use Lacan and his work, use Freud and his work, but without being bound—as it were—to it. Would they adhere, to the letter, to Lacan's work on psychosis from the 1950s, they would not have arrived at the formulation of Ordinary Psychosis. If they were to imaginarize it as the consistent (in reference to R.S.I.) form of psychosis, they would not have derived the formulation of Ordinary Psychosis.

My sense is that many psychoanalysts of other orientations, in the face of the Real of the twenty-first century, a Real that is not the Real of Freud, realize—rightly—that psychoanalysis as formalized by certain readings of Freud will not work and are gloomy in their assessment of psychoanalysis today. This neurasthenia that they feel is in fact linked to this adherence to a certain formalization of their practice itself derived from a formal, Imaginary adherence to the Name of the Father as semblant, to a certain Freudianism.

For the Lacanians, however, we note that the formulations from the 1950s are not discarded, however, or even surpassed (as Rivka warns us not to believe), but used in a different way. It is this "use of the Name of the Father" that supports our work and is the hallmark of the Lacanian practice. With the invention we accomplish in its use, we will not see the neurasthenia that Rivka is rightly concerned about.

CHAPTER NINETEEN

Countertransference is the symptom of the analyst*

I wish to develop something now about Countertransference. I will present several different theses on Countertransference, but want to at the outset alert you to three different aspects of the Countertransference that I want to address throughout this paper. The first is the source of Countertransference—whether it results from the analysand or the analyst or some combination of the two. The second is the judgment we make of the Countertransference—is Countertransference, put most simply, bad—some unanalyzed dimension of the unconscious of the analyst, for example—or good, and somehow productive, a dimension of successful psychoanalytic treatment? Finally, I wish to ask— does the Countertransference exist? While this seemingly ontological question would seem primary and worthy of addressing at the outset— I wish to bracket this—and will proceed initially as if it is a given, but I will address this at the end.

Rather than discuss these issues directly through a theoretical discussion, I wish to go directly to casework, so that we can see how

---

*"Countertransference is the symptom of the analyst" was presented at the Workshop "(En)countering transference" sponsored by the Center for Psychoanalysis and Psychotherapy in Omaha, Nebraska, April 16, 2004.

these issues may work their way out in the treatment. I have chosen two cases—previously published cases, one of Owen Renik's and one of Thomas Ogden's. These are, of course, not psychoanalysts of the Lacanian orientation, though both are familiar to some degree with the work of Lacan. Both are members of the American Psychoanalytic Association and the IPA, and I think that they are two of the leading psychoanalysts of the San Francisco Psychoanalytic Institute. I chose these cases for a series of very particular reasons, for in both of these cases, it is a particular use of Countertransference that is advocated for, and I wish to examine in these cases the specific details of the case as presented and the claims made within the cases for the utility of the Countertransference in the direction of the treatment. Ogden's case is the case of Mrs. B., from his well known paper "The analytic third" (1994). It is a classic theoretical and technical paper in American Psychoanalysis, which has also drawn the attention of Jacques-Alain Miller, as we shall see later (Miller, 2004c).

I will look at the Renik case first. I have chosen this case also in part because of the somewhat seminal role that this case played in a shift in the theorization and use of the Countertransference in the San Francisco Psychoanalytic Institute, as described to me in conversation by Mitch Wilson.

In his paper, Renik presents the case of a young male whose treatment he described as stuck (1993). There was an initial period within the case where a first stage in the analysis of the analysand's severe obsessions and compulsions indicated that they were serving to protect the analysand from a series of violent and sadistic fantasies that were disturbing to him. However, once brought to light, Renik was experiencing what he termed as frustration, with the treatment becoming "bogged down." He did not feel he was making progress in elucidating the cause for the now less hidden anger in this seemingly timid man. He detected as well, within the transference, a combination of demandingness and a superficial compliance.

At a critical juncture within the treatment, Renik himself becomes increasingly impatient—particularly with the complaints from the patient seeking recognition (in this case for discontinuing use of hypnotics prescribed by another provider). In the midst of this Renik stated to his patient: "It's as if you feel like the only person who was ever weaned from the breast." Renik describes his emotions at the time as frustrated and impatient, as noted above, but adds also resentment (feeling sorry for himself and comparing his past to the analysand's, whose degree of distress he felt was disproportionate to his so-called real suffering by comparison). He comments further that the intervention was not kindly meant and was delivered without self-conscious self-analysis of his feelings, but rather was there to fulfill his own needs.

Renik goes on to note that the analysand was apparently affected by this intervention (by virtue of a brief pause). Renik then comments that the analysand did not respond to the hostility apparent within the interpretation, nor did Renik himself comment on it (out of a continued denial—he states—of his Countertransference). What happened was that the analysand responded to the "face value" of the intervention and associated to the content of it. This led to some associations on the part of the analysand to his own son's weaning several years before. Then (significantly, in spite of, Renik claims, both of their avoidance of Renik's hostility), the analysand offered some acknowledgment that others have been weaned from the breast and substituted "Gary" for his son's name in his statement. This slip—with some pressure on Renik's part—leads to the analysand commenting that "the only Gary I can think of is the younger brother my parents told me about that was stillborn when I was a year and a half old." This important fact had apparently (to the analysand's surprise) never been discussed in the analysis at all, and Renik felt that this was extremely relevant to their attempts to identify the origin of the analysand's sadistic fantasies. In any case, this represented a significant turning point in the analysis and led to the production of much valuable work—most notably additional early childhood memories of the analysand's mother, her depression, a subsequent separation from the mother because of this depression, and the replacement of the mother with a very generous and adoring aunt who idealized him.

Renik goes on to interpret the patient's expectations of him within the transference as allied to his attempt to recreate the relationship he had with the aunt and indicates that his deflating remark to the analysand derailed that transference (or, separated the position of the analyst from the Ideal, for example, as I detailed above in the chapters on *Seminar 20*), in that through it he came to re-experience his relationship to his rejecting mother within the treatment. He also goes on to comment on the valuable character of the Countertransferential aspect of that intervention he made for the progress of the case.

I want to offer a different interpretation of this particular moment in the analysis and the impact it had.

Before doing so, I want to take a look at the intervention itself from within another framework. For starters, I would certainly agree with Renik as to the importance of this intervention. One of the simplest standards we might use to evaluate our technical interventions (by this I mean any way in which we directly intervene in the treatment—scansion, interpretation, repetitions of words or phrases of the analysand, and so forth) relates to their effect on the generation of new material. The source for this theory is, of course, the Rat Man case. In the sixth session with the analysand, Freud delivers a fairly lengthy discourse to the Rat Man on the nature of love, a veritable pedagogical lesson, and seemingly very much discordant with the austere and restrained view of the analyst's intervention ascribed to the analyst. Commenting on his technique here, Freud notes that:

> It is never the aim of discussions like this to create conviction. They are only intended to bring the repressed complexes into consciousness, to set the conflict going in the field of conscious mental activity, and to facilitate the emergence of fresh material from the unconscious. A sense of conviction is only attained after the patient has himself worked over the reclaimed material, and so long as he is not fully convinced the material must be considered as unexhausted. (Freud, 1909d, p. 181)

I wish to argue that we might expand on Freud's thoughts on this as elucidating one dimension of the successful intervention of the analyst—those interventions are successful which lead to the production of new unconscious material (dreams, further slips, and so forth). In this case, not only did this particular intervention lead to the production of new material, but it dealt with the particular problem Renik was facing of the "rut" into which he felt regarding the case, in the sense that it led the analysis into a new direction. Thus, I would agree the intervention was quite successful.

But, why is this intervention successful? Renik will argue that it has something to do with the way in which his Countertransference is implicated in it. But, before examining his views on that, let me draw attention to another aspect of his commentary. He says that—and I wish to quote him here directly—"what happened was that the patient took my interpretation at face value, and began to associate to the content of it." I think this is most critical, for the very success of the interpretation derived from its productivity, and that productivity was itself clearly derived from the actual face value or content of the intervention. Without wanting to digress too far from the topic of the transference, I would simply note that Renik dismisses in a sense the truth impact of the intervention—we might say—in its significatory value, the way in which its signification—what he refers to as its "face value"—led to further significatory activity within the analysis. This observation on Renik's part attests to a point which he will not make here, namely that of the power of speech, the very words used within the treatment, to convey meaning and enjoyment and to propel the treatment, beyond any search for any so-called depth beneath the intervention. But, this is the subject of another discussion.

Back to the case: Renik attributes much of the importance of this intervention to the feelings that he had at the time of the intervention, his affects ("feeling sorry for myself," "resentment toward the patient," "grandiose self-pity," and so forth) and analyses in some detail his own feelings about the case and his analysand. Regarding these feelings and thoughts on Renik's part, I think that it is easy to agree that Renik is very self-aware, in this sense, and attuned to the various things operating intrapsychically. This, I would argue, is not without value. And here, I would argue, following Lacan's earliest sustained comments on the Countertransference (1988), that the goal of the analyst is not necessarily to be without feelings. In other words, in contrast to what I think we could only characterize as a kind of straw-man view of the psychoanalyst in which the analyst—following his own analysis—is without any feelings or passion, the analyst after an analysis should, if anything, be more sensitized and aware of his feelings.

Let us digress and examine Lacan's discussion. The comments of Lacan are made in his *Seminar 1* and are offered apropos of a case of Margaret Little's, published in a well-known paper on Countertransference (1951). In this paper, Little offers a clinical vignette:

> A patient whose mother had recently died was to give a wireless talk on a subject in which he knew his analyst was interested; he gave him the script to read beforehand, and the analyst had the opportunity of hearing the broadcast. The patient felt very unwilling to give it just then, in view of his mother's death, but could not alter the arrangement. The day after the broadcast he arrived for his analysis in a state of anxiety and confusion.

The analyst (who was a very experienced man) interpreted the patient's distress as being due to a fear lest he, the analyst, should be jealous of what had clearly been a success and be wanting to deprive him of it and of its results. The interpretation was accepted, the distress cleared up quite quickly, and the analysis went on.

Two years later (the analysis having ended in the meanwhile) the patient was at a party which he found he could not enjoy, and he realized that it was a week after the anniversary of his mother's death. Suddenly it came to him that what had troubled him at the time of his broadcast had been a very simple and obvious thing, sadness that his mother was not there to enjoy his success (or even to know about it), and guilt that he had enjoyed it while she was dead had spoilt it for him. Instead of being able to mourn for her (by canceling the broadcast) he had had to behave as if he denied her death, almost in a manic way. He recognized that the interpretation given, which could be substantially correct, had in fact been the correct one at the time for the analyst, who had actually been jealous of him, and that it was the analyst's unconscious guilt that had led to the giving of an inappropriate interpretation. Its acceptance had come about through the patient's unconscious recognition of its correctness for his analyst and his identification with him. Now he could accept it as true for himself in a totally different way, on another level—i.e. that of his jealousy of his father's success with his mother, and guilt about himself having a success which represented success with his mother, of which his father would be jealous and want to deprive him. The analyst's behavior in giving such an interpretation must be attributed to counter-transference. [...] what happened was that the analyst felt the patient's unconscious repressed jealousy as his own immediate experience, instead of as a past, remembered, one. The patient was immediately concerned with his mother's death, feeling the necessity to broadcast just then as an interference with his process of mourning, and the pleasure proper to it was transformed into a manic one, as if he denied his mother's death. Only later, after the interpretation, when his mourning had been transferred to the analyst and so become past, could he experience the jealousy situation as an immediate one, and then recognize (as something past and remembered) his analyst's counter-transference reaction [...].

Failures in timing such as this, or failures to recognize transference references, are failures of the ego function of recognizing time and distance. (Little, 1951, pp. 32–35)

In his commentary on this vignette, Lacan notes that he does not believe that the analyst was necessarily mistaken in his intervention, but states that it is not clear that Countertransference was at issue in this case. In fact, the very content of the interpretation may well have been accurate, according to Lacan. Lacan even goes so far as to say that:

If the only analyzing subject, the analyst, had even felt some jealousy, it is up to him to take it into account in an appropriate manner, to be guided by it as by an extra needle on the dial. No one has ever said that the analyst should never have feelings toward his patient. But he must know not only not to give in to them, to keep them in their place, but how to make adequate use of them in his technique.

In this particular instance, it is because the analyst thought he should look first in the *hic et nunc* for the reason for the patient's attitude that he found it in something which, without a shadow of a doubt, really existed in the intersubjective fields shared by the two characters. He was well placed to recognize it, because he felt some hostility, or at the very least irritation in connection with the patient's success. What is serious is to have believed himself authorized by a certain technique to make use of it straightaway and in a direct manner. (1988, p. 32)

Thus, in this sense—following what we might refer to as a first formulation of Lacan—what we might term the intersubjective Lacan—we can say that Countertransference exists, and it is up to the analyst to decide what to make of it. The analyst's responsibility in the treatment is to make the right use of it. Lacan will reformulate this, but let's stay with this for now.

So, going back to Renik, let us look at the case and in particular Renik's use of this. Renik notes that the patient somehow denied and failed to recognize this affective value, and he felt this is important, and he further subtly critiques himself for failing to act based on this affect that he (as analyst) was experiencing. Thus, in contrast to my thesis that the effect of the interpretation rested on its significatory value, and that the affect, while important in some sense, did not have impact on the treatment, Renik ascribes importance to the affect. Let us look further at this.

Regarding the affect which Renik ascribes to the intervention, it may well be that this Countertransference affect meant more to Renik than to the analysand. The analysand, it is certainly reasonable to suppose, may not even have noticed the affective charge to the intervention. Perhaps the analysand's pause at the intervention (to which Renik gives significance) had nothing to do with the affect, and more to do with the content (which Renik acknowledges was what led to the productivity). One piece of evidence is that the analysand himself ignored the affect. We can also hypothesize that had the affect on the part of the analyst been noticed by the analysand, perhaps any attempt to immediately interpret the affect would have disrupted the productive stream of associations which subsequently resulted from the intervention. Let me elaborate further on this point. Many analysts, especially with regard to a number of trends within the Kleinian school, would have quickly advocated an intervention on the part of the analyst to clarify the issue of what had transpired in the *hic et nunc* of the analytic session. Such a type of work is demonstrated in some of the numerous clinical vignettes provided by Betty Joseph in her work (1989; 1992). This type of approach—characteristic of certain of the neo-Kleinians—would have led—in this case—to a discussion on the part of Renik of how, perhaps, he had been "forced" through projective identification to having the very feelings which he was aware of, and how the analysand needed to become aware of the process by which he was dealing with them, via an analysis of how projective identification had "worked" in this case. By my view, this would only have destroyed the setting through which this very successful intervention on Renik's part succeeded, in other words, by destroying the possibility for productive association on the part of the analysand.

To take another approach to this, I would suggest an examination of what we might term the next stage in Lacan's work, in which the concept of desire comes to the forefront in his elaboration of transference and Countertransference. This would be the proposal Lacan advances in his seminar on the Transference (2015). Here, in the chapter "Critique of countertransference," Lacan argues, in the context of a long discussion of Money-Kyrle's well-known paper "Normal countertransference and some deviations," that, again, yes indeed, the analyst does have passions, wishes, whims, prejudices, and so forth, with regard to the analysand in treatment. The analyst has desires, as it were. But, the analyst also a stronger desire, a desire brought about by the change in his desire through the very process of analysis, which has been dubbed the desire of the analyst. And, further, it is the desire of the analyst, a desire focused on the treatment—the exigencies of the treatment—that maintain the treatment purified, as it were, from these other more pedestrian desires.

It is in this context that I would argue that approaches which focus the analyst's attention to his passions—his pedestrian or pathological (in the Kantian sense) desires—only detract from the analyst's ability to sustain the desire of the analyst, for the treatment itself. And here, an example of this kind of direction frequently given to analysts, can be identified in many non-Lacanian schools of psychoanalysis. As a characteristic example of this kind of practice, I will draw here from a classic paper of the British middle-school, Winnicott's "Hate in the countertransference" (1949). In this paper, we see Winnicott exhorting analysts to pay special attention to their hate, and points out the baleful effects of unrecognized hate. This type of recommendation is often given in practice associated with object relations, a drawing of attention, as it were, from the treatment to the analyst's own affects, which—in the case vignette which we are currently examining—might only distort the very progress of the case in a way analogous to the neo-Kleinian approach.

In this way, what I wish to introduce is the notion that Countertransference—if we're going to stay with that term, i.e., assume it exists in the way in which we have developed it up to now—is constantly in operation. In other words, the analyst has a continuous set of both conscious and unconscious mental processes in operation during the course of any session. In fact, I think that it's fair to say that many of these are in fact unconscious and that the ideal of the unconscious of the analyst as being analyzed away through the course of the analysis seems far-fetched, not only from the contemporary relational perspectives, but more so from the critical point that the unconscious is structural, a function of the organization of the mental apparatus (at least in neurosis). Thus, there are certainly a full range of emotions, thoughts, affects, memories, and so forth constantly in play in the analyst, and to direct attention to them in some prescribed way—as Winnicott would have us do—would only potentially divert us from our desire—and responsibility—as analyst. In fact, another way of conceiving Renik's success in his intervention was his very disregard for such advice as to the proper attention to and use of his Countertransferential affective experience and mobilization of them in the treatment.

I will take up another point of Renik's regarding this intervention. That relates to the importance of the affective "charge" given to his interpretation. Certainly, affective coloring by the analyst can certainly draw attention to an intervention—and may well have had some impact here, even when not intended—but other means exist through which this can be accomplished, such as the sparse content of interpretative material or the enigmatic character of the intervention, which can further bring attention to an intervention. But, here again, we would digress on the matter of the nature and forms of psychoanalytic interventions.

I would like, rather, to suggest in fact an alternative view as to the importance of Countertransference in this particular case. What if, in fact, the impact of Countertransference was more operative—more significant—in the development of the case *prior* to Renik's brilliant interpretation. In introducing the case, Renik comments on the beginning of the case leading to this moment as follows: "After two years or so, our analytic work together had gotten to the point at which we were able to understand that these activities [intrusive thoughts and obsessive rituals] served to prevent him from being aware of violent, sadistic fantasies that would come to his mind and disturb him very much" (1993, p. 145). In as much as this formulation was in some ways partial or inadequate, perhaps even mistaken, perhaps the focus on it as a formulation (a static representation of the case at the very point of stagnation), a misrecognized "successful" formulation, in opposition to the very treatment itself, represents the more powerful example of Countertransference in operation in the case.

In making this assertion, I wish to reclaim Lacan's well-known definition of Countertransference from the height of his intersubjective period, that of Countertransference as "sum total of the analyst's prejudices, passions, and troubles, or even of his inadequate information, at any given moment in the dialectical process" (Lacan, 2005, p. 183). Lacan offers this definition in the course of his examination of the Dora case, in which he attributes Freud's failure in the case to Freud's Countertransference, to Freud's failure to recognize Dora's love for Frau K as a function of his Countertransferential belief that Dora ought to have fallen for Herr K, instead of Frau K. Freud's failure—according to

Lacan, however, is two-fold—and relates to his failed construction of this aspect of the case, but also—even more significantly—to his failure to put this "Countertransferentially driven" construction into play in an appropriate intervention. In other words, Lacan notes that had Freud utilized this "wrong" material in a transference interpretation (relating Dora's relationship to Freud to that of Herr K), it would have kept the case moving by virtue of her response to it. Thus, Freud's mistake here is twofold: one, the wrong "understanding" of the case, caught up in the limitation of Freud's view of the case; and, more importantly, two, the failure to act decisively, even with that, in his interventions.

I wonder if Renik's account of the rut he was in with this case does not represent a similar (counter)transference in play—his own sense of being stuck, failure for the case to progress and so forth, much in the same way Lacan describes Freud in the case. I will quote here again from Lacan on the Dora case: "In other words, transference is nothing real in the subject if not the appearance, at a moment of stagnation in the analytic dialectic, of the permanent modes according to which she constitutes her objects" (Lacan, 2006a, pp. 183–184). Noting this, I think that we can say that perhaps "something" was going on in this treatment at this point of stagnation Renik alludes to, and that the ways in which Renik "felt" he was being affected by the treatment speak to something operative within the treatment. And, in this sense, perhaps what is "Countertransferential" was perhaps *not* the intensity of Renik's affect at the time, but his inhibition, we might say, with regard to acting, of making some intervention all the while he was feeling that sense of stagnation. It is in this sense that we might say—my first thesis: Countertransference is the inhibition of the analyst.

In fact, let me emphasize again that the very success of the intervention Renik finally made may have very little to do with the Countertransference. The success related to the content of the intervention as relayed to the analysand, and the fact of the strong affect associated with it may well be irrelevant to the progress of the analytic treatment (though perhaps of some relevance to Renik). In fact, his Countertransference may well be what delayed—through inhibition—the delivery of this effective intervention and what kept the critical material that this intervention brought to the treatment out of the treatment for so long. I do not believe it was integral to the generation of this intervention.

I wish to comment in brief on another, yet more well-known example, of so-called Countertransference, the case of Mrs. B. in Thomas Ogden's paper on "The analytic third," to demonstrate a similar logic in place (Ogden, 1994). In this case, Ogden was treating Mrs. B for various vague complaints with her life and describes the initial several years of treatment also as "vague," along with a sense of "surprise" on his part that she kept showing up. The sessions proceeded to fall apart with longer silences, to which Ogden responded with various attempts at interpretation of transference. He noted that around that time, he would sometimes forget her name, and—more notably—developed a series of somatic feelings of fatigue (which included as well thoughts he might have a brain tumor), a series of anxieties and sensations that occurred only during his sessions with Mrs. B. One day, reaching for a glass of water (a frequent move within a session, he states), Mrs. B turned around and stared at him, which had not happened before. He then felt the conviction that the somatic feelings and anxiety he was feeling were caused by Mrs. B. At the moment she turned, he immediately said to her that he thought "she had been afraid that something terrible was happening to me and that I might even be dying." She responded affirmatively, that she thought he was having a heart attack, and that she was afraid for him. This subsequently was a turning point in the analysis, brought on, Ogden believes, by the richness of the Counter-transferential experiences he was feeling. Examining Ogden's description of his work here, my second thesis is that Countertransference is the anxiety of the analyst.

In his recent analysis of this vignette, Jacques-Alain Miller makes a number of important points worth noting (Miller, 2004c). The first is that he accepts the fact that this intervention was truly generative of the impact that Ogden attests to (Much in the way that Renik's intervention truly was deft). However, he also observes that, in contrast to Ogden's claim that this type of work represents a dialectical practice, there is in fact nothing dialectical about this process. Ogden's argument is that through the analytic process and the intersubjective relationship between the analyst and the analysand, a third subjectivity is generated which is somehow a product of the two subjects and an intermediary between them, a process that he refers to as dialectical and that results in the generation of what he terms—following André Green—the "analytic third" (Green, 1997). However, as Miller has observed, the fact remains that the type of practice that Ogden is describing here is hardly dialectical at all, not generative of some new subjectivity, but rather one in which his failure as analyst to properly identify and interpret to the patient her position as an unwanted child (this is, after years of analysis) forces her—in a sense—to this regression in which she acts out within the treatment this very state—her very shutting down in the sessions—a state that Ogden himself grows to feel as a kind of shutting down himself, as if he is dying. This state that Miller identifies as one of fusion, a state of fused emotions in which the analyst's very symptoms are perceived as being caused by the analysand, hardly represents the creation of a new subjectivity, but rather a shared emotional state based on an Imaginary identification between the two subjects in the treatment (The much-valued projective identification—a central theoretical model of analysis in the IPA tradition—is certainly in a sense what is at play here, and this too demonstrates the limitation to this construct as a theoretical model operative only at the Imaginary level). In this treatment (or at least in this segment of the treatment as presented), we do not see the transference in play, in Ogden's use of the very important clinical material presented to him (Much as Renik may well have been missing critical transference issues in his own sense of stagnation in that case). I would argue that Ogden gives us plenty of details about the transference operative in this case, transference that we could define in the most basic Freudian—not Lacanian—sense as a repetition of certain infantile positions. The analysand presented herself as an unwanted child, which Ogden failed to note, only to end up in the situation in which he as analyst didn't want her as analysand by virtue of his being late for sessions, forgetting her name, and other parapraxical details. He failed to make use of this critical material (at least as presented). If one wants to retain this notion of an Analytic Third, we might hypothesize (more clinical material would be necessary) that it was actualized through the transference—a creation of Ogden as an object who did not want the analysand, the unwanted child. Again, Ogden seemed to miss this transference. Failing to interpret this Transference, this analysand ends up acting out the various regressive symptoms within the treatment itself, staging a performance for Ogden in which she shows him that she is unwanted (through her shutting down in the Treatment). This too demonstrates Lacan's theory on Acting Out, in that it is something staged for an Other to create an object and represents Transference without Analysis, or Transference missing an Interpretation (Lacan, 2014). We might even generalize beyond this case and conjecture that the importance of regression emphasized in some analytic orientations is a technical imperative to be theorized in this way. In this case, instead of making some proper use of the Transference in his interventions and moving the case forward, the treatment stagnated and he eventually ended up in this state of identification with the analysand through his (Ogden's) symptoms, which is the basis for my claim here—my third thesis—that the Countertransference is the symptom (the Freudian symptom, not the Lacanian) of the analyst. Ogden's failures within the treatment, his very Countertransferential blind spots (which he honestly recognizes and attributes to a series of unconscious fantasies about his position as analyst), present here as a series of symptoms. And finally, when he eventually was able to make use of those, and the case moved forward, rather than claim that this was the moving force of the case as an ideal representation of good practice, I think we must recognize this as a reasonable save of a treatment that was stagnating due to Ogden's Countertransference.

But, as we can see here, in discussing this case, and the Renik case, we end up falling back to the issue of Transference itself, rather than Countertransference. And, in fact, this becomes Lacan's final statement on Countertransference, first hinted at in the paper on the Dora case, then more fully articulated later in his extended discussion on Countertransference from *Seminar 8* cited above (his last lengthy discussion of Countertransference—which subsequently disappears as a critical concept in his work), and occasionally cited, through to the end of his work (see his brief comment on Michel Neyraut's book on Transference in *Seminar 21* [Lacan, 1974, Session of March 19, 1974]). This is his statement that the countertransference doesn't exist. There is only one transference operative in psychoanalysis, between the analysand and the analyst, a transference in which the analyst drops the position of the Ideal and comes to occupy the position of object *a*, the Real object as object-cause of the desire of the patient, as supported by the fundamental fantasy of the patient (as elaborated in Chapter Five). To the extent that the analyst can enable to the fantasy to manifest itself in the treatment, to properly recognize his placement as object *a*, and be presumed as someone who knows something about what to do with this in the subsequent management of the treatment, the Transference will be operative. Everything else to the analyst—inhibitions, symptoms, and anxieties with regard to the treatment—do not have a relationship to the treatment as such—and in this sense I think we can say: Countertransference does not exist in the treatment, but relates to the analyst as person, and not as analyst.

CHAPTER TWENTY

There is no situation in the United States

J ust after the turn of the century, a psychoanalyst colleague asked
me about "the evolution of the situation in the US." The reference
was political, to the politics of the psy field in the US, and most
specifically, in comparison to France, which had just seen at that moment
the appearance of a new work—*Le livre noir de la psychanalyse*. This book
is about, of course, psychoanalysis, an attack on psychoanalysis, and
had caused quite a stir in France, with debates and responses appearing
in the newspapers and the popular media and, of course, in the various
electronic communications of the psy world.

Now, this question about the "evolution of the situation in the US"
came as a shock to me, I was a bit stunned by it, especially with regard
to the word "situation." Something about this word situation struck
me, and the first thing that I could articulate from this was the fact that
"there is no situation in the United States." If we are to think of situation in the way in which it has developed and is played out in France,
for example, such a situation—which I understand in reference to psychoanalysis, or perhaps to the psy field in general—simply does not
exist in the United States. With regard to psychoanalysis at the start of
this twenty-first century, there is no public debate or media positioning
in the forms of books or essays or whatever in the United States that

221

is comparable to what is happening in France, and in other parts of Western Europe and, to an extent, South America. The most immediate conclusion drawn from that is often that Americans are somehow not interested in intellectual matters or psy matters, do not care about such things. I think that this is a mistake.

The reason for this is rather that in the United States, psychoanalysis— psychoanalysis as understood by Americans—is defunct, bankrupt, in decline. The matter of psychoanalysis in the United States is, to generalize here, settled—in fact, it was settled and is seen as a twentieth century abberation. It's on the way out. And, well, perhaps this is not a bad thing, if we recall that American psychoanalysis is the psychoanalysis of *Ego psychology*, which rejected not only Lacan, but, in its heyday, even the work coming out of England. And this is not just historical: the prejudice against the Lacanians is alive and well in the American psychoanalytic establishment. Further, as I noted in Chapter Seventeen, it is the American psychoanalysts who insisted that an analyst must be—first and foremost—a physician, a belief that they held onto as vigorously as possible, until after a prolonged legal battle, the American establishment was forced by the courts to accept as analytic candidates those who were not physicians. These two fundamental facts—one related to beliefs and practices, one related to institutional issues—were the defining characteristics of American psychoanalysis, in contrast to what developed in the rest of the world.

In the last quarter century, the fall of American psychoanalysis has been marked by the very same distinguishing characteristics. For example, we have the very unique licensure situation in the United States, a consequence of this. In many states, the very groups previously marginalized by the American establishment have turned to the States (each individually responsible for licensure) to establish new licensure laws for psychoanalysis. Thus, somewhat unlike the situation in some European settings, the very intrusion of the State into psychoanalysis was in fact a request of some psychoanalytic groups for such involvement, in response to their previous marginalization by the establishment, which itself has been blindsided by many of these political developments, such as in New York State.

I think we can also examine some of the theoretical developments in American psychoanalysis in the same light, such as, for example, the turn to neuroscience. Now, there may well be some level in which relations between developments in biology—such as neuroscience, or evolutionary theory, or genetics—and psychoanalysis could be explored, or developed, or investigated. What has impressed me, however, about this turn, is the way in which it is perceived, understood, and subjectified by psychoanalytic colleagues—as the very condition for the possibility of "proof" for psychoanalysis. It is as if work in this field will somehow prove the theories of psychoanalysis and its efficacy. Having lost faith themselves in their very work, American psychoanalysts look elsewhere for external support to prop it up. The great irony in all of this is that I have yet to see any real demonstration of what psychoanalysis "gets" from neuroscience—how it has led to any development in theoretical constructs (most of what happens is merely a re-writing of theory) or especially, any change in practice. That is not to say that this has not benefited science, however, as it does strike me that important psychoanalytic constructs have invigorated some research programs.

The rise of cognitive therapies (to be developed in the next chapter), including the oddly linked cognitive-behavioral therapy (behavioral therapy not having any necessary relation to cognitive therapy), is another very consequence of this decline. Figures such as Aaron Beck and Albert Ellis, the very founding figures of the CBT movement, came out of American psychoanalysis. Their beliefs and practices were a response to their sense of the failure of American psychoanalysis in their clinical work.

Thus, we see two responses to the failure of psychoanalysis by American psychoanalysts, one a turn to neuroscience (or, developmental psychology, or statistical outcome studies, or other fields) to prop up a discipline that is felt as lacking. The other, the path of Beck and Ellis, is a turn away from psychoanalysis, experienced as deficient in their clinical work.

So, psychoanalysis has declined to the point of the non-situation of psychoanalysis in the United States, and we are faced with the deleterious consequences of such—in the form of licensure debates, psychoanalysis' offspring (CBT, rising like the Phoenix from the ashes of American psychoanalysis), and the very lack of a public debate on psychoanalytic matters.

Well, the lack of public debate does not necessarily mean that the public is happy about what is going on in the psy field. Most recently, we have seen a series of public outrages in the psy field—serious examination of the risks of psychiatric medications when prescribed to children; concerns about suicide and antidepressants; and, exposure of the financial ties linking research scientists to the pharmaceutical industry and the consequently biased quality of research. There is a recognition of the limitations of psychopharmacology as a cure for all ills. There are the periodic debates on diagnosis that we see with new editions of the *DSM*. We also see the popularity of certain pop-therapists—clinicians who serve in the media on television, on the radio, and in the newspapers. While their approach is, more often than not, a combination of simple advice and various exhortations to shore up crumbling family and authority structures, their popularity is an indicator, I believe, of a great dissatisfaction with what is available from the so-called professionals.

The lack of a great space of public debate, however, is not an indicator of a lack of debate. In fact, it is only the decline of psychoanalysis in its American form (which I hesitate to even call psychoanalysis—Freudianism is a more appropriate term here) that gives us an opportunity. This is the opportunity we have in our clinical work with those who come to us—one by one; in our conversations with colleagues and peers; in our positions in hospitals, clinics, and universities; and, in the development of study groups and cartels and seminars. This is the opportunity we have to redefine what Americans will think of when they think of psychoanalysis and what people will experience in their encounters with psychoanalysts. And this debate may not occur on the public stage, there will be no situation in the United States (at least not for now—though we will strive to develop this and we will join in solidarity with our colleagues throughout the world). But this debate will occur as we go about our work. And the success of our work on that scale will determine the future of psychoanalysis in the United States in the twenty-first century.

PART VIII

REMARKS ON THE
MENTAL HEALTH FIELD

CHAPTER TWENTY-ONE

The American plague*

L et us see what we can learn from rats. They play a curiously
   prominent role in the origins of both psychoanalysis and behavioral psychology. With psychoanalysis, I am referring, of course,
to the case of Ernst Lanzer, the Rat Man. With regard to behaviorism,
I refer not to the experimental rats, but to another case, a case from the
same decade as the Ratman and which played a more seminal role as a
case study in the development of behaviorism than the Rat Man did in
psychoanalysis. This is the case of Albert, reported in 1920. The case is
not one of a treatment, but rather an experiment. Experimenters placed
a rat near this nine-month old boy, and he showed no fear. However, he
was afraid of a hammer struck near his head on a steel bar, which caused
a reaction of fear and violent panic. The experimenters then induced a
fear of rats in Albert by banging the steel bar whenever he was placed
near a rat, which they claimed demonstrated the role of *conditioning* as
the cause of emotion. Note that the experimenters further hypothesized

---

*"The American plague" was presented May 22, 2005, at the London Psy Forum of the
Congress of the New Lacanian School of the World Association of Psychoanalysis, in
London, United Kingdom.

that the boy could be deconditioned as well (for example, they stated, by showing him the rat and stimulating his erogenous zones), but did not do that, creating in him an animal phobia they did not treat.

The experimenters here were John B. Watson and one of his students. Now, much attention has regarding behaviorism has been given to B. F. Skinner, who rightly deserves it. In his ceaseless promotion and universalist expansion of the behaviorist paradigm to all domains of psychology as well as sociology, politics, education, and clinical practice, Skinner was the greatest advocate on behalf of behaviorism. Well, before Skinner, we have Watson, whose *Psychology as the Behaviorist Views It* is certainly the foundational text of the behaviorist movement. Well, comparing Freud and Watson here, we can see a different ethical impulse in place—Freud directing his attention to an elaboration of the truth of the Rat Man's symptom and with some goal in mind of an alleviation of suffering, and Watson seeking merely to master knowledge and demonstrate something, with what we can only call remarkable cruelty in his treatment of Albert. We have Ernst's obsessions alleviated by Freud, and Albert's phobias induced by Watson. And it is here that we also see one of the great ironies of the psy debate today as it is typically construed, Freud's psychoanalysis a veritable empirical practice (directed in so many ways to the particularity of the symptom of the Rat Man), while it is Watson's behaviorism that is in fact the speculative practice.

But, with regard to the clinic and the practice of therapy, Watson had modest impact and Skinner's impact was mostly felt in the practice of *behavioral modification* in educational or institutional settings. It is in fact Joseph Wolpe who brought behaviorism into the clinic. Wolpe developed the practice now known as *systematic desensitization*, first constructed with regard to phobias, in which a patient is taught how to alleviate anxiety through deep-muscle relaxation and subsequently to apply that anxiolytic state to imagined thoughts closer and closer to the feared object. The real genius of Wolpe was to generalize this model, to reconfigure the vast array of human suffering into phobias and in doing so generalize this practice to a variety of forms of human suffering. This—along with Skinner's behavioral modification—is the basis for much of behaviorist practice in the United States today.

The interesting thing is that many in American academic psychology will in fact claim that behaviorism is dead, and that academic psychology has rejected the fundamental behaviorist premise that all behavior

THE AMERICAN PLAGUE   229

is a function of learning, claiming that they are beyond that (and, thus, beyond association with the more unsavory aspects of Watson—such as his racially motivated beatings—and Skinner—the baby boxes among other things). Psychology proclaims that cognitive and perceptual structuration of reality play a more significant role than the behaviorists recognize, and that there are genetically programmed behaviors as well. I do not think we ought to be deceived, however, by this stated rejection of behaviorism. I think that this is a case where so much of the behaviorist tradition has become so generally accepted (for example, the fundamental notion of reflex) that it has become part of the theoretical background and is no longer recognized as behaviorist as such, and it is here that I believe we can look at theories such as *social learning theory* or other developments in social psychology as not fundamentally new theories as such but mere modifications of behaviorism. Take the latter and the work of someone like Robert Cialdini, whose analyses of mating rituals, advertising, business practice and an expansive array of social phenomena demonstrate through the general principle of *compliance management* nothing more or less than what Watson did with poor Albert.

But then, there is cognitive psychotherapy, certainly at first glance a truly different theory and practice. Indeed, it is truly cognitive therapy that dominates CBT as practiced in the US. Unlike behaviorism, which developed out of academic psychology, cognitive psychotherapy—which came along much later, in the 1960s—developed outside of the academy, and not in response to academic psychology, but to American practices in psychoanalysis. Both Aaron Beck and Albert Ellis were psychoanalysts and spoke of their frustration with the then existing practices in American psychoanalysis as motivation for the development of practices that they saw as speedier, thus more efficient, and perhaps more effective as well, indeed a reaction to the very failure of American ego psychology practices in psychoanalysis (as articulated in Chapters Two and Seventeen). Certainly both of these practices at least appear on the surface as somewhat closer to psychoanalysis with, say, the critical notion of *automatic thoughts* put forth as a kind of substitute for the unconscious, a compatibility made much of today in those researchers who claim to have identified the *common factors* in all psychotherapeutics or those who promote an integration of cognitive therapy into psychoanalysis now seen at times in the American Psychoanalytic Association.

Beck's work derived from his confrontation in his clinical practice with patients identified as depressed and the contradictions he felt between how he had been trained to work with these patients psychoanalytically and his own clinical experience. He replaced an emphasis of his earlier practice on the patient's wishes he saw implicated in the suffering with a view of depression as a series of *cognitive distortions* that need to be replaced with different cognitive structures, ones which would subsequently alleviate the suffering. Now, this treatment has also been generalized for many different psychiatric diagnoses.

One critical question, however, relates to this notion of CBT, of cognitive-behavioral therapy, namely—how have cognitive psychotherapy and behavioral psychotherapy, with apparently radically different beliefs and practices, ended up being lumped together? Certainly, my sense is that Beck and his daughter Judith Beck look at their treatment as cognitive therapy only, and the radical behaviorist paradigm does not intersect with the cognitive one. Many practitioners do not necessarily see them together, though of course in the US today, many therapists describe their practice as *eclectic* in orientation, which can mean anything from a rigorous selection of different techniques for different patients to lack of focus within the treatment for any patient. But, regardless, there they are—cognitive therapy and behavioral therapy—linked, as if this is a natural alliance.

In some ways I think this is quite true. One dimension of this is the issue of control—the management of cognitive beliefs and of behaviors. This is the Taylorist dimension of contemporary psychotherapy practices—an extension of the ideology of management and control into the psyche itself (a true characteristic of postmodernism, according to Fred Jameson)—not unrelated to Lacan's musings on the role of psychology in the service of the master, nor I would venture to Watson's choice of career path in advertising after he was kicked out of the academy.

Now, we can extend this notion a bit further and note that within the practice of CBT itself—in any of its guises—we see a powerful and veritable pseudo-rectification in play. But, unlike rectification in psychoanalysis (see Chapter Six above) where the symptom in all its singularity is brought on the stage, CBT promotes a practice in which a symptom is named as a general symptom—depression, phobia, and so forth— a general nomination—in contrast to the oracular process of rectification in psychoanalysis with the indeterminateness that subjectifies the analysand. This general nomination concretizes the suffering in a name brought forward by the clinician as master, or the name-dispensing Father. But, further, unlike psychoanalysis in which the subject ultimately will handle the symptom in one way or another, the whole point of this nomination in CBT is to create something to eliminate in the treatment, a disposable symptom (so American as well!).

On his way to Clark University, Freud famously described his only trip to the United States as bringing the plague to America. Freud, however, miscalculated. Americans did not accept psychoanalysis as psychoanalysis, but as Freudianism, a practice modeled after Freud's ego, or Freud's desire, as Lacan argues in *Seminar 17*. Describing himself to the American psychiatrist Abram Kardiner, Freud once said that he was a bad analyst: he was impatient, too interested in playing the Father, and more interested in theory than practice. It is an interesting exercise to view the history of American psychoanalysis in similar terms, and it has always seemed to me that those traits of Freud's which form the basis for Freudianism in all its forms from ego-psychology to neuro-psychoanalysis to relational psychoanalysis resonated more strongly in the United States than psychoanalysis itself. America proved itself quite resistant to this plague Freud imagined, but its adoption of Freudianism truly plagued the history of psychoanalysis in the United States, leading to its internally programmed self-destruction and granting space in the psy field now for the truly American plague—CBT—to grow and prosper and now spread, we see, to Europe and throughout the world. And, as students of biology know, it is the rats that are the vectors, the carriers, of the plague.

CHAPTER TWENTY-TWO

A comment on the segregation in the clinic today

It is certainly commonplace these days to observe that we are seeing patients with unusual and different symptoms, or that some kinds of symptoms or diagnoses previously thought rare are no longer quite so uncommon. These observations are certainly made by some clinicians of a sufficient age to have accumulated the perspectives of decades of practice, but are also reflected in clinical literature in various places. With regard to new symptoms, we can easily enumerate a list of these—self-mutilation and other self-injurious behavior; anorexia and bulimia; and, dissociative symptoms of various types, from multiple personalities to various symptoms associated with derealization and depersonalization. Now, certainly, case reports of these exist in the past, but in many ways these previously unusual symptoms and diagnoses are now a significant part of many clinical settings, especially in institutions. And also, in addition to this, we have the veritable new "epidemics" of everything from drug use and additions, to so-called post-traumatic stress disorder, to bipolar disorder.

While some of these symptoms and diagnoses have worked their way in the contemporary diagnostic system used by many in the psy field today—the *DSM* (whose growth is a veritable reflection of this historical change and growth of symptoms—I will return to this)—many of these symptoms and diagnoses stand out from our classical diagnoses used in the psy field. Our traditional diagnostic systems evolved, of course, from the clinical practice of the psychiatric tradition of Western Europe and the United States, over the last two hundred years. Whether based on careful examination of the natural history of various types of presentations understood in terms of presentation, such as Kraepelin; or, as diagnoses whose specificity related to etiological theories regarding the clinical presentations that they represented, such as Morel and degeneration theory; it is easy enough to note a certain prudence in terms of the numbers of diagnoses in most of these systems. The modern version of traditional clinical psychiatric diagnosis in biological psychiatry is certainly the famous text *Psychiatric Diagnosis* of Goodwin and Guze, which presents a diagnostic system that includes a modest number of diagnoses.

In the development of psychoanalysis, Freud adopted several of these psychiatric diagnoses, reformulating them in terms of psychic structure, but also keeping the numbers relatively limited—hysteria, obsessional neurosis, phobia, paranoia, traumatic neurosis, anxiety nervosa. With Freud and psychoanalysis, the key is no longer simply an enumeration of symptoms and their evolution over time. While Freud adopted the classical psychiatric diagnostic terms, he attempted to articulate a logic about each one of the diagnostic structures. The logic defined the structure as a form of mental organization, which exists regardless of the symptoms or forms of suffering that an individual presented with. This approach to diagnosis—while dropped by Kleinians and other post-Freudians—was preserved by Lacan, whose major effort we could describe as an effort to better formalize the diagnoses, as based on a notion of psychic structure—a relationship of the subject (e.g., the person) to the Other (language, the body, the social body) and the object (the partial drive object, or the object causing desire); or, alternatively as a formalization of the ways in which certain fundamental structures link together the Symbolic (roughly, language), the Imaginary (ego and object representations), and the Real (the ineffable, drive, libido).

Thus, we see two traditions having evolved, one that of classical psychiatry—with a certain identification of a small group of syndromes (statistically commonly linked symptoms), whether or not linked to certain etiological theories about the psychiatric diagnoses—and that of psychoanalysis, in which a certain set of psychic structures, or forms of mental organization, are elaborated, which can articulate in any number of ways with any individual symptoms.

Now, I would argue that we have seen two periods of significant change in our clinical diagnostics in the last fifty years.

We can look at the first shift in psychodiagnostics as a consequence of the development of cognitive-behavioral therapy. The contribution of CBT to the clinic is profound in its simplicity (see the previous chapter for a summation of this history). Let's look at the work of Joseph Wolpe as a model here. With Wolpe, there is only one diagnosis—phobia. No matter what the specific problems are of any individual patient, the problem can be reconstructed and reformulated as a phobia. For example, a patient may have difficulty speaking in public—he has agoraphobia. A patient may have difficulty with a relationship with his spouse or sexual intimacy—he has a phobia of intimacy. A patient may describe depressive symptoms—he has a fear of happiness. In all these cases, we see, if not a collapse of the previous diagnoses, then at least the dismantling of the former diagnostic systems in terms of their efficacy in the clinic. With regard to the clinic, the former diagnoses fall to the side of the rewriting of the entire clinic into the clinic of phobia.

We note as well here a collapse of the levels of symptom and diagnosis as well, into one clinical category. In the psychoanalytic approach, the diagnosis and the symptomal (or, phenomenological) presentation remain on two different levels (and are to be distinguished from yet a third, that of the psychoanalytic symptom particular to each subject). With the diagnostic revolution of CBT, we see not only a universal diagnosis, but a collapse of the veritable levels of symptom and diagnosis itself.

I would identify the second major shift in diagnostics as the one proper to what we now refer to as postmodernity. This is the shift to the segregated clinic of addictions and is reflective of the most current developments in diagnosis we see in the general psy world today (including psychiatry and some forms of psychoanalysis, but excluding the Lacanian orientation). In this second shift in diagnostics, diagnosis is reformulated as addition. A person's diagnosis is that which he "gets off" from—be it drugs or alcohol, gambling, love or sex, self-mutilation, or even work (i.e., the workaholic). Interestingly, while the diagnostic clinic of CBT required an effort of the clinician to name the diagnosis (some logical gymnastics were required in some cases to identify the phobia in certain situations), in our postmodern clinic of addictions, the "naming" of the diagnosis is often made by the patient himself, in the willing adoption of a label with which he identifies himself. Treatment then becomes a matter of segregation. The alcoholics and the gamblers and the workaholics are separated from one another and then sent to, either, specialists who claim a unique knowledge of the group in question, or to self-help groups, who claim the knowledge is unique and specific to their group. In all cases, the treatment often hinges on the subject acceding to the diagnosis in question.

The great irony of this segregation is that, while people are subsequently separated into these various groups, the treatment for all of the conditions is relatively the same (some mix of cognitive therapy and twelve-step approaches and SSRI medications). Thus, while the patients are separated into these different groups, the separations have often little treatment impact as the treatments are fairly similar to one another.

A more subversive impact relates to the effects of this segregation on the clinicians themselves. This segregation of patients leads to a resultant segregation of clinicians, who are then called to task for their own segregated specialization. In some cases, this comes in the form of demands from hospitals or insurance companies for "evidence" of specialized training or practice experience to treat a particular group. Even more alarming is the development of attitudes among clinicians of their inability and lack of experience or knowledge that they feel disables them from dealing with patients with any of these new symptoms. These observations hold mostly for nonpsychotic disorders, as, certainly, in psychiatry, the issue of serious mental illness, or chronic psychotic conditions, is configured differently—some residue of the classical Freudian distinction between neurosis and psychosis is preserved.

I think that we can look at this effect on clinicians from several different perspectives. The usual one in Schools of Medicine is that this is the shift from the position of paternalism to that of an evidence-based (and also, often linked, consumer driven) practice. In other words, the physician clinician is less the master giving names to things and suggestions about what to do about them, but rather merely offering recommendations based on the evidence and doing his or her best to ensure compliance management. The straw-man here in this argument is the role of the physician as master. What is often missed in this development is the fact that the clinician becomes then what we might refer to as an apparatchik or a bureaucratic agent of the Evidence (what, in Lacanian terms, we would configure as a shift from the discourse of the master to the discourse of the University—no longer is the word of the master the dominant agent in discourse, but rather the role of knowledge itself). These bureaucratic clinicians, however, can be just as malevolent in their relations as the old "master," but all the while skirting the responsibility for their actions ("well, I'm just letting you know the current practices of today").

And, in fact, that is indeed the most important dimension of this shift we see in the typical configurations in the psy field today, a veritable absence of subjectivity on the part of the clinician in this new position of the clinician-bureaucrat. But, in contrast to this usual dichotomy of the patriarch and the bureaucrat, we also have the position of the clinician within the discourse of the analyst, where the clinician takes on the role of the *object a* for the patient, allowing an articulation of the object cause of desire specific for each individual patient within the treatment, an articulation of the specificity of the subject for each treatment that is determined within the logic of the treatment itself, and not driven by external standards. This is the essence of the psychoanalytic approach, most often left out in such discussions about the role or position of the clinician.

I want to close out these observations on diagnosis in our clinic today with some reflections on what this has to say about larger issues of our society, about the particular structure of society and culture in this era of postmodernity. I think that this rise of addictions as the model of diagnosis is in fact pathognomonic of the very rise of *object a* as the central point for identification for subjects today, as developed in the chapters above on addictions. People identify themselves on the basis of how they enjoy themselves, on the basis of what objects induce a state of desire in them. Now, certainly much as been made of this in contemporary accounts of the role of our contemporary media in the formation of individuals today, in the production of ready-made objects of desire in the movies, music, the internet and other forms of our contemporary socio-cultural formation.

But, to shift our perspective on this a bit, we can also see an expansion of psychosis today—perhaps not the full-blown psychoses of schizophrenia, but more subtle manifestations of psychosis—misrecognized in the *DSM*, which relies on overt symptomatology. These can present in very varied phenomenological forms in the psychiatric clinic, from the so-called micropsychotic breaks of some patients with Borderline Personality Disorder, to the "extended spectrum" of Bipolar Disorder, to the language troubles and difficulties with interpersonal relationships seen in some cases of addictions and even Attention-Deficit Hyperactivity Disorder, and so on. In any case, the sheer phenomenological variety captured in the *DSM* covers over the key distinction between psychosis and non-psychosis, which has important consequences for treatment positioning of the clinician. I have found the concept of Ordinary Psychosis elaborated in the work of the World Association of Psychoanalysis singularly helpful at deploying a structural approach with which to grapple with these diverse presentations and in the orientation of the treatment. In fact, looking back to 1938 in *Les complexes familiaux dans la formation de l'individu*, we see Lacan in fact predicting that with the decline of the role of the Father in society, we will see an increase in psychosis.

This very general observation has been subsequently developed by Jacques-Alain Miller and Éric Laurent (in the seminar "The Other who doesn't exist and his ethical committees") and, more recently, in a dramatic summary statement by Miller delivered in Brazil in 2004 as "A fantasy." The key notion of these positions is that with postmodernity, we have witnessed a significant change in the basic identification in psychic and social structure. Previously, psychic structure was organized around identifications with *Ego ideals*—representations of the Father, Country, God, and so forth—and these Ego ideals also serves the role as the driving agent in society, organized within the discourse of the master, with the word of the master in the position of agency. With postmodernity, the key point of identification in psychic structures is the varied objects *a*—as object causes of desire—as we have noted above in our observations on the clinic, and society itself (and our observations on the psy field of today also bear witness to this) also is structured around object *a*, which takes the place of the agent in the organization of society, in the very segregation we see in the clinic today.

CHAPTER TWENTY-THREE

Realist, modern, and postmodern diagnosis in the psychiatric field*

I think that there are two questions at stake here on the relationship of diagnosis and science in the field of psychiatry. The first is—Do we have a scientific diagnostic system now? The second is—Is a scientific diagnostic system someday possible in the psychiatric field?

With regard to the first question, I think that it is quite clear—we do not have a scientific diagnostic system, one grounded in science. I think that the *DSM* is dressed up to look like science, with criteria and numbers and so forth, but this is pseudo-scientific. This is, of course, not only my opinion, but the conclusion drawn by the National Institute of Mental Health, which has developed a comprehensive research program to construct a scientific basis for psychiatric diagnosis, the so-called RDOC project, one they hope to be based on objective measures in the body, the so-called biomarkers. Now, this does not mean that there is no science at all in the psychiatric use of diagnosis. I think that a condition such as Alzheimer's disease is one in which we have

---

*"Realist, modern, and postmodern diagnosis in the psy field" was presented at the Creighton University Department of Psychiatry Grand Rounds, Roundtable Series on Psychiatric Diagnosis, on February 15, 2006.

a diagnosis with a direct relationship to science. And, further, there are other conditions where a relationship exists between the diagnosis and science, but the relationship is not nearly so well defined. Take the case of bipolar disorder, in which there is convincing evidence of a genetic dimension to its presentation. The exact nature of this connection, however, has not been elucidated.

In Alzheimer's, we have the neurofibrillary tangles and amyloid plaques—we can see them—and directly relate their presence in the body to a pathological syndrome. In this case, I would argue that we have science, because we have touched something of the body directly. We might simply say that there is a Thing there in the body—these tangles and plaques—and that they function as a cause of or marker of the syndrome of dementia as we see in Alzheimer's. This, I would argue, is the huge exception in the psychiatric field. And, further, as has been pointed out earlier, when we tend to find these Things in the body—as in Epilepsy and Syphilis—the psy syndrome associated with it tends to be taken out of the psy field into General Medicine or Infectious Disease or Neurology and so forth.

In the case of so-called bipolar disease, however, we do not have the Thing in the body. There's nothing that anyone can point to now—like in Alzheimer's—as the Thing, the cause. We understand from the complicated genetics studies that there are relationships, but that's it. There is the possibility of a science with regard to diagnosis here.

Nonetheless, psychiatrists and psychologists and others in the psychiatric field practice as if there is a science of diagnostics—this pseudoscience evoked earlier. I think that there are some dangers here. The first: in putting this forward as science, we have clinicians degrading science, cheapening science in an elevation of their practice to the status of science. This is a discredit to science and damages the reputation of those making the claims.

There is a second danger, which is that the supposedly scientific diagnoses are then linked to a supposed scientific theory of disease, creating a whole set of scientific explanations for human suffering that may not have scientific validity, but which are promulgated as such, along with a set of scientifically validated recommendations for treatment. For example, a patient presents with suffering and is given the diagnosis of depression, informed that the reason for this is some dysfunction in his serotonin system which can be corrected with this

SSRI type medication. This all sounds very scientific, like going to a doctor, having one's blood sugar checked, and being prescribed insulin. The problem is that the diagnosis is not scientific, the supposedly scientific explanation that accompanies it is merely a theory, a guess (and we have seen the biological theories of depression change many times over the last several decades), and that such a scientific guess has a set of explicit links with certain treatments, i.e., meds targeted for that condition. This whole pseudo-scientific explanatory system—used ubiquitously in psychiatric practice today—should be recognized for what it is—neuro-mythology (to adopt a term of Bill Burke's): a neuro-mythology used to support a practice as scientific while truly it is not, used to support certain diagnostic and therapeutic treatment options, and to attack, at times viciously, other treatment options. Now, it is true that we do have these outcome studies to direct psychopharmacological treatment (but, see the next chapter for an explication of the limitations of these), but in clinical practice these sets of empirical observations about response to drug treatment are extrapolated well beyond the scope of the studies themselves, and are quite rapidly linked by most practitioners to etiological theories without justification. Further, it is clear that, in the case of depression at least, the majority of the treatment benefit cannot be attributed to the specific medication prescribed, but only to the placebo effect of the experience of treatment itself.

So, thus, in response to the first question, we have a first thesis—With a few isolated exceptions, we do not have a scientific diagnostic system.

Let me briefly address this second question—will we have a scientific diagnostic system someday? I don't know—and nobody knows. We will have to wait and see what happens, as with the RDOC project of the National Institute of Mental Health. I think we ought not to act as if it's around the corner, though, for that certainly is not the case. In any event, I am skeptical that we will ever have one. And this is for a simple reason, namely that I think the brain is complex enough that it will elude our ability to represent the psychic apparatus and the ways of suffering—whether behaviors, mood, affect, thoughts, whatever—in any simple way. But, here we head into speculation, and a speculation that does not help us address the clinical exigencies of our practice today.

So, my second thesis—We do not know if we will ever have a scientific system of diagnosis.

Well, beyond the recognition that our current system is pseudo-scientific at best and downright misleading at worst, how do we make sense of diagnosis in the psychiatric field?

I think that one way of approaching this issue is by looking at diagnoses and diagnostic systems as systems of representations, systems of organization of psychopathology or psychic structure. We use these representational systems in the psychiatric world for a very specific reason—to guide us in our treatment. A diagnosis is useful in our encounter with the suffering patient in as much as it provides such a guide. All the other uses—administrative, legal, research and so forth—are secondary in as much as they support this primary use of diagnostics.

Having perhaps set aside any argument about the scientific dimension to these representational issues, I think we might take a different view of diagnostics. I want to take a more historical approach to this question, and assert that we can divide psychiatric diagnostics into three great phases, a tripartite periodization—which I will label as realism, modernism, and postmodernism.

The classical psychiatric diagnostics—from the eighteenth century through the early twentieth century—is a diagnostics of realism. Psychopathology is observed, recorded, organized, and presented as a set of things out there in the world that the psychiatrist is making note of. The existence of the observations is not called into question, the status of the psychiatrist as author or creator of a system is essentially not called into question, and the assumption is clearly that the diagnostic system is a type of accurate representation of the world. The quality of the representations may be argued or debated or discussed, but mostly in terms of the way in which the different elements are organized or combined—or, in terms of the quality of the narrative presentation, the way in which it is organized. In my choice of the term "realism" for this period, I want to draw attention to the closeness of these diagnostics to the literary form of realism, the realist novel (of, say, Dickens or Balzac or some other nineteenth century novelist).

This is in contrast to Modernism. Here in literature, the names are Joyce, Kafka, Proust, Musil, Eliot, and so forth. A simple way of organizing these diverse literary developments is to note that in all these cases, the representation of reality is called into question, the simple straightforward representations of reality no longer seem to function as clearly. There is some type of recognition of a more complicated reality out there, one requiring a very different literary form to represent it with. Furthermore, the position of the author as the guarantor of the work is called into question, and we get the development in Modernism of very distinct literary styles, seemingly idiosyncratic to the particular authors, easily recognizable. Finally, the entire realist project is thrown out. While Modernism was once popular, my sense is that these works are mostly read by academics now, or people with unusual literary interest. Modernism is certainly not much in fashion these days.

This striking shift from Realism to Modernism in literature does, in fact, have an obvious correlate within the realm of psychiatric diagnostics—Behaviorism. I think that the work of Pavlov and Watson, brought to clinical fruition by Skinner and Wolpe, can only be understood within that context. For, indeed, with Behaviorism, we see a wholesale rejection of the Realist approach to diagnostics: its approach and categories, its form of presentation, and so forth are completely discarded in favor of a reworked conceptualization of psychic structure and psychic suffering. Put simply, with Skinner, the only relevant data is behavior—normal or otherwise. Everything else is irrelevant and not worthy of representation. Further, behavior is understood as a function of environmental conditioning, conditioning to be modified through the pedagogical and rehabilitative techniques theorized in operant conditioning. Thus, much of the information incorporated in classical psychiatric diagnostics is of no utility in the practice, and the entire, slowly evolved set of diagnostic structures is no longer of interest in the treatment. Or, with Wolpe, we see a similar situation where all forms of suffering are rewritten as phobia—from phobias and anxiety itself to depression (phobia of happiness) and even such things as marital strife (a phobia of intimacy). The patient is then simply taught how to relax and that state of relaxation is then linked to objects closer and closer to the phobic object through systematic desensitization. With both of these systems, we have a rejection of the complex richness of the realist diagnostics in favor of a very idiosyncratic diagnostic system (easily recognizable and attributed to its founder—as would be a literary work of Kafka or Joyce), one that discards in its entirety the Realist diagnostics, and one in which the position of the clinician is highlighted: the subjective stance of the clinician in assigning the diagnosis is highlighted in contrast to the seemingly transparent position of the clinician in realist diagnostics.

Well, as with modern novels, this Modernist diagnostics has fallen out of favor, and there are few today who would fully adhere to this system. But, before leaving this, I think it's worth drawing attention to one other dimension of Modernist diagnostics, the Nietzschean dimension. The figure here is, of course, Thomas Szasz, who proposed a wholesale rejection of realist diagnostics (and any transcendental scientific or pseudo-scientific basis for it) in favor of a view of human activity as an experience to be understood in moral terms and a view of psychiatric therapeutic practices in terms of power relations—arguments fully congruous with the philosophical Modernism of Nietzsche.

But, what about today, what about the *DSM*? Here, too, I want to continue with this periodization drawn from literature and would like to quickly survey some of the features that are used to described postmodernity in literature: a breakdown of the barriers between high and low culture; a loss of depth or a certain superficiality in style; a mix of styles from different historical eras; a debasement of literature itself; a general mode of heterogeneity (Jameson, 1991). Now, of course, there are many who are critical of postmodern literature and art forms, and one of the very interesting things is that those criticisms of postmodernism are precisely some of the same criticisms that we hear of the *DSM*: too superficial, a loss of the depth or richness of classical psychiatric diagnosis, a debasement of diagnosis in its formulaic approach, and heterogeneous—with a mix of more classical appearing diagnoses such as schizophrenia and a whole range of mono-symptomatic diagnoses modeled after addictions (eating disorders, pathological gambling, all the addictions diagnoses), whose form resembles a type of modernist diagnosis in the mode of Wolpe, with Addiction replacing phobia as the new template. And, indeed, the *DSM* is the properly postmodern form of diagnosis.

I would like shift for a moment to psychoanalysis—what about psychoanalysis and diagnosis? How does the Freudian enterprise fit in? I will just make one comment about this here. On the one hand, Freud would seem to fit among the Modernists, with a novel system of explanation in stark contrast—many would say—to the classical psychiatric tradition of Realism. The problem with that thesis is that, for the most part, Freud maintained the classical psychiatric diagnoses. He really, in many ways, did not create a new diagnostic system, and he continued to uphold the importance of diagnosis, in contrast to the Modernist behaviorists (or, within psychoanalysis itself, to the post-Freudian disinterest in diagnosis). I think that what Freud did with regard to diagnoses here is to add an explanation, a causal system, which organized—in a sense—the diagnoses. He supposed a certain unconscious structure necessary for the formation of a certain psychic structure and pattern of psychopathology. But, unlike science, which will directly touch, or image, or index that causal Thing in the body—like the tangles and plaques in a brain of someone with Alzheimer's—Freud's unconscious is a Thing that is fundamentally not representable, but whose existence must be supposed as a logical corollary to a certain psychic structure. This is a key difference between psychoanalysis and science on the issue of diagnostics (which brings up the question raised by Lacan—will we ever have a science adequate for psychoanalysis?). This also hints at the key difference and an inherent incompatibility in the overall approach of science today and psychoanalysis to the psyche and psychic suffering. But, note that the body returns in the final phase of Lacan's work in a very strong way, distinct, though, from the scientific approach to the body—a development articulated in various ways in Chapters Eight–Thirteen above, but developed more comprehensively in Éric Laurent's *L'Envers de la Biopolitique: Une Écriture pour la Jouissance* (Laurent, 2016).

But, if we don't have science to guide us much in our diagnostics, what about psychoanalysis? I would assert it is the most useful guide in diagnostics and understanding psychic structure, whether or not one practices psychoanalysis. And, I don't think I am alone on this. Eric Kandel is certainly one of the great biological psychiatric researchers of our era. The Nobel laureate, who is not a psychoanalyst, delivered a series of assessments and critiques of psychiatry and psychoanalysis in several articles. One point he emphasized I will sum up with a direct quote from his article in the April 1999 *American Journal of Psychiatry*, where he states that: "This decline [of psychoanalysis] is regrettable, since psychoanalysis still represents the most coherent and intellectually satisfying view of the mind" (Kandel, 1999). Kandel argues that research scientists must turn to psychoanalysis as guides in their work. Certainly we have seen evidence of the benefits of such an approach in Kandel's work and other work from researchers over the last ten years. I argue that clinicians may want to consider following a similar path. As we wait to see what science will turn up—a long wait I argue, do not turn to pseudo-science—for whatever reason, but look at different models of diagnosis—psychoanalysis first and foremost among them. And, further, in light of the absence of a science to guide clinicians, perhaps there ought to be other systems put in play—maybe there will not be a single diagnostic system, but different systems, systems to guide the clinician in treatment as a function of the treatment that is practiced: a diagnostic system for psychoanalysts, a diagnostic system for psychopharmacologists, a diagnostic system for other practices.

There is considerable frustration with the *DSM*, and not just from psychoanalysts, but from many quarters—researchers, clinicians, and so forth. When one finds it substantially lacking, cynically holding onto the *DSM*—because it is what's out there, and necessary, and without alternatives—is of no service to the patients coming to us with their suffering.

CHAPTER TWENTY-FOUR

The crumbled building blocks of evidence-based medicine

Certainly one of the greatest trends in medicine over the last decade has been the rise of a new mode of medical practice and medical education: Evidence-Based Medicine, the promulgation of practice guidelines, and other associated developments. Speaking, perhaps, in an overly simplistic way, we might say that there was once a notion of an academic physician as a master of the profession—whose mastery was characterized by experience, judgment, knowledge and clinical know-how, and other more or less ineffable aspects of the practice. There was a subjective and ethical aspect to the practice, and schools arose in medicine around the style of their great leaders, something that was passed onto those studying the practice.

That notion of transmission of medical practice has been replaced by a new one, where the frame is no longer defined by experience and judgment, but a new system in which, through a process of isolation and measurement, medicine (and the patient him- or her-self) is reduced to that which can be broken into bits, quantified, and evaluated in an application that—in adopting a style from science—at least appears to be objective and scientific. In this model, what cannot be quantified and reduced is relegated outside of the field of scientific medicine, making, in such a way, the doctor-patient relationship in

247

clinical practice (transference, as it is known for the psychoanalyst), or the teacher-student relationship in education (another form of transference, for sure) no longer part of the practice or education. In this whole process, physicians give up responsibility and control for the practice to a varied group—payers, insurers, the government, groups of so-called physician experts, all operating now as Committees (see, e.g., Laurent & Miller, 1997), who have now assumed (or, been handed over) responsibility for decision-making about practice and education.

While some grumbling about this certainly occurs among older doctors, physicians as a group are remarkably complacent about these developments, accepting them without any significant critical examination. We must note, however, that this reduction and quantification within the realm of medicine has occurred at precisely the same time that we see a developing interest in non-Western or alternative therapies in medicine, as if people are seeking to pick up what is lost in "ordinary" medicine with a different doctor, a complementary doctor, where the physician-patient relationship and the "ineffable" aspects of care are captured with a different relationship.

But, again, while on a whole, mainstream medicine has accepted these developments without question, there is a serious literature within psychoanalysis (at least, psychoanalysis of the Lacanian orientation) that has attempted to carefully scrutinize these developments and examine their influence on clinical practice, especially in Europe, where a small groups of ideologues are attempting to eradicate an entire tradition of clinical practice in mental health care (Sauvagnat, 2007; Laurent, 2007; Miller, 2007; Miller, J.-A., Burgoyne, B., & Grigg, R , 2005; Miller & Milner, 2004).

It was something of a surprise, then, to come upon the remarkable study done by Erick Turner and colleagues on "selective publication of antidepressant trials and its influence on apparent efficacy," published in the *New England Journal of Medicine* (2008). In this study, Turner demonstrated that of a total of seventy-five or so studies completed on newer generation antidepressants, almost all of the thirty-seven studies that demonstrated a positive result were published in the medical literature. Of the studies that demonstrated negative results of the medication, the majority were not published. Of those negative results that were published, the significant majority of those were distorted in such a way that what was originally (per the study design) a negative outcome was reported as a positive outcome. Using a complex statistical tool on effect size, Turner then demonstrated that, as a group, these medications, which have a fairly modest clinical effect as based on the published trials, in fact have a far more modest clinical effect when all the data (negative and positive) gathered about their clinical effect is factored into the analysis. The implication of the study is very clear: important information about these medications was withheld from physicians and the public, groups that based their decisions about the use of these medications on a distorted and overly positive sample of the data that was selectively released into the literature.

In and of itself, this does not come as too much of a surprise. Any clinician with familiarity with this class of medications is aware that they just are not all that effective. And, in light of all the information that has come out about pharmaceutical companies withholding information about medications (such as cardiac mortality in newer anti-inflammatory drugs; suicide risk in antidepressants; and, weight gain in some antipsychotics), only the most naïve person would be surprised by the revelation of a failure of the companies to release these data. And, even for the more scientifically minded physician, the statistical findings should not be too much of a surprise. After all, in all of the selectively released positive studies, the randomly controlled trials show about a sixty-five percent efficacy of the medication in comparison to a fifty percent or so efficacy for the placebo. Seeing that slimmest of margins in the published data will lead the astute reader to hypothesize the existence of studies that do not show the margin (after all, like many phenomena, these studies are distributed along a kind of Gaussian curve: we only got to see one side of the curve).

What I found most remarkable about Turner's work is the extreme rigor and dispassion with which he approached the subject, using the very tools and techniques of this contemporary development of Evidence-Based Medicine to demolish one of the core foundational building blocks of Evidence-Based Medicine, namely the randomly-controlled trials that form the bedrock on which are built the practice guidelines that physicians are told they must follow to deliver quality care. The published literature, which forms the basis for the whole enterprise of Evidence-Based Medicine, contains a significant misrepresentation. It is not an "objective" source of knowledge about these treatments, but a carefully manipulated presentation of the data gathered by a Medical-Industrial Complex keen on controlling what is promulgated as "science" itself. This is most obvious in the "Supplementary appendix" to Turner's article (found on the website of the *New England Journal of Medicine*) that demonstrates the degree of outright deception in the ways in which some of the negative studies were subsequently reworked and manipulated into positive studies. If these randomized controlled trials are not to be trusted, this whole edifice needs to be re-examined.

Turner's work on publication of drug trials, however, is not the only evidence that has come out that should lead physicians to call into question the ways in which practice standards and recommendations regarding treatments are transmitted to physicians in practice. Indeed, while Evidence-Based Medicine and the Practice Guidelines that are developed based on scientific evidence are an important means for education of medical students and residents in training and are followed especially closely among younger physicians, they are not the only ways in which physicians in practice acquire information about treatments, especially new treatments. Many physicians rely on talks by local experts in their field and on visits by pharmaceutical reps (which may include mental health professionals) to get information on new treatments.

In the first decade of the twenty-first century, a great deal of attention has been drawn to the ways in which these local experts (the so-called "thought leaders") and pharmaceutical representatives are instructed by the pharmaceutical industry to deliver deceptive messages about the products that the industries are selling. Once of the greatest examples of this within the psychiatric field has been the promotion of the drug Neurontin (a brand name of gabapentin, developed by the Parke-Davis division of Warner-Lambert) (Landefeld & Steinman, 2009). Neurontin was a drug developed in the 1970s that was approved by the Food and Drug Administration (FDA) in the early 1990s in doses up to 1800 mg per day as an adjunctive treatment for partial complex seizures. In the United States, once a drug is approved for use by the FDA, a physician may prescribe it for any reason and at any dose that he feels is in the best interests of his patients. The companies, however, are only allowed by law to promote the drug for the specific indication (or, diagnosis) that the drug was approved for by the FDA. As a drug for the adjunctive treatment of partial complex seizures, this particular drug had a very small market. Parke-Davis initiated a marketing strategy that was blatantly against these federal regulations. One of their "medical liaisons" (scientific representatives that meet with physicians to discuss products) was told:

> I want you out there every day selling Neurontin. […] We all know Neurontin's not growing for adjunctive therapy, besides that's not where the money is. Pain management, now that's money. Monotherapy [for epilepsy], now that's money. We don't want to share these patients with everybody, we want them on Neurontin only. We want their whole drug budget. […] We can't wait for them [physicians] to ask, we need [to] get out there and tell them up front. Dinner programs, CME [Continuing Medical Education] programs, consultantships all work great but don't forget the one-on-one. That's where we need to be, holding their hand and whispering in their ear, Neurontin for pain, Neurontin for monotherapy, Neurontin for bipolar, Neurontin for everything. […] I don't want to see a single patient coming off Neurontin before they've been up to at least 4800 mg/day. I don't want to hear that safety crap either, have you tried Neurontin, every one of you should take one just to see there is nothing, it's a great drug. (Franklin, n.d., p. 11)

Parke-Davis executives not only exhorted their representatives to push the drugs to physicians, but organized an expansive and comprehensive strategy to sell the drug to the medical community. Parke-Davis contracted with medical education companies to create articles about the expansive range of uses of Neurontin for a wide range of conditions, many of the articles ghost written by the industry following its specific guidelines, but promoted as academic and educational. Research directed by the company was deceptively presented to physicians and the academic medical community overstating the efficacy of Neurontin for conditions for which it was not effective. Sadly, many physicians participated in this outright deception regarding this drug. The results, however, were dramatic. Annual sales for this product went from $98 million in 1995 to nearly $3 billion in 2004. Clearly, this strategy was effective in getting physicians to prescribe the drug for a range of conditions for which it was not effective. In May 2004, the company agreed to settle criminal and civil charges associated with the promotion of this medication and pay fines of more than $430 million (Gilpen, 2004, May 13).

This type of activity on the part of the pharmaceutical industry to manipulate the ways in which their drugs are received in the greater psychiatric community are by no means limited to this particular company and medication. Indeed, following a series of investigations, Senator Charles Grassley (Iowa) released documentation detailing how numerous so-called "thought leaders" in psychiatry have received extensive payments from the pharmaceutical industry. The allegations involve some of the leading psychiatrists in the United States. Charles Nemeroff is probably the most notable case (Harris, 2008, October 4). Nemeroff is the former Chair of the Psychiatry Department at Emory University; recipient of millions of dollars of federally funded research grants (from the National Institutes of Health); the author of several major textbooks in psychiatry and over 850 scientific publications; the Editor-in-Chief of a major journal in the field; and, a widely admired speaker. Nemeroff received more than $2.8 million in fees from consultation with pharmaceutical corporations and failed to report at least $1.2 million to his university and to the federal government, in violation of federal research rules. These actions put $190 million of federal research funding at Emory in jeopardy, and he resigned from the position of Chair of his Department. These reporting mechanisms are designed so that the government can "manage" potential conflicts of interest and to promote transparency in the relationships between academia and industry. The system fails to do that, and, as Gardiner Harris reported:

> In one telling example, Dr. Nemeroff signed a letter dated July 15, 2004, promising Emory administrators that he would earn less than $10,000 a year from GlaxoSmithKline to comply with federal rules. But on that day, he was at the Four Seasons Resort in Jackson Hole, Wyo., earning $3,000 of what would become $170,000 in income that year from that company—17 times the figure he had agreed on. (Harris, 2008, October 4)

Nemeroff is hardly the only "thought leader" with significant so-called conflicts of interest. Many in the mental health field have noted a significant increase in the diagnosis of bipolar disorder since the introduction of atypical antipsychotics. Two leaders in this field also have been under scrutiny for their industry relationships. Frederick Goodwin— an Adjunct Professor at George Washington University; an author of a textbook on bipolar disorder; former Director of the National Institute of Mental Health; and, the host of an influential radio program on the mind that received federal support—has allegedly failed to disclose significant relationships with pharmaceutical corporations that promoted products in the fields he was discussing, supposedly from an objective scientific perspective. The amounts were again substantial—a failure to disclose $1.3 million over a seven year period, including more than $329,000 he received from GlaxoSmithKline just to promote lamotrigine for bipolar disorder in one twelve month period. (Harris, 2008, November 22)

Similarly, while Goodwin's work related largely to adult bipolar disorder, Harvard University psychiatrist Joseph Biederman is widely seen as one of the country's leading experts in childhood bipolar disorder, and in fact has been a promoter of a wider use of the diagnosis in children and adolescents (the diagnosis was previously used quite rarely in children, but its use has expanded dramatically since the end of the 1990s). Biederman founded an institute at Harvard—the Johnson and Johnson Center for the Study of Pediatric Psychopathology—that was largely supported by Johnson and Johnson, a pharmaceutical company. Emails produced in the course of a lawsuit against the company document an academic entity that seems to be nothing other than a front for the corporation (Armstrong & Mundy, 2008, November 25). Indeed, the documents list in the annual report that one of the criteria listed as an "essential feature of the center" is moving "forward the commercial goals of J&J." The company also apparently stated that it helped fund the center "with an objective to conduct rigorous clinical trials to clarify the appropriate [*sic*] use and dosing of Risperdal [an antipsychotic medication of Johnson and Johnson under investigation for bipolar disorder] in children." A physician panel convened by the FDA has determined that antipsychotics such as Risperdal have been overprescribed to children (there were 390,000 children on Risperdal in 2007, 200,000 of them less than twelve years old). At the same time as this Center was operating, Biederman was receiving direct payments from the company ($58,000 in 2001, though he only reported $3500). Like the other thought leaders, Biederman received over $1.6 million in a seven year period, and reported only several hundreds of thousands to his university and federal authorities.

Given all of the controversy within the mental health community about the appropriate diagnosis of bipolar disorder (especially in children) and the appropriate use of antipsychotic medications (given all of the side-effects and risks and the high cost), it is alarming to see the extent to which some of the so-called though leaders in that particular field are linked to various industry interests.

Turner's careful research demonstrated a serious deception and manipulation in the presentation of scientific data to physicians, academics, and the general public. These reports cited above about the ways in which the industry paid off academic leaders in the field may point in one direction to understanding how this deception was sustained. Money may have been the glue that held together the blocks of Evidence-Based Medicine that seem to be crumbling away.

In his January 1961 Farewell Speech, President Eisenhower, while recognizing the importance of the military, offered cautionary words about the dangers of a "military-industrial complex," which would pose a threat for the "disastrous rise of misplaced power" and threaten to "endanger our liberties or democratic processes" and that must be guarded against by "an alert and knowledgeable citizenry." Within psychiatry and medicine, the work of Turner and his colleagues indicates that we are seeing nothing less than the rise of a similarly dangerous "Medical-Industrial Complex," at least in the United States today, one which also holds an immense amount of power and poses similar threats to our liberties and to the democratic processes which are the basis of the social bond that is medicine and the work of physicians. Physicians, especially academic physicians, must reconsider the nature of their relations with this Medical-Industrial Complex and the extent to which they want to be complicit in deceptions such as those promulgated in the work that Turner has carefully studied.

CHAPTER TWENTY-FIVE

Depression screening as the latest avatar of moralism in American public mental health

When we think of the world as "globalized"—implying a kind of uniform standardization of practices, especially in something such as the psy field, the mental health field—it can be a shock to realize the significant differences between two such equally "advanced Western capitalist" countries such as France and the United States on a matter such as depression screening. Depression screening is currently under debate in France, as a number of forces are pushing France to adopt this practice.

The shock is that depression screening in the United States is something of a *fait accompli*, an established part of the practice of so many clinicians and clinics, schools and universities, and workplaces and community agencies. There is no debate in the United States on this topic, it has been decided—it is a good practice for the mental health field.

Depression screening in the United States can be traced back to 1991, the first National Depression Screening Day. This day was established by Screening for Mental Health, Inc., with the financial backing of major pharmaceutical corporations. The non-profit corporation responsible for guiding the NDSD is currently led by a Board of Directors, largely comprised of academic psychiatrists. This practice of depression

255

screening was initially promoted to clinicians, but screening—either in person or by the completion of questionnaires, now even online—has been extended to mental health clinicians and clinics, primary care clinics, schools, and workplaces. It is taught in psychiatry residencies and promoted by the US Preventative Services Taskforce recommendations as a "best practice" in medical practice.

Interestingly, while many academics and administrators wish to resolve debates in mental health practice on the grounds of evidence—this whole movement for Evidence-Based Medicine attempts to apply a very reduced Anglo-American "empiricism" in the care of patients to the exclusion of any other values or ethics—there is little significant evidence to support this practice of depression screening. One of the major resources in the analysis of scientific evidence is the Cochrane Library, which provides an online database reviewing the medical literature. In a comprehensive meta-analysis of all the published studies on depression screening to date, they concluded that there is little evidence in support of this practice. The Summary is unambiguous: "The use of depression screening or case finding instruments has little or no impact on the recognition, management or outcome of depression in primary care or the general hospital" (Gilbody, House, and Sheldon, 2005).

That said, the practice remains in place, well established. There is little debate on this within the psychiatric literature. In the popular literature, such as on the internet, the only critical discussion of this topic can be found in the Scientology literature—with its strong anti-psychiatric positions—and in some comments suggesting that this whole endeavor is supported and funded by the pharmaceutical industry as a way of promoting the diagnosis of depression and subsequent prescription of antidepressants.

Certainly, this latter relationship is important. The Medical-Industrial Complex (of corporations and the physicians who work for them, consult for them, and receive funding from them for their research—see the previous chapter) has come under increasing scrutiny in the United States in the beginning of the 21st century—for hiding negative effects of medications; suppressing unfavorable studies and data that failed to support its products; promoting "off-label" uses of medications for treatments without established benefit; providing excessive payments to physicians by corporations in money and gifts; and, creating a loss of critical scrutiny of the scientific literature due to the overly close relations of researchers to the corporations. We might certainly look upon the pharmaceutical connection to depression screening as just another effort to market their drugs to the public under the rubric of a public health effort, something which would have been necessary in the 1990s, as it was only recently that corporations were allowed to market their drugs directly to the general population through the media.

But there is yet another dimension of this that we must take into account, namely the support of employers—including and especially some very large corporations—for this screening. The 1990 Global Burden of Disease Project identified depression as the number one cause of disability in the world and suggested that psychiatric diagnoses were significantly underestimated as a cause of disability. This study has led to additional research in psychiatry in what we might refer to as psycho-economics, namely the effect on productivity of psychiatric diagnoses such as depression. Large corporations have taken significant notice of this and have implemented depression screening into their workplaces to promote better productivity, enhance workplace safety, and reduce medical and disability expenses.

While the goals of better health and fewer accidents is certainly laudable, we cannot fail to notice another dimension to these practices, which I would identify as an extension of Taylorism into the psyche or mind. In the first industrial era, workers were hired and worked perhaps several different positions within a factory, passing on their knowledge of production to each other. The innovations of Frederick Taylor were to improve efficiency within the factory through scientific management, especially in the analysis of the activities of the workers within the factory, who should subsequently be trained precisely what to do, which often led to increasing specialization of tasks within the factory and greater control by the corporation of their activity. Depression screening, as part of the wellness movement in general so prevalent today in the US, is nothing other than an extension of the Taylorist doctrine into the minds of the workers themselves—their mental activity is to be monitored, analyzed, and studied. And, furthermore, workers will be instructed as to the proper state of mind for their jobs. What Fredric Jameson in *Postmodernism, or the Cultural Logic of Late Capitalism* described as one of the last of the precapitalist enclaves (the unconscious, along with nature) is now directly territorialized by corporations.

There is yet another dimension, however, to depression screening. One of the sponsoring groups for depression screening is Mental Health

America. This non-profit group is an extensive network of organizations with the mission "of promoting mental health, preventing mental disorders and achieving victory over mental illness through advocacy, education, research and service." The organization sponsors mental health awareness programs, is a major promoter of screenings, and advocates for care for people with mental illness. The group is one of the largest non-profit groups in the mental health field, and one of the oldest, having been founded originally as the National Committee for Mental Hygiene in 1909 by Clifford Beers. Beers' story is strikingly close to that of Daniel Paul Schreber. He was a very intelligent and educated man, hospitalized in 1900 for a number of years for paranoia. He was subsequently released and wrote an autobiographical account of his life and the poor treatment by the staff in the hospitals where he was confined, *A Mind that Found Itself*. This text led to significant reform in mental health practices and the promotion of a notion of mental hygiene (See Edward Shorter's *A History of Psychiatry* for a brief discussion with references [Shorter, 1997]).

This mental hygiene movement, of which depression screening is the latest manifestation, can be squarely situated within that movement in turn of the century (nineteenth to twentieth) American history described as the Progressive Era (Hofstadter's 1954 *The Age of Reform* remains a key reference). One aspect of the Progressive agenda that we find in Beers' work and the mental hygiene movement is the notion of social justice and equality for all, with a special focus and reliance on organization and bureaucracy, with the support of science, to achieve these changes. The Progressive Era is often described as a response to the rapid changes occurring at that time in history, mostly associated with industrialization. For example, Upton Sinclair's 1906 *The Jungle*, which chronicled the abuses of the meat packing industry, led to bureaucratic initiatives such as the Food and Drug Administration, which regulated food through a systematization of food production as an industry. Beers' book similarly took issue with the increasingly "factory-like" nature of the American asylums of the time, where he was confined. The crucial logic for all of these efforts, however, was a notion of what we might even term an Aristotelian Sovereign Good, be it in the care of animals or patients in asylums, that holds true for society—for everyone in society—and one which must be secured through the action of government, enlisting the help of science, in promotion of this Good for all.

There is yet a further historical antecedent for this in the first half of the nineteenth century in the US—the period known as the Second Great Awakening. The history of the United States has been marked by various periods of heightened religious activity, periods of great interest in protestant evangelism, times that are often referred to as Great Awakenings. The second one, though, from 1800–1835, is most notable, however, for in addition to the personal religious dimension present in the earlier Great Awakening, this latter movement is notable for various reform causes: efforts to bring rights and equality to women and blacks (through the women's suffrage movement and the abolition movement) and, important in the context of depression screening, the development of the temperance movement and movements against masturbation and sexuality as such, which brought religion into personal behavior in a public and universal way for all (and eventually resulted, in the later Progressive Era, in the Constitutional Amendment of Prohibition, which banned the production and sale of alcohol for a number of years).

A review article by Jill Lepore on the Second Great Awakening discussed the historical debate on the relationship of these reform efforts to the growth of egalitarian Jacksonian democracy and the expansion of American business (Lepore, 2007). Cited in Lepore, Charles Sellers' *The Market Revolution: Jacksonian America, 1815–1846* argues for the importance of this moment as the critical moment of a shift from an agrarian to a market capitalist economy, during which "Establishing capitalist hegemony over economy, politics, and culture, the market revolution created ourselves and most of the world we know." Sellers' thesis is strongly disputed by Daniel Walker Howe's *What Hath God Wrought: The Transformation of America, 1815–1848*, but both acknowledge a historical transition during this period. As Lepore succinctly summarizes it: "Sellers thinks that poor, drunk, lusty, impious eighteenth-century Americans were freer, and happier, than their wealthier, sober, prim, devout nineteenth-century grandchildren; Howe thinks it's the grandchildren who were better off. "

What strikes one immediately with a chronology such as this, however, from the Second Great Awakening to the Progressive Era to the depression screening of today, is how each of these moral reform efforts—within the mental health field: from temperance and movements against sexuality to mental hygiene to depression screening— each occur at a pivotal moment in American economic history: the transition to a market economy, the transition to monopoly capitalism and, now, the development of advanced or global capitalism. Each moment carries within it one more effort for greater morality for all, in a well-nigh Weberian logic, extending moral control from that of behaviors such as drunkenness into the psyche itself, with an increasing alliance with science to bolster these programs, even when science itself offers no support for practices such as depression screening.

This is moralism, writ large on the political stage, and is indeed something that Jacques Lacan warned about, in 1960, in *The Ethics of Psychoanalysis*, stating that:

> There is absolutely no reason why we should make ourselves the guarantors of the bourgeois dream. A little more rigor and firmness are required in our confrontation with the human condition. That is why I reminded you last time that the service of goods or the shift of the demand for happiness onto the political stage has its consequences. The movement that the world we live in is caught up in, of wanting to establish the universal spread of the service of goods as far as conceivably possible, implies an amputation, sacrifices, indeed a kind of puritanism in the relationship to desire that has occurred historically. The establishment of the service of goods at a universal level does not in itself resolve the problem of the present relationship of each individual man to his desire in the short period of time between his birth and his death. The happiness of future generations is not at issue here. (Lacan, 1992, p. 303)

Lacan may well have been describing moralism in mental health in its American manifestations. It is a valuable cautionary note for all clinicians today, whether psychoanalysts or not.

REFERENCES

Adams, S. (1906). *The Writings of Samuel Adams, Vol II, 1770–1773*. New York: G. P. Putnam's Sons.

Alvarenga, E. (2011). What is the importance of dreams in psychoanalysis today? *LCExpress, 2.1*: 1–6.

Armstrong, D., & Mundy, A. (2008, November 25). J&J emails raise issues of Risperdal promotion. *The Wall Street Journal*. Available online at: http://online.wsj.com/article/SB122755237429253763.html?mod=testMod

Badiou, A. (2003). *St Paul: The Foundation of Universalism*. Stanford: Stanford.

Berrios, G. E. (1996). *The History of Mental Symptoms: Descriptive Psychopathology since the Nineteenth Century*. Cambridge: Cambridge.

Borch-Jacobsen, M. (1996). Neurotica: Freud and the seduction theory. *October, 76*: 15–43.

Brousse, M.-H. (2005). Vers une nouvelle clinique psychanalytique. *Mental, 15*: 28–40.

Brousse, M.-H. (2009). Ordinary psychosis in the light of Lacan's theory of discourse. *Psychoanalytical Notebooks, 19*: 7–20.

Brown, P. (1988). *The Body and Society*. New York: Columbia.

Cosenza, D. (2005). La psychanalyse et les transformations contemporaines du symptôme. *Mental, 16*: 57–64.

De Saussure, F. (1994). *Course in General Linguistics*. New York: Columbia.

Deleuze, G. & Guattari, F. (1983). *Anti-Oedipus: Capitalism and Schizophrenia.* Minneapolis: University of Minnesota.

Edelman, G. (1992). *Bright Air, Brilliant Fire: On the Matter of the Mind.* New York: Basic Books.

Ellmann, R. (1982). *James Joyce, New and Revised Edition.* Oxford: Oxford.

Fink, B. (1997). *A Clinical Introduction to Lacanian Psychoanalysis: Theory and Technique.* Cambridge: Harvard.

Fonagy, P., Gergely, G., Jurist, E., & Target, M. (2002). *Affect Regulation, Mentalization, and the Development of the Self.* New York: Other Press.

Franklin, D. P. (n.d.). Disclosure of information by relator David P Franklin: Pursuant to 31 USC 3730 b(2). Franklin v. Parke-Davis. Accessed on June 6, 2016. Available online at: www.industrydocumentslibrary.ucsf.edu/drug/docs/zgyd0217.

Freeman, K. (1995). *Ancilla to the Pre-Socratic Philosophers.* Cambridge: Harvard.

Freud, S. (1896c). The aetiology of hysteria. *S.E., 3:* 192–193. London: Hogarth.

Freud, S. (1900a). *The Interpretation of Dreams. S.E., 4:* 148–150. London: Hogarth.

Freud, S. (1905a). On psychotherapy. *S.E., 7:* 260–261. London: Hogarth.

Freud, S. (1905d). *Three Essays on the Theory of Sexuality. S.E., 7:* 125–243. London: Hogarth.

Freud, S. (1905e). Fragment of an analysis of a case of hysteria. *S.E., 7:* 3. London: Hogarth.

Freud, S. (1909d). Notes upon a case of obsessional neurosis. *S.E., 10:* 153–318. London: Hogarth.

Freud, S. (1910k). Wild psycho-analysis. *S.E., 11:* 121. London: Hogarth.

Freud, S. (1915e). The unconscious. *S.E., 14:* 161 204. London: Hogarth.

Freud, S. (1917e). Mourning and melancholia. *S.E., 14:* 243–258. London: Hogarth.

Freud, S. (1919d). Introduction to *Psychoanalysis and the War Neuroses. S.E., 17:* 205–210. London: Hogarth.

Freud, S. (1919e). A child is being beaten: a contribution to the study of the origins of sexual perversions. *S.E., 17:* 175–204. London: Hogarth.

Freud, S. (1920g). *Beyond the Pleasure Principle. S.E., 18:* 7–64. London: Hogarth.

Freud, S. (1921c). *Group Psychology and the Analysis of the Ego. S.E., 5:* 69–143. London: Hogarth.

Freud, S. (1925d). *An Autobiographical Study. S.E., 20:* 3–76. London: Hogarth.

Freud, S. (1926e). *The Question of Lay Analysis. S.E., 20:* 179–258. London: Hogarth.

Freud, S. (1930a). *Civilization and Its Discontents. S.E., 21:* 115–116. London: Hogarth.

Freud, S. (1937c). Analysis terminable and interminable. *S.E., 23:* 209. London: Hogarth.

Freud, S. (1937d). Constructions in analysis. *S.E., 23:* 255–270. London: Hogarth.

Freud, S. (1950a). Project for a scientific psychology. *S.E., 1:* 281–387. London: Hogarth.

Freud, S. (1953). *On Aphasia: A Critical Study.* New York: International Universities Press.

Freud, S. (1954). *The Origins of Psycho-analysis: Letters to Wilhelm Fliess, Drafts and Notes: 1887–1902.* New York: Basic.

Freud, S. (1955c). Memorandum on the Electrical Treatment of War Neurotics. *S.E., 17:* 211–216. London: Hogarth.

Freud, S. (1985). *The Complete Letters of Sigmund Freud to Wilhelm Fliess, 1887–1904.* Cambridge: Harvard.

Freud, S. (1999). *The Interpretation of Dreams.* Oxford: Oxford.

Gilbody, S., House, A. O., & Sheldon, T. A. (2005, October 19). Screening and case finding instruments for depression. *Cochrane Database of Systematic Reviews, 4.*

Gilpen, K. (2004, May 13). Pfizer to pay $420 million in illegal marketing case. *The New York Times.* Available online at: http://www.nytimes.com/2004/05/13/business/13CND-DRUG.html?ex=1233378000&en=3f23c61636301b91&ei=5070.

Gorostiza, L. (2010). From the instant of the fantasy to the desire of the psychoanalyst. *Hurly-Burly, 4:* 39–54.

Green, A. (1997). The intuition of the negative in playing and reality. *International Journal of Psychoanalysis, 78:* 1071–1084.

Grigg, R. (2007). The concept of semblant in Lacan's teaching. Unpublished. Accessed June 6, 2016. Available online at: www.lacan.com/griggblog.html.

Guéguen, P.-G. (2009). The plunge of the symptom in hypermodernity. *Lacanian Compass, 1, 14:* 5–12.

Guéguen, P.-G. (2011). Hypermodern families. Unpublished paper, delivered at the Paris USA Lacan seminar in New York.

Harris, G. (2008, October 4). Top psychiatrist didn't report drug maker's pay. *The New York Times.* Available online at: www.nytimes.com/2008/10/04/health/policy/04drug.html.

Harris, G. (2008, November 22). Drug makers paid radio host $1.3 million for lectures. *The New York Times.* Available online at: http://query.nytimes.com/gst/fullpage.html?res=9806EEDC153DF931A15752C1A96E9C8B63&sec=&spon=&pagewanted=1.

Heidegger, M. (1987). *Nietzsche (Volume 4: Nihilism)*. New York: Harper Collins.

Herman, J. (1992). *Trauma and Recovery*, New York: Basic.

Hoornaert, G. (2011). Womanliness: Defamation, fantasy, semblance. *Hurly-Burly, 5:* 93–98.

l'Instance de réflexion sur le mathème analytique. (1997). *La Conversation d'Arcochon: Cas rares: les inclassables de la clinique*. Paris: Agalma—Le Seuil.

l'Instance de réflexion sur le mathème analytique. (2005a). *Le Conciliabule d'Angers: Effets de surprise dans les psychoses*. Paris: Agalma—Le Seuil.

l'Instance de réflexion sur le mathème analytique. (2005b). *La psychose ordinaire: La Convention d'Antibes*. Paris: Agalma—Le Seuil.

Isaacs, S. (1948). The nature and function of phantasy, *International Journal of Psycho-Analysis, 29:* 73–97.

Jackson, J. H. (1996). On affectations of speech from disease of the brain. In: *Selected Writings*. Nijmegen: Arts and Boeve. Volume 2: 155–204.

Jameson, F. (1991). *Postmodernism; or, the Cultural Logic of Late Capitalism*. Durham: Duke.

Jameson, F. (2002). *A Singular Modernity: Essay on the Ontology of the Present*. London/New York: Verso.

Jameson, F. (2011). *Representing Capital: A Reading of Volume 1*. London/New York: Verso.

Jameson, F. (2015). The aesthetics of singularity. *New Left Review, 92:* 101–132.

Joseph, B. (1989). *Psychic Equilibrium and Psychic Change: Selected Papers of Betty Joseph*. London: Routledge.

Joseph, B. (1992). Psychic change: Some perspectives. *International Journal of Psychoanalysis, 73:* 237–243.

Kandel, E. (1999). Biology and the future of psychoanalysis: a new intellectual framework for psychiatry revisited. *American Journal of Psychiatry, 156(4):* 505–523.

Kernberg, O. (1986). *Severe Personality Disorders*. New Haven: Yale.

Lacan, J. (1962). *Le Séminaire de Jacques Lacan: IX, L'identification, 1961–1962*. Unpublished.

Lacan, J. (1965). *Le Séminaire de Jacques Lacan: XII, Problèmes cruciaux pour la psychanalyse, 1964–1965*. Unpublished.

Lacan, J. (1966). *Le Séminaire de Jacques Lacan: XIII, L'objet de la psychanalyse, 1965–1966*. Unpublished.

Lacan, J. (1967). *Le Séminaire de Jacques Lacan: XIV, La logique du fantasme, 1966–1967*. Unpublished.

Lacan, J. (1970). Discussion of the paper by C. Morazé. In: R. Macksey & E. Donato (Eds.). *The Structuralist Controversy: The Languages of Criticism and the Sciences of Man*. Baltimore, The Johns Hopkins Press, 1970, pp. 41–44.

Lacan, J. (1973). *Télévision: Psychanalyse I et II* (Videocassette). Paris: Éditions du Seuil/INA.

Lacan, J. (1974). *Le Séminaire de Jacques Lacan: XXI, Les Non-Dupes Errent, 1973–1974*. Unpublished.

Lacan, J. (1975a). *De la psychose paranoïaque dans ses rapports avec la personnalité. Suivi de Premiers écrits sur la paranoïa*. Paris: du Seuil.

Lacan, J. (1975b). *Le Séminaire de Jacques Lacan: XXII, R.S.I., 1974–1975*. Unpublished.

Lacan, J. (1976). Intervention in the "Journées des cartels de l'École freudienne de Paris." *Lettre de l'École freudienne, 18*: 263–270.

Lacan, J. (1977a). *The Four Fundamental Concepts of Psycho-Analysis*. New York: Norton.

Lacan, J. (1977b). *The Seminar of Jacques Lacan: Book XXV*. Unpublished, session of Dec 20, 1977.

Lacan, J. (1978a). Du discourse psychanalytique: Discours de Jacques Lacan à l'Université de Milan le 12 mai 1972. In: G. Contri (Ed.). *Lacan in Italia 1953–1978. En Italie Lacan* (pp. 32–55). Milan: La Salamandra, 1978.

Lacan, J. (1978b). La psychanalyse dans sa reference au rapport sexuel: Conférence donnée au Musée de la science et de la technique de Milan, le 3 février 1973. In: G. Contri (Ed.). *Lacan in Italia 1953–1978. En Italie Lacan* (pp. 58–77). Milan: La Salamandra, 1978.

Lacan, J. (1979a). The neurotic's individual myth. *Psychoanalytic Quarterly, 48*: 405.

Lacan, J. (1979b). Lacan pour Vincennes. *Ornicar?, 17/18*: 278.

Lacan, J. (1988). *The Seminar of Jacques Lacan: Book I, Freud's Papers on Technique 1953–1954*. New York: Norton.

Lacan, J. (1990). *Television*. New York: Norton.

Lacan, J. (1992). *The Seminar of Jacques Lacan: Book VII, The Ethics of Psychoanalysis 1959–1960*. New York: Norton.

Lacan, J. (1993). *The Seminar of Jacques Lacan: Book III, The Psychoses 1955–1956*. New York: Norton.

Lacan, J. (1994). *Le Séminaire de Jacques Lacan: Livre IV, La relation d'objet et les structures freudiennes 1956–1957*. Paris: Éditions du Seuil.

Lacan, J. (1998a). *The Seminar of Jacques Lacan: Book XX, Encore 1972–1973*. New York: Norton.

Lacan, J. (1998b). *Le Séminaire de Jacques Lacan: Livre V, Les formations de l'inconscient 1957–1958*. Paris: Éditions du Seuil.

Lacan, J. (2001). *Autres écrits*. Paris: Éditions du Seuil.

Lacan, J. (2005). *Le Séminaire de Jacques Lacan: Livre XXIII Le Sinthome 1975–1976*. Paris: Éditions du Seuil.

Lacan, J. (2006a). *Écrits: The First Complete Edition in English*. New York: Norton.

Lacan, J. (2006b). *Le Séminaire de Jacques Lacan: Livre XVIII, D'un discourse qui ne serait pas du semblant, 1971*. Paris: Éditions du Seuil.

Lacan, J. (2007). *The Seminar of Jacques Lacan: Book XVII, The Other Side of Psychoanalysis*. New York: Norton.

Lacan, J. (2013). *The Triumph of Religion, preceded by Discourse to Catholics*. Cambridge: Polity.

Lacan, J. (2014). *The Seminar of Jacques Lacan: Book X, Anxiety*. Cambridge: Polity.

Lacan, J. (2015). *The Seminar of Jacques Lacan: Book VIII, Transference*. Cambridge: Polity.

Lacan, J., Aubert, J., Godin, J.-G., Millot, C., Rabatt, J.-M., & Tardis, A. (1997). *Joyce avec Lacan*. Paris: Navarin.

Landefeld, C. S. & Steinman, M. A. (2009, January 8). The neurontin legacy—marketing through misinformation and manipulation. *The New England Journal of Medicine, 360, 2*: 103–105.

Laurent, É. (2000). From saying to doing in the clinic of drug addiction and alcoholism. *Almanac of Psychoanalysis, 2*: 129–141.

Laurent, É. (2006). *Where Has the Name of the Father Gone Today?* Tel-Aviv: DORa Project.

Laurent, É. (2007). Blog-notes: The psychopathology of evaluation. *Psychoanalytical Notebooks, 16*: 45–75.

Laurent, É. (2014). *Lost in Cognition: Psychoanalysis and the Cognitive Sciences*. London: Karnac.

Laurent, É. (2016). *L'Envers de la Biopolitique: Une Écriture pour la Jouissance*. Paris: Navarin.

Laurent, É. (n.d.). Ordinary psychosis. Unpublished paper.

Laurent, É. & Miller, J.-A. (1997). L'Autre qui n'existe pas et ses comités d'éthique. *La Cause freudienne, 35*: 7–20.

Leguil, C. (2011). Lacanian uses of ontology. *Psychoanalytical Notebooks, 23*: 107–116.

Lepore, J. (2007, October 29). Vast designs: How America came of age. *The New Yorker*.

Liddell, H. G. (1889). *An Intermediate Greek-English Lexicon*. Oxford: Clarendon.

Little, M. (1951). Counter-transference and the patient's response to it. *International Journal of Psychoanalysis, 32*: 32–40.

Lipovetsky, G. (1994). *The Empire of Fashion: Dressing Modern Democracy*. Princeton: Princeton.

Lipovetsky, G. (2005). *Hypermodern Times*. Cambridge: Polity.

Lyotard, J.-F. (1984). *The Postmodern Condition: A Report on Knowledge*. Minneapolis: University of Minnesota.

Miller, G. (2011). Video. *Rendez-vous chez Lacan*. Paris: Éditions Montparnasse.

Miller, J.-A. (1988). Extimité. In: Bracher, M., Alcorn, Jr., M. W., Corthell, R. J., & Massardier-Kenney, F. (Eds.). *Lacanian Theory of Discourse: Subject, Structure and Society*. New York: New York University, pp. 74–87.

Miller, J.-A. (1995). E = UWK: towards the ix international encounter of the Freudian field. *Analysis, 6:* 14–31.

Miller, J.-A. (1999). Of semblants in the relations between sexes. *Psychoanalytical Notebooks, 3:* 9–26.

Miller, J.-A. (2000). Paradigms of jouissance. *Lacanian Ink, 17:* 8–47.

Miller, J.-A. (2001a). Psychanalyse pure, psychanalyse appliquée, et psychothérapie. *La cause freudienne, 48:* 7–36.

Miller, J.-A. (2001b). The ironic clinic. *Psychoanalytic Notebooks, 7:* 9–26.

Miller, J.-A. (2003). Lacan et la politique. *Cités, 16:* 105–126.

Miller, J.-A. (2004a). Sigma(X), *The Symptom, 5:* (2004): online. Available online at: www.lacan.com/newspaper5.htm.

Miller, J.-A. (2004b). Introduction à la lecture du Séminaire de L'angoisse de Jacques Lacan. *La Cause freudienne, 58:* 61–100.

Miller, J-A. (2004c). Countertransference and Intersubjectivity. *Lacanian Ink, 23:* 8–53.

Miller, J.-A. (2005). A fantasy. *Lacanian Praxis: International Quarterly of Applied Psychoanalysis, 1:* 6–17.

Miller, J.-A. (2006). AMP 2008. Les objects *a* dans l'expérience analytique. *La Lettre mensuelle, 252:* 8–12.

Miller, J.-A. (2007). The era of the man without qualities. *Psychoanalytical Notebooks, 16:* 7–42.

Miller, J.-A. (2008). Semblants et sinthomes. *La Cause freudienne, 69:* 124–131.

Miller, J.-A. (2011). Reading a symptom. *Hurly-Burly, 6:* 143–156.

Miller, J.-A. (2014a). The Real for the 21st Century. In: World Association of Psychoanalysis (Eds.). *Scilicet: A Real for the 21st Century*. Paris: NLS Publication, 2014, pp. 25–36.

Miller, J.-A. (2014b). The child and the object. *Psychoanalytical Notebooks, 28:* 11–17.

Miller, J.-A. (2015). The unconscious and the speaking body. In: World Association of Psychoanalysis (Eds.). *Scilicet: The Speaking Body. On the Unconscious in the 21st Century*. Paris: NLS Publication, 2015, pp. 27–42.

Miller, J.-A., & Milner, J.-C. (2004). *Voulez-Vous Être Évalué?: Entretiens sur une machine d'imposture*. Paris: Bernard Grasset.

Miller, J.-A., Burgoyne, B., & Grigg, R. (2005). *The Pathology of Democracy: A Letter to Bernard Accoyer and to Enlightened Opinion*. London: Karnac.

Naparstek, F. (2002). Toxicomania of yesterday and today. *Psychoanalytical Notebooks, 9:* 151–162.

Nietzsche, F. (2001). *The Pre-Platonic Philosophers*. Urbana: University of Illinois.

Nobus, D. (2000). *Jacques Lacan and the Freudian Practice of Psychoanalysis.* London: Routledge.

Ogden, T. (1994). The analytic third: Working with intersubjective clinical facts. *International Journal of Psychoanalysis, 75:* 3–19.

Palombo, S. (1992). Connectivity and condensation in dreaming. *Journal of the American Psychoanalytic Association, 40:* 1139–1159.

Pally, R. (2000). *The Mind-Body Relationship.* London: Karnac.

Renik, O. (1993). Countertransference enactment and the psychoanalytic process. In: M. J. Horowitz, O. F. Kernberg & E. M. Weinshel (Eds.). *Psychic Structure and Psychic Change. Essays in Honor of Robert S. Wallerstein, M.D.* Madison, CT: Inter. Univ. Press, pp. 135–158.

Sauvagnat, F. (2007). The Current State of 'evidence-based medicine': Recent reductionist trends in psychiatry and some of their drawbacks. *Psychoanalytical Notebooks, 16:* 85–95.

Shorter, E. (1997). *A History of Psychiatry: From the Era of the Asylum to the Age of Prozac.* New York: John Wiley and Sons.

Sollers, P. (2011, August 10). Le Corps Sort de la Voix. *Lacan Quotidien, 8:* 1–6.

Solms, M. & Saling, M. (1986). On psychoanalysis and neuroscience: Freud's attitude to the localizationist tradition. *International Journal of Psycho-Analysis, 67:* 397–416.

Svolos, T. (2001). The past and future of psychoanalysis in psychiatry. *The Symptom, 1:* electronic journal.

Svolos, T. (2005, April 12). Lacan in the US. *Agence Lacanienne de presse, Nouvelle série, n° 78.*

Tarrab, M. (2005). Produire de nouveaux symptoms. *Quarto, 85:* 48–51.

Tarrab, M. (2007). Testimony of the pass in New York. *Lacanian Compass, 1.11:* 26–36.

Thurston, L. (2004). *James Joyce and the Problem of Psychoanalysis.* Cambridge: Cambridge.

Turner, E. H., Matthews, A. M., Linardatos, E., Tell, R. A., & Rosenthal, R. (2008). Selective publication of antidepressant trials and its influence on apparent efficacy. *New England Journal of Medicine, 358:* 252–260.

Vanheule, S. (2004). Neurotic depressive trouble: Between the signifier and the Real. *Journal for Lacanian Studies, 2, 1:* 34–53.

Ventura, O. (2011). Without nostalgia. Unpublished paper. Transcription of the lecture given at the EOL on 19th April 2011. Available online at: www.congresoamp.com/en/template.php?file=Actividades-preparatorias/Resenas/11-04-19_Sin-nostalgia.html.

Wajcman, G. (1982). *Le maître et l'hystérique.* Paris: Navarin.

Wallace, D. (2003). *Everything and More: A Compact History of Infinity.* New York: Norton.

Warshawsky, R. (2005, November). "Meaning is use" but nonetheless, one may question the use. *Papers of the School One Action Committee, New Series, 11:* electronic journal.

Wikipedia. (2016). Entry on "Soapbox." Accessed June 3, 2016. Available online at: https://en.wikipedia.org/wiki/Soapbox.

Winnicott, D. W. (1949). Hate in the counter-transference. *International Journal of Psychoanalysis, 30:* 69–74.

Wolfram, S. (2002). *A New Kind of Science.* Champaign, IL: Wolfram Media.

Zinberg, N. (1965). Psychoanalysis and the American scene: A reappraisal. *Diogenes, 13:* 73–111.

Žižek, S. (2012). *Welcome to the Desert of the Real.* London: Verso.

INDEX

271